Private Market Financing for Developing Countries

**Prepared by a Staff Team in the
Policy Development and Review Department**

**Steven Dunaway
Robert Rennhack
Brian Aitken
George Anayiotos
David Andrews
Jahangir Aziz
Juan Jose Fernandez-Ansola
Shogo Ishii
Thomas Laursen
Paul Mylonas
Susan Prowse
Alejandro Santos
Anne Jansen
Jolanda Heemskerk
Louis Pauly**

INTERNATIONAL MONETARY FUND
Washington, DC
March 1995

HG
3891.5
P75
1995
March

Charts and Cover Design: IMF Graphics Section

ISBN 1-55775-456-X
ISSN 0258-7440

Price: US$20.00
(US$12.00 to full-time faculty members and
students and universities and colleges)

Please send orders to:
International Monetary Fund, Publication Services
700 19th Street, N.W., Washington, D.C. 20431, U.S.A.
Tel.: (202) 623-7430   Telefax: (202) 623-7201

recycled paper

Contents

Contents

The following symbols have been used throughout this paper:

. . . to indicate that data are not available.

— to indicate that the figure is zero or less than half the final digit shown, or that the item does not exist;

– between years or months (e.g., 1992–93 or January–June) to indicate the years or months covered, including the beginning and ending years or months;

/ between years (e.g., 1992/93) to indicate a crop or fiscal (financial) year.

"Billion" means a thousand million.

Minor discrepancies between constituent figures and totals are due to rounding.

The term "country," as used in this paper, does not in all cases refer to a territorial entity that is a state as understood by international law and practice; the term also covers some territorial entities that are not states, but for which stat.istical data are maintained and provided internationally on a separate and independent basis.

Preface

This study was prepared in the Policy Development and Review Department of the International Monetary Fund, under the direction of Steven Dunaway, Chief of the Debt and Program Financing Issues Division, with Robert Rennhack, Deputy Chief of the division. Its authors are Brian Aitken, George Anayiotos, David Andrews, Jahangir Aziz, Juan Jose Fernandez-Ansola, Shogo Ishii, Thomas Laursen, Paul Mylonas, Susan Prowse, and Alejandro Santos, economists in the division; Anne Jansen, research officer in the division; and Jolanda Heemskerk, an intern at the IMF during the summer of 1994. The study updates information and analyses contained in *Private Market Financing for Developing Countries,* World Economic and Financial Surveys (Washington: IMF, December 1993).

The work benefited from comments by staff in other departments of the IMF and by members of the Executive Board. Opinions expressed, however, are those of the authors and do not necessarily represent the view of the IMF or its Executive Directors. The study was completed in October 1994 and reflects developments to that time.

Louis Pauly prepared the text for publication. The authors are also grateful to Delrene Alvis, Lucia Buono, Ida Jenkins, and Anne-Barbara Hyde for their valuable word-processing services. Juanita Roushdy of the External Relations Department, gave the manuscript a final edit and coordinated production.

I

Overview and Current Issues

Over the period since the end of 1992, steady progress has been achieved toward resolving the commercial bank debt problems of middle-income countries.[1] By the end of 1994, most of the major debtor countries in this group will have completed restructurings of their bank debt. At the same time, a number of developing countries—including some of the former major debtors—have expanded their access to spontaneous private financing, as investor interest in developing country bonds and equities broadened significantly. The markets for these securities ran into substantial turbulence at times during the first half of 1994, however, reflecting higher interest rates in international markets prompted by the tightening of monetary conditions in the United States and by adverse developments in some developing countries.

Progress with Commercial Bank Debt Restructuring

Recent Experience

Over the past year, Brazil, Bulgaria, the Dominican Republic, Jordan, Poland, Sao Tome and Principe, and Zambia completed bank-debt-restructuring packages with support from the Fund, the World Bank, and bilateral official agencies. Ecuador also is expected to complete an arrangement with its bank creditors before the end of 1994. By that time, a total of 21 countries will have concluded bank debt- and debt-service-reduction operations. Debt worth approximately $170 billion will have been restructured, representing roughly 75 percent of bank debt outstanding at the end of 1989 for the group of heavily indebted developing countries (Table A1). Panama and Peru are the most heavily indebted middle-income countries that have not yet regularized relations with their commercial bank creditors; both are engaged in negotiating restructuring agreements.

South Africa continued to address its external debt problems through a rescheduling of obligations to commercial banks. Agreement on a fourth and final arrangement following the 1985 payment "standstill" was reached in September 1993. In the case of Russia,

talks have focused on rescheduling its stock of bank debt and capitalizing a declining share of interest arrears. A preliminary agreement was reached in July 1993, but its implementation was delayed pending resolution of issues regarding Russia's waiving sovereign immunity and designation of the official agency that would be the signatory to the agreement. These issues were resolved in September 1994, and the agreement is to come into effect by the end of the year, after Russia makes a previously agreed payment of $500 million with respect to past due 1993 interest obligations.

A growing number of low-income countries also are making efforts to resolve their debt problems, often aided by the resources of the debt reduction facility for countries of the International Development Association (IDA). Progress for most, however, remains slow. With the backing of IDA resources and assistance from official bilateral sources, debt buy-backs have been concluded by Bolivia, Guyana, Mozambique, Niger, Sao Tome and Principe, Uganda, and Zambia. Preliminary discussions on similar operations are under way with several other countries.

Further innovations in debt operations have occurred over the past year. Bulgaria's discount bond, for example, involves a much steeper discount than has been the case in previous debt packages. In addition, Poland's agreement provided for some debt reduction for interest arrears and did not include interest collateral. Packages now generally include limits on the use of certain options or explicit rebalancing clauses to provide countries with more certainty as to the up-front costs of an operation and the profile of debt-service relief ultimately provided. The Fund and the World Bank have also shown increased flexibility in the use of their own resources by eliminating the segmentation provisions in their guidelines governing support for bank debt operations.

Over the past year, bank debt operations for Brazil and Jordan were financed entirely by the debtor countries themselves. While not directly involved in these deals, the international financial institutions have provided some indirect support. The bank deal with Jordan was predicated on the existence of a Fund arrangement with the country. In the case of Brazil, the country's stabilization program, which was expected to be monitored by the Fund, and continuing discussions on a Fund arrangement were considered sufficient assurance to enable completion of negotiations with creditors.

---

[1]For earlier periods, see Collyns and others (1993, 1992, and 1991). For information on official financial flows to developing countries, see Kuhn and others (1994).

Prospects

Notwithstanding recent progress, certain developments appear likely to make future negotiations between indebted developing countries and the holders of their commercial bank obligations more complex. Nonbank investors now have purchased significant amounts of bank debt in the secondary market. Difficulties in persuading them to accept certain aspects of the debt packages negotiated by bank advisory committees have contributed to delays in completing some recent restructuring operations. Negotiating committees in the future will have to take better account of the diverse interests of these investors.

Another possible complication arises from the market impact of speculation that a country will conclude a debt- and debt-service-reduction operation. For example, so-called pre-Brady speculation has contributed to the run-up in the secondary market prices for the bank debt of Panama and Peru. In recent years, such price run-ups have tended to be earlier and larger than was the case for countries that concluded debt packages in 1989 and 1990 (Chart 1). As a consequence, secondary market prices may not always fully reflect a country's medium-term capacity to service its debt and the up-front costs of completing a debt-restructuring agreement may be bid up significantly. The potential effects of such speculation will need to be taken into consideration in negotiating the terms of bank packages in the remaining cases.

While most of the major bank debt cases have been resolved, attention still needs to be focused on the problems of low-income countries. In many of these countries, the process of debt restructuring has been delayed owing to economic and political difficulties. Although the amounts owed by these countries are small compared with the debt of the large middle-income debtor countries, individual debt burdens for many are severe. In some cases in the past, commercial banks have accepted steep discounts on these debts, particularly when they had no significant longer-term business interests and had already made provisions for losses. Additional flexibility will be needed in the future. There will also be a continuing substantial need for concessional assistance to finance debt operations. For some low-income countries, the total amount of assistance required to buy back bank debt, even at very steep discounts, is likely to be relatively large. Resources from the debt reduction facility for IDA countries and from other official agencies may not be sufficient. In such cases, it may not be enough to organize simple buy-backs of commercial bank debt. Instead, more complex operations may have to be considered that reduce up-front costs but still provide debt and debt-service reduction in line with a country's payments capacity over the medium term. Such deals might involve options that include larger discounts on discount bonds, par bonds bearing lower interest rates, more favorable treatment of past due interest, and less than full collateralization of principal.

Private Financial Flows

Recent Experience

The resurgence in private market financing to developing countries that began in the late 1980s continued during 1993 as both portfolio flows and net foreign direct investment rose sharply.[2] The strong expansion in international bond and stock placements was fueled in large part by a broadening of the investor base to include a wider group of institutional investors.[3] Medium- and long-term commercial bank lending, however, remained limited. Moreover, while total private market financing for developing countries as a group increased strongly in 1993, much of these flows continued to go to a small number of countries, primarily in Asia and Latin America.

Toward the end of 1993 and in early 1994, spreads on bonds narrowed appreciably, and demand for developing country bonds, as well as equities, began to fall dramatically. This coincided with increases in U.S. interest rates and adverse developments in several borrowing countries. In addition, highly leveraged·investors were reported to have liquidated their positions in developing country securities in an effort to meet margin requirements or to take profits. The slide in demand for these bonds and equities continued through April 1994, before recovering moderately in May and June.

While countries with weaker economic performance experienced cutbacks in market access somewhat earlier than others, financing flows to all developing countries, including those in Asia and stronger performers in Latin America, fell to very low levels by April 1994. Both issuers and purchasers pulled back sharply in the wake of overall market uncertainties. Bonds placed after February 1994 tended to be from only the better credit risks and to carry floating interest rates and shorter maturities. While highly leveraged investors unwound most of their positions, it appears that institutional investors generally maintained their holdings, even if they curtailed their demand for new bond and equity issues.

Durability of Market Re-Entry and Pricing of Risk

The increase in private financing to developing countries over the past few years and the market's abil-

---

[2]International bond and equity flows amounted to $71 billion in 1993 ($33 billion in 1992); net foreign direct investment flows amounted to $58 billion in 1993 ($39 billion in 1992). Direct purchases of equity and bonds by nonresidents in local markets are not included because of the lack of sufficient data.

[3]The expansion of the investor base is discussed further in Goldstein and others (1994).

Chart 1. Selected Developments in Secondary Market Prices During Negotiations of Bank Restructuring Packages

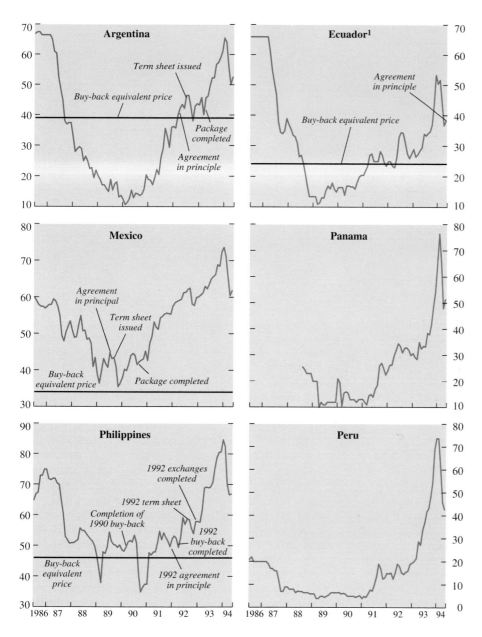

Sources: Salomon Brothers; ANZ Grindlays Bank; and IMF staff estimates.
[1]Per unit of claim.

ity to rebound from a moderate correction in 1992 engendered optimism about the sustainability of the process of market re-entry.[4] While the sharp correction in early 1994 raised fresh doubts, the emergence of a recovery later in the year reinforced that optimism. As noted in previous reports in this series, three conditions appear basic to sustaining private flows to developing countries: an expanded investor base, appropriate pricing and assessment of risk, and continued implementation of sound policies that help match future debt-servicing requirements to payments capacity. Progress continues to be made along these lines.

---

[4]The 1992 market correction is described in Goldstein and others (1993).

The expansion of the investor base in 1993 was part of a trend toward the globalization of portfolios. Relative stability of the investor base in 1994, despite the market correction, has been encouraging. As new investor groups come into the market, flows and prices of developing country securities could nevertheless be subject to considerable volatility, especially if new investors have poorer information and different liquidity preferences than existing investors. Although a number of developing countries have experienced increased volatility in security prices following the opening of local stock markets to foreign investors, a diversified and stable investor base can be expected over time to promote reduced fluctuations in asset prices, particularly as information becomes more widely disseminated.

The sharp run-up in the prices of developing country securities in late 1993 and early 1994 raises questions about the pricing of risk. It appears that the market ranks countries in a manner that is broadly consistent with their recent economic performance and immediate prospects. It is unclear, however, whether investors differentiate carefully among different borrowers. In general, and as would be expected, issuers from countries that previously rescheduled their debt tend to pay higher spreads, while those from countries with stronger growth and better inflation performance tend to pay lower ones. Beyond such broad differentiations, however, the market may be slow to make finer distinctions. For example, yield spreads on bonds of countries that ran into difficulties in late 1993 were slow to react to the deterioration in their economic performance until it was widely recognized; at that point, the response was quite significant. Investors also have been attracted to developing country securities because returns historically have not closely tracked price developments in industrial country financial markets. Under these circumstances, the diversification of portfolios by including developing country securities could raise the portfolios' expected returns for a given level of risk. Experience during the market turbulence in 1994, however, suggests that asset returns of developing and industrial countries tend to become more closely related in turbulent periods.

To maintain market access on reasonable terms, countries need consistently to implement strong macroeconomic and structural policy programs. Maintenance of such programs is likely to be particularly important in the period ahead, given the high degree of uncertainty with regard to interest rate movements in the industrial countries. Developing countries are also now entering a period of rising debt amortization as the bullet repayments on bonds issued earlier this decade are beginning to fall due (Chart 2). The increasing integration of international financial markets also means that interest rates and equity prices in developing coun-

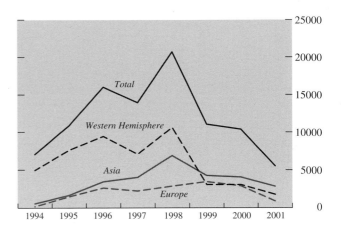

Chart 2. Maturing Bonds of Developing Countries
(In millions of U.S. dollars)

Sources: *International Financing Review; EuroWeek;* and IMF staff estimates.

tries will become more sensitive to developments in asset prices in the major industrial countries. A more open international environment will have to be taken into consideration by developing countries in determining the appropriate stances of monetary, fiscal, and exchange rate policies. While at times it might appear tempting to supplement such policies with capital controls, such actions would ultimately tend to be counterproductive. To provide a basis for sustained portfolio capital flows, continued efforts are also needed to strengthen financial markets in developing countries. Structural reforms to increase market transparency and reduce transaction costs and risks are important in fostering investor confidence. Intermediation of capital flows through the banking system points as well to the need for adequate banking regulation and supervision.

Developing countries can improve the mix of external financing by taking steps to remove obstacles to non-debt-creating capital flows. In recent years, international equity placements and direct purchases of equities by foreigners in domestic stock markets have risen sharply. At the same time, there has also been a surge in foreign direct investment inflows. These flows generally entail longer-term commitments on the part of foreign investors. Nevertheless, foreign direct investment flows, taking into account reinvested and repatriated earnings, also exhibit some of the same characteristics as other flows during periods of domestic macroeconomic instability. While investment positions are rarely liquidated rapidly, the totality of transactions associated with foreign direct investment may give rise to net outflows of funds.

II

Commercial Bank Debt Restructuring

Overview

Progress has been made by a number of the heavily indebted middle-income developing countries in regularizing their relations with commercial bank creditors. To many observers, the conclusion of the Brazilian debt package in April 1994 is seen as marking the end of the debt crisis that began in August 1982 when Mexico announced its inability to service its external obligations to commercial creditors. Along with Brazil, Bulgaria, the Dominican Republic, Jordan, Poland, Sao Tome and Principe, and Zambia completed debt- and debt-service-reduction operations or comprehensive debt buy-backs over the past year. Ecuador and its bank creditors also reached agreement, and the restructuring package is scheduled to be completed before the end of 1994. By that time, 21 countries will have concluded debt- and debt-service-reduction operations restructuring $170 billion of original commercial bank claims (Tables 1 and A2), or 75 percent of commercial bank debt owed by heavily indebted developing countries at the end of 1989.[5] Debt reduction achieved will amount to an estimated $76 billion at a cost of about $25 billion.

Allocations to the different options available in bank packages have varied depending (among other things) on explicit limits imposed by debtor countries, on interest rate developments following the issuance of term sheets, on creditors' perceptions of country creditor risks, and on the prospect of capital gains (Tables 2 and A3). In general, packages have been cost-effective in that the cost per unit of debt reduction obtained has been broadly in line with prices prevailing in the secondary market at the time agreements in principle were reached (Tables 3 and A4).

Following the trend of previous years, debt conversion activity was less buoyant in 1993. This partly reflected a shift in emphasis in the privatization program in Argentina, which accounted for about half of debt conversions in 1992, as priority shifted from reducing foreign commercial bank debt to reducing foreign currency denominated domestic debt instruments. In addition, the decline in debt conversions reflected the rise in secondary market prices for the debt of many countries and the reduced scale of privatizations, owing to countries having substantially completed their schemes.

Recent Bank Packages

While *Argentina's* debt- and debt-service-reduction package closed on April 7, 1993, about 6 percent of eligible principal (amounting to $19.4 billion) and 100 percent of past due interest ($8.6 billion) were exchanged at a later date because of reconciliation problems. All collateral and guarantees (totaling $3.1 billion), however, were deposited with the collateral agent (the Federal Reserve Bank of New York), and the downpayment on past due interest ($0.7 billion) and the bonds related to unreconciled debts were deposited with the escrow agent (the Bank of England) on the closing date. Reconciliation of the remaining principal was completed on September 27, 1993, and the release of bonds covering past due interest and the corresponding cash payments was made in four tranches: the first on October 29, 1993 (83 percent); the second on December 29, 1993 (14 percent); the third on February 28, 1994 (3 percent); and the fourth and last on April 28, 1994 (negligible amounts).

Brazil completed one of the largest and most complex debt- and debt-service-reduction operations on April 15, 1994. Completion of the deal came almost two years after the agreement in principle was reached, following four extensions of the closing date. Since an arrangement with the Fund was not likely to be in effect at closing (this had been a condition in the term sheet), a waiver from bank creditors had to be requested. This waiver was granted on March 24, 1994. The process was also delayed because of problems in obtaining full creditor participation.[6]

The deal restructured $40.6 billion in eligible principal and $6.0 billion in past due interest. Out of a menu of six options, only five were actually used. Creditors accepted the May 1993 limits suggested by the authorities on the amount of debt allocated to the par and new

---

[5]A further 10 percent of the stock of commercial bank debt outstanding in 1989 has been extinguished through debt conversions and other mechanisms. Of the remaining debt that has not been restructured, Peru and Panama account for more than 20 percent, and four low-income countries (Cameroon, Congo, Côte d'Ivoire, and Nicaragua) account for another 17 percent.

[6]In the end, one major creditor, a large nonbank investor holding roughly $1.4 billion of Brazil's debt, refused to participate in the deal. That creditor subsequently filed a law suit in the United States to force payment of past due interest on Brazil's original debt and to accelerate payments of principal arrears.

Table 1. Commercial Bank Debt- and Debt-Service-Reduction Operations, 1987–July 1994[1]

(In millions of U.S. dollars)

		Debt and Debt-Service Reduction (DDSR)[2]						Total Debt and Debt-Service Reduction/	
	Debt Restructured Under DDSR Operation[3]	Debt reduction		Debt-service reduction		Prepayments through collateral-ization	Total	Debt Restructured	Cost of Debt Reduction
		Buy-back	Discount exchange[4]	Principal collateralized par bond[4]	Other par bond[4]				
	(1)	(2)	(3)	(4)	(5)	(6)	(7)=(2)+..+(6)	(7)/(1)	
	(Concluded agreements)								
Argentina (1992)	19,397	—	2,356	4,291	—	2,739	9,386	48.4	3,059
Bolivia	643	331	232	29	—	20	612	95.2	61
(1987)	473	253	182	—	—	7	442	93.5	35
(1993)	170	78	50	29	—	13	170	100.0	26
Brazil (1992)	40,600	—	4,974	3,996	337	3,891	13,198	32.5	3,900
Bulgaria (1993)	6,186	798	1,865	—	421	443	3,527	57.0	652
Chile (1988)	439	439	—	—	—	—	439	100.0	248
Costa Rica (1989)	1,456	991	—	—	101	36	1,128	77.5	196
Dominican Republic (1993)	776	272	177	—	—	63	511	65.8	149
Ecuador (1994) [6]	4,520	—	1,180	826	—	595	2,600	57.5	583
Guyana (1992)	69	69	—	—	—	—	69	100.0	10
Jordan (1993)	736	—	84	111	—	117	312	42.5	118
Mexico	51,902	—	7,953	6,484	—	7,777	23,173	44.6	7,677
(1988)	3,671	—	1,115	—	—	555	1,670	45.5	555
(1989)	48,231	—	6,838	6,484	—	7,222	20,544	42.6	7,122
Mozambique (1991)	124	124	—	—	—	—	124	100.0	12
Niger (1991)	111	111	—	—	—	—	111	100.0	23
Nigeria (1991)	5,811	3,390	—	651	—	352	4,393	75.6	1,708
Philippines	5,812	2,602	—	516	116	467	3,701	63.7	1,795
(1989)	1,339	1,339	—	—	—	—	1,339	100.0	670
(1992)	4,473	1,263	—	516	116	467	2,362	52.8	1,125
Poland (1994)	9,918	2,454	2,401	779	72	602	6,309	63.6	1,866
Sao Tome and Principe	10	10	—	—	—	—	10	100.0	1
Uganda (1993)	152	152	—	—	—	—	152	100.0	18
Uruguay (1991)	1,608	633	—	160	—	95	888	55.2	463
Venezuela (1990)	19,700	1,411	511	2,012	471	1,639	6,043	30.7	2,585
Zambia (1994)	200	200	—	—	—	—	200	100.0	22
Total	170,170	13,986	21,733	19,855	1,519	18,835	75,927	44.6	25,146

Source: IMF staff estimates.

[1]Debt and debt-service reduction are estimated by comparing the present value of the old debt with the present value of the new claim, and adjusting for prepayments made by the debtor. The methodology is described in detail in Annex I of *Private Market Financing for Developing Countries* (Washington International Monetary Fund, December 1992). The amounts of debt reduction contained in this table exclude debt extinguished through debt conversion.

[2]The figure for debt-service reduction represents the expected present value of the reduction in future interest payments arising from the below-market fixed interest rate path on the new instruments relative to expected future market rates. The calculation is based on the estimated term structure of interest rates at the time of agreement in principle.

[3]Includes debt restructured under new money options for Mexico (1989), Uruguay (1991), Venezuela (1989), and the Philippines (1992); the Philippine (1989) new money option was not tied to a specific value of existing debt.

[4]Excludes prepayment of principal and interest through guarantees.

[5]Cost at the time of operation's closing. Includes principal and interest guarantees, buy-back costs, and for Venezuela, resources used to provide comparable collateral for bonds issued prior to 1990. Excludes cash downpayments related to past due interest.

[6]Closing of the operation has been delayed and is expected to take place in the first quarter of 1995.

money options and the minimum allocation for the discount bond. The final allocation was (1) 35 percent for the discount bond; (2) 32 percent for the par bond; (3) 22 percent for the capitalization bond with temporary interest reduction; (4) 6 percent for the new money option; and (5) 5 percent for the front-loaded interest reduction bond (FLIRB). No allocation was made to the restructuring option.

The cost of the enhancements required for the operation is estimated at $3.9 billion, of which $2.8 billion in collaterals was delivered at closing, with the rest to be phased in over a two-year period in four semiannual installments. Phase-in bonds and partly collateralized bonds were issued at closing and were to be exchanged for fully collateralized instruments over the next two years.[7] The Bank for International Settlements is serving as the collateral agent. Financing for the operation comes from $0.4 billion collected in the new money

[7]These phase-in and partly collateralized bonds apply only to the par and discount bond options. The FLIRBs were fully collateralized at closing, and the other options did not require collateral.

Table 2. Bank Menu Choices in Debt-Restructuring Packages

(In percent of total eligible bank debt)

	Debt Reduction		Debt-Service Reduction			Other Non-Debt- and Debt-Service-Reduction Options
	Buy-back	Discount exchange	Principal collateralized par exchanges	Other par exchanges	New Money	
Argentina	—	34	66	—	—	—
Bolivia	46	35	19	—	—	—
Brazil	—	35	32	5	6	22
Bulgaria	13	60	—	27	—	—
Costa Rica	63	—	—	37	—	—
Dominican Republic	35	65	—	—	—	—
Ecuador	—	58	42	—	—	—
Jordan	—	33	67	—	—	—
Mexico	—	43	47	—	11	—
Nigeria	62	—	38	—	—	—
Philippines (1989)[1]	100	—	—	—	—	—
Philippines (1992)	28	—	42	17	13	—
Poland	25	54	18	—	4	—
Uruguay	39	—	33	—	28	—
Venezuela	7	9	38	15	31	—
Total[2]	8	34	39	5	9	5

Sources: National authorities; and IMF staff estimates.
[1]The agreement included new money but was not tied to a specific amount of eligible debt.
[2]Weighted average.

option and from Brazil's own resources. Zero-coupon U.S. Treasury securities used as collateral for the deal were purchased by Brazil in the secondary market.

In one of the fastest completions of a menu-based debt- and debt-service-reduction operation, *Jordan* concluded a deal with its banks on December 23, 1993, two weeks after the formal signing of the agreement and less than six months after reaching an agreement in principle. The package covered eligible principal of $740 million and past due interest of $120 million. Following considerable official buy-backs in the secondary market before the commitment date (about 12 percent of the total bank debt outstanding), the final allocation of eligible principal was (1) 67 percent for the par bond; (2) 33 percent for the discount bond; and (3) negligible amounts for the (below-market price) buy-back. The $150 million cost of the operation included $29 million for cash payments on past due interest. Financing was covered entirely by the country's own resources.

Bulgaria reached an agreement in principle with its commercial bank creditors on November 24, 1993. A term sheet was distributed to banks on March 11, 1994, and the package was completed on July 29, 1994. Eligible principal amounted to $6.2 billion, including $1.9 billion in short-term debt. The menu consisted of three options: (1) a 50 percent discount exchange; (2) a FLIRB; and (3) a buy-back at 25¾₆ cents on the dollar per unit of claim. Partial interest payments were resumed shortly after the agreement in principle was

reached. Retroactive to March 1993, the rate paid was 5 percent of amounts due, or roughly $30 million a quarter.

The discount bond involves a 30-year bullet repayment and bears an interest rate of ¹³⁄₁₆ over the London interbank offered rate (LIBOR). The principal is fully collateralized, and there is a 12-month rolling interest guarantee at 7 percent. The FLIRB carries an 18-year maturity with eight years of grace. The interest rate starts at 2 percent in the first year and increases in steps each year, reaching 3 percent by year seven; subsequently, it reverts to a market rate of ¹³⁄₁₆ over LIBOR until maturity. There is no principal guarantee, but the bond has a 12-month rolling interest guarantee at 2.6 percent (for the seven years of interest reduction), capitalizing earned income until it reaches 3 percent. Equal amortization payments are due semiannually. Special issues of discount and FLIRB bonds will be made to cover 30 percent of the short-term debt allocated to the different options. These bonds carry an interest rate ½ of 1 percent higher than that on bonds exchanged for medium- and long-term debt. Some debt reduction on past due interest is achieved through a lowering of the interest rate for capitalization purposes. The package also includes a value recovery clause on the discount bonds linked to the overall performance of the Bulgarian economy.

The term sheet limited the allocation for the FLIRBs to 30 percent. Rebalancing was not needed by the commitment date (May 18, 1994), since the allocation was

Table 3. Buy-Back Equivalent Prices in Debt- and Debt-Service-Reduction Operations[1]

(In percent of face value)

| | Debt Reduction | | Debt-Service Reduction | | | Secondary Market Price at Time of Agreement in Principle |
	Buy-back	Discount exchange	Principal collateralized par exchange	Other par exchanges	Overall package	
Argentina	—	25	32	—	30	37
Brazil	—	26	36	19	30	35
Bulgaria	25	18	—	8	18	27
Costa Rica[2]	16	—	—	29[3]	18	19
Dominican Republic	25	28	—	—	26	23
Ecuador	—	19	29	—	24	23
Jordan	39	25	41	—	35	39
Mexico[2]	—	33	39	—	36	44
Nigeria[2]	40	—	36	—	39	40
Philippines (1989)	50	—	—	—	50	50
Philippines (1992)	52	—	45	28	48	53
Poland	41	14	22	—	25	39
Uruguay[2]	56	—	45	—	53	54
Venezuela[2]	45	35	38	25	38	46
Total[4]	41	27	36	21	33	37

Source: IMF staff estimates.

[1]The buy-back equivalent price for a debt exchange is the total value of enhancements as a proportion of the total reduction in claims payable to banks, including effective prepayments through collateralization, evaluated at prevailing interest rates at time of agreement in principle. This is the price at which the debt reduction achieved through a debt exchange is equivalent to the debt reduction under a buy-back at this price.

[2]The calculations include estimates of value recovery clauses.

[3]Weighted average of the buy-back equivalent price of the series A par bond (33 cents), the series B par bond (0 cents), and the series A past due interest bond (119 cents).

[4]Weighted average.

(1) 60 percent for the discount bond; (2) 27 percent for the FLIRB; and (3) 13 percent for the buy-back. Interest arrears estimated at about $1.9 billion were included in the operation. A cash payment of 3 percent was made, with remaining amounts (other than amounts purchased in connection with the buy-back option) rescheduled in the form of a 17-year uncollateralized bond bearing a market interest rate of ¹³⁄₁₆ over LIBOR and a grace period of seven years. Amortization is in semiannual installments on a back-loaded schedule. The cost of the operation was $716 million, which was initially financed by the country's own resources. However, after the closing of the operation, Bulgaria requested and received additional financial assistance from the Fund and the World Bank in support of the debt- and debt-service-reduction operation.

On February 14, 1994, the *Dominican Republic* formally signed an agreement to restructure $1.1 billion of its commercial bank debt, including interest arrears of $320 million. The operation closed on August 31, 1994. After an initial allocation failed to provide the 50 percent debt reduction included in the term sheet, creditors were asked to rebalance their commitments. The final allocation on eligible principal was 65 percent to the discount exchange, 35 percent to the buy-back, and no allocation to the FLIRB. The up-front cost of the

operation was about $190 million, financed entirely by the country's own resources.

A highly innovative and somewhat controversial agreement in principle was reached between *Poland* and its bank advisory committee on March 10, 1994. The larger-than-anticipated debt reduction entailed in the agreement produced a significant decline in the price of Polish debt in the secondary market after the announcement. The agreement restructured $12.7 billion, comprising virtually all of Poland's outstanding commercial bank debt. A term sheet was distributed to banks on May 23, 1994, and commitments were due on June 29, 1994. That date was subsequently extended to improve chances that approval of a waiver for a buy-back would be received from creditors holding 95 percent of the debt. That figure was achieved, and the deal was completed on October 27, 1994. Eligible principal amounted to $9.9 billion, of which $1.1 billion was short term. The menu for eligible principal included six options, four for medium- and long-term debt and two for short-term debt. The options for medium- and long-term principal were (1) a buy-back at 41 cents on the dollar per unit of claim; (2) a 45 percent discount bond exchange; (3) a below-market interest rate par exchange; and (4) a new money option, whereby in exchange for 35 percent of new money, old claims are rescheduled on somewhat more favorable terms than in the other options. The options for short-term principal were (1) a buy-back at 38 cents on the dollar per unit of claim and (2) a below-market interest rate par bond exchange, with an interest rate profile marginally higher than that for the par bond exchange for medium- and long-term principal.

The discount bond in the Polish package involved a 30-year bullet repayment bearing a market interest rate of $^{13}/_{16}$ over LIBOR. Principal was fully collateralized. The par bond also involved a 30-year bullet repayment carrying a prearranged interest rate profile starting at 2.75 percent in year one, rising in increments to 5 percent in year twenty-one, and remaining at that level thereafter. The interest rate profile on the short-term par exchange was somewhat higher, in that the interest rate rises at a somewhat faster rate after year one. Both par bonds included full principal collateral. The new money option involved the exchange at par of up to 5 percent of eligible principal for a debt conversion bond, with the creditor providing $35 in new money for each $100 in debt tendered. The 25-year debt conversion bond had no principal collateral and carried a sub-market interest rate starting at 4.5 percent in year one, increasing to 7.5 percent in year eleven and thereafter. This was an innovative feature of the package; in the past, these types of bonds involved no debt- or debt- service reduction. This bond has a grace period of 20 years with equal semiannual amortization payments. The 15-year new money bond also has no principal collateral. It carries a market rate of $^{13}/_{16}$ over LIBOR, a grace period of ten years, and an even amortization schedule. None of the bonds in the package is covered by interest guarantees.

Bank creditors allocated their medium- and long-term debt as follows: (1) 24.6 percent to the buy-back; (2) 60.8 percent to the discount exchange; (3) 10.3 percent to the par exchange; and (4) 4.4 percent to the new money option. Allocation of the short-term debt was as follows: (1) 26.1 percent to the buy-back and (2) 73.9 percent to the par exchange.

In the Polish package, past due interest of $3.5 billion was effectively subject to debt and debt-service reduction. Debt reduction of about 15 percent was obtained by reducing the capitalization rate on interest arrears. Debt-service reduction was also obtained through a below-market interest rate for the associated bond. In theory, there were five modalities for dealing with past due interest, two for interest arrears on short-term principal and three for interest arrears on medium- and long-term principal. The options for short-term interest arrears are exactly the same as the options for short-term principal. The three options for interest arrears on medium- and long-term principal included (1) a cash payment corresponding to 85 percent of interest due in December 1989 to regularize previous anomalies and catch up on payments of interest due on medium- and long-term principal accruing since May 1993 (about $160 million); (2) a buy-back

at the same price as medium- and long-term principal; and (3) a bond covering past due interest at below-market rates. The latter bond has a 20-year term and is uncollateralized; it carries an interest rate that starts at 3.25 in year one and rises to 7 percent in year nine and thereafter. The amortization schedule on these bonds provides for eight years grace followed by back-loaded semiannual payments. Starting in March 1994, partial interest payments on medium- and long-term principal were increased to 30 percent of interest due. The final agreement did not include a rebalancing clause, except for the limit of 5 percent of eligible principal on the new money option and an undetermined maximum on the buy-back in the event that insufficient financing was available. There was no currency option or value recovery clause. Implementation of a debt-conversion program is expected. The cost of the operation was $2.1 billion, financed with resources from the Fund, the World Bank, the new money option, and Poland's own contribution.

Ecuador reached an agreement in principle with its bank advisory committee on May 2, 1994, to restructure debt amounting to $7.4 billion. A termsheet was circulated to banks on June 14, 1994. The menu of options for eligible principal, amounting to $4.5 billion, includes (1) a 45 percent discount exchange; and (2) a par exchange at a submarket interest rate. The discount bond has a 30-year term with a bullet repayment; it bears a market interest rate of $^{13}/_{16}$ over LIBOR and includes full principal collateral and a 12-month rolling interest guarantee at 7 percent. The par bond also involves a 30-year bullet repayment; it bears a predetermined below-market interest rate profile starting at 3 percent in year one, increasing to 5 percent by year eleven, and remaining at that rate for the balance of the bond's maturity. As with the discount bond, the principal of the par bond is fully collateralized, but the 12-month interest guarantee was fixed at 3.75 percent in year one, with income earnings capitalizing until 5 percent is achieved. The termsheet does not include any mandatory allocation or rebalancing clauses. It also does not include a currency option or a value recovery clause. Creditors have chosen to allocate 58 percent of their exposure to the discount exchange and 42 percent to the par exchange.

Interest arrears on *Ecuador's* bank debt is estimated at $2.9 billion. Implicitly, this estimate involves some debt forgiveness, because past due interest is calculated from the end of October 1986 to the end of December 1993 at three-month LIBOR plus $^{13}/_{16}$, instead of the interest rates on the original loan agreements.[8] From January 1994 through the closing date, interest will accrue at a 4 percent fixed rate. The agreement calls for interest arrears to be treated separately through (1) a cash payment of $75 million; (2) issuance of a 10-year uncollateralized interest equal-

---

[8]Original contractual interest rates on Ecuador's debt were generally higher, with some loans priced at LIBOR plus 2¼.

ization bond for $191 million to regularize previous discriminatory payments to creditors; and (3) a 20-year uncollateralized past due interest bond bearing a market interest rate of $^{13}/_{16}$ over LIBOR and a ten-year grace period. The amortization schedule on the latter bond consists of back-loaded semiannual payments. The PDI bond also introduces the innovation of having the option to capitalize a declining fraction of interest due in the first six years. Partial interest payments were resumed in May 1994 at a rate of $5 million a month (retroactive to January 1994). The up-front cost of the operation has been estimated at about $658 million. Financing is expected to come from the Fund, the World Bank, official bilateral sources, and the country's own resources. The deal is scheduled to close in December 1994.

Sao Tome and Principe concluded a comprehensive buy-back of commercial bank debt covering $10.1 million of claims (about 87 percent of eligible debt) at 10 cents on the dollar in August 1994. The $1.0 million cost of the buy-back was entirely financed by the Debt Reduction Facility for IDA countries.

Zambia completed a comprehensive buy-back at 11 cents per dollar of principal and past due interest in two transactions, the first on July 26, and the second on September 14, 1994. Eligible principal covered amounted to about $200 million (about 79 percent of eligible debt) and included commercial bank debt, as well as trade and supplier credits. The cost of the operation thus far has been roughly $25 million, financed by a $13 million grant from the debt reduction facility for IDA countries and grants from Germany, the Netherlands, Sweden, and Switzerland. Further buy-backs could take place by the end of 1994, which is the expiry date for Zambia's grant facility to finance the operation. An innovation in this buy-back operation is that, due to initially low levels of creditor participation, the operation has taken place in several tranches, instead of the usual single transaction.

South Africa agreed on a fourth and final rescheduling arrangement with its commercial banks at the end of September 1993. The arrangement, which became effective at the beginning of 1994, rescheduled those debts (some $5 billion) that were still subject to the "standstill" on repayments imposed in 1985. The arrangement involved a cash payment of 10 percent of outstanding debt, with the remainder being rescheduled for eight years on a graduated schedule. Interest margins were to be negotiated between South African debtors and foreign creditors, with margins in excess of 2.5 percent over the relevant base rate requiring approval by the authorities under exchange control arrangements.

A rescheduling agreement between *Gabon* and its commercial bank creditors was signed on May 26, 1994 and became effective on July 1, 1994. The agreement covers the principal on debts contracted before September 1986 (which amounts to $100 million). These debts are rescheduled for ten years with 2½ years

of grace. Interest arrears accumulated since 1986 (estimated at $50 million) were also rescheduled but at shorter maturities. This operation covered most of the country's commercial bank debt.

On July 30, 1993, a preliminary rescheduling agreement was reached between *Russia* and its bank creditors. This agreement rescheduled the entire stock of pre-cutoff date debt with a ten-year maturity and a five-year grace period. Russia agreed to pay $500 million toward interest accrued but unpaid through the end of 1993. Remaining interest arrears were expected to be rescheduled on the same terms as pre-cutoff date principal. In the event, Russia did not make payments on interest, and the agreement did not come into effect. Major stumbling blocks included the Russian authorities' refusal to waive sovereign immunity and questions regarding which official Russian agency should sign the agreement. These issues were finally resolved in October 1994, and the agreement was scheduled to come into effect by the end of 1994, following Russian payment of $500 million on past due interest in 1993, as was previously agreed.

Debt-Conversion Activity

After reaching a peak in 1990, debt conversions fell over the last three years. In 1993, debt conversions were at their lowest level since the outbreak of the debt crisis over a decade ago (Table 4). High debt prices in the secondary market, regularization of relations with commercial bank creditors, and advances already made in most privatization programs were responsible for declining conversion activity.

Argentina, which accounted for two thirds of conversion activity in 1992, shifted its privatization program to encourage exchanges involving foreign currency denominated domestic debt. With buoyant equity markets worldwide, Argentina also elected to privatize part of the state oil company, Yacimientos Petroliferos Fiscales (YPF), through an international share placement, rather than by means of conversions made with commercial bank debt. Despite these developments, Argentina still accounted for about one fourth of total bank debt conversions in 1993. While involving only small amounts, debt conversions more than doubled in *Brazil* during 1993, reflecting some pickup in interest by foreign investors in the country's privatization program. Debt conversion activity in *Chile* fell by one fourth during 1993, with the high price of commercial bank debt in the secondary market continuing to curtail demand for debt conversions under the formal mechanisms. All conversion activity took place through "informal" schemes, under which residents retire their debt to the Central Bank by delivery of Chilean debt acquired in the secondary market.

Among other countries, conversions in the *Philippines* declined by about 15 percent as investors' interest dropped and debt prices edged up. Activity was negligible in *Mexico* and *Nigeria* owing to the suspen-

Table 4. Debt Conversions[1]

(In millions of U.S. dollars)

	1987	1988	1989	1990	1991	1992	1993	First Quarter 1994
Argentina	—	1,146	1,534	6,464	132	2,825[2]	371	5
Brazil	336	2,096	946	283	68	95	219	30
Chile	1,979	2,940	2,767	1,096	828	385	298	2
Costa Rica	89	44	124	17	2	—	—	—
Ecuador	127	261	32	45	20	50	2	—
Honduras	9	14	35	33	52	39	—	—
Jamaica	1	9	23	22	36	14	3	—
Mexico	1,680	1,056[3]	532	221	1,956	344	—	—
Nigeria	—	40	257	217	119	122	35	—
Philippines	450	931	630	378	489	379	349	. . .
Tanzania	—	—	—	11	21	33	52	. . .
Uruguay	—	60	27	4	44	34	48	. . .
Venezuela	—	50	544	595	343	148	87	—
Yugoslavia	—	135	1,369	681	631	. . .	. . .	. . .
Total	4,671	8,782	8,820	10,067	4,741	4,468	1,464	37

Sources: Central Bank of Argentina; Central Bank of Brazil; Central Bank of Chile; Ministry of Finance of Mexico; Central Bank of the Philippines; Bank of Jamaica; Central Bank of Venezuela; and IMF staff estimates.

[1]Face value of debt converted under official ongoing schemes. Figures do not include large-scale, one-off cash buy-backs and debt exchanges.

[2]Excludes $0.3 billion from the privatization of the state power company deposited in a trust fund for later debt conversion as well as $0.5 billion in foreign currency bonds of the Argentine Government (BOCONES) retired with the privatization of the state gas and power companies.

[3]Does not include an estimated $6-8 billion related to payment at a discount of private-sector debt following the August 1987 signing of an agreement to restructure debt of the foreign exchange risk coverage trust fund (FICORCA).

sion of conversion programs. In *Venezuela,* political and financial uncertainties were factors behind a further reduction in conversion activity in 1993.

Secondary Market Developments

After remaining stable in the first quarter of 1993, secondary market prices for bank claims and Brady bonds rose sharply later in the year and into early 1994 (Chart 3). The weighted average of prices for claims on 15 heavily indebted countries peaked in January 1994 at about 70 cents on the dollar (compared with 51 cents in December 1992), its highest level in the last seven years. The strength in secondary market prices reflected improving economic situations in major developing countries and greater investor interest in emerging market securities. Subsequently, prices fell sharply in response to higher interest rates in the United States and market reactions to adverse economic and political developments in some major countries. Moreover, during the 1993 run-up in prices, some investor groups built up some highly leveraged positions; their subsequent need to unwind these positions added to the drop in debt prices during the first half of the year. By the end of June 1994, the weighted average price for the 15 countries had fallen to 58 cents on the dollar.

The stripped price of *Argentina's* restructured bank claims rose by 82 percent in 1993, reaching about 80 cents on the dollar by the end of the year.[9] Completion of the debt- and debt-service-reduction operation, good economic prospects, the privatization of the largest public enterprise (YPF), and Congressional approval of the social security reform accounted for the solid performance of Argentine debt prices. By the end of June 1994, the price of Argentine claims had declined in line with overall market developments to 62 cents on the dollar.

Following market trends, the price of claims on *Brazil* also performed well in 1993. Debt prices climbed by 62 percent in 1993, reaching about 50 cents on the dollar by the end of the year, despite political uncertainties and difficulties in completing the debt deal. By the end of June 1994, the price of Brazilian claims had fallen back to 41 cents on the dollar. In *Mexico,* while the stripped price of its claims did not change much over the first three quarters of 1993, prices jumped in the last quarter by about one third following the approval of the North American Free Trade Agreement. By year end, Mexican Brady bonds were trading at almost 90 cents on the dollar. Concerns resulting from an uprising in Chiapas and the assassination of the leading presidential candidate, together with the tightening of monetary policy in the United

---

[9]The stripped price is a measure of country risk. It is the ratio of the market value of unguaranteed payments to the present value of such payments discounted at a risk-free interest rate.

Chart 3. Secondary Market Prices of Bank Claims on Selected Countries

(In percent of face value)

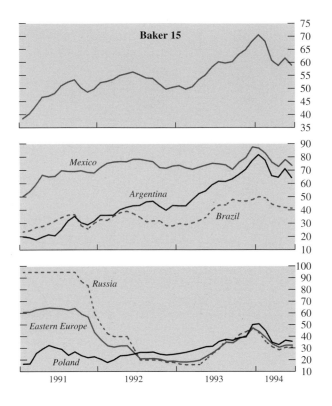

Sources: Salomon Brothers; and ANZ Grindlays Bank.

States, led by June 1994 to a decline in the stripped price of Mexican bonds to 73 cents. The stripped prices on *Venezuela's* debt increased by about one fourth to reach about 69 cents on the dollar at the end of 1993, despite political uncertainties. Concerns about the health of the banking system in the wake of the failure of a major bank and more generally about the country's economy, contributed to a sharp decline in Venezuelan claims in the first half of 1994. By June, they had fallen to 42 cents on the dollar.

In 1993 and early 1994, considerable price speculation accompanied reports that various countries were making progress in their discussions with commercial banks on restructuring agreements. In the case of *Ecuador,* the price of its debt (including past due interest) increased by 84 percent in 1993 to reach a level of about 53 cents on the dollar at the end of the year. For *Peru,* expectations of a debt-conversion program linked to privatization ran prices up sharply; the price of Peruvian claims (including past due interest) rose by about 250 percent in 1993 and closed the year at 69 cents on the dollar. In both cases, prices slid in the first half of 1994, falling to 40 cents and 48 cents, respectively, by the end of June.

Price developments on *Eastern European* countries' debt resembled the behavior of debt prices for other indebted countries. Prices of claims on Eastern European countries increased by about 150 percent to reach almost 50 cents on the dollar by the end of 1993, before declining by one third in the first half of 1994. The announcement of *Bulgaria's* agreement in principle with commercial banks in November 1993 produced a 50 percent increase in the price of its claims to about 44 cents on the dollar; it fell to 33 cents by the end of June 1994. Expectations of a bank debt agreement for *Poland* contributed to a rise in the price of Polish debt, which peaked at 51 cents on the dollar in January 1994. It then dropped in line with the general fall in debt prices; the decline accelerated following the announcement of the restructuring agreement in March 1994. After falling to 32 cents, it recovered to 35 cents by the end of June.

There were indications of significant growth in the volume of debt instruments trading in the secondary market during 1993. These instruments continue to be relatively liquid, as reflected in relatively tight bid-ask spreads. Market analysts estimate that trading volume reached nearly $2 trillion in 1993.[10] For short periods of time during the turbulence in bond markets during the first half of 1994, however, trading was reported to have slowed appreciably, with bid-ask spreads widening and dealers at times being reluctant to quote prices.

---

[10]The Emerging Markets Traders Association (EMTA) estimated volume at $733.7 billion in 1992. EMTA is planning to implement a computerized trade-clearing system to verify bond and loan trades. The system is expected to be in place by January 1995 and will provide uniform pricing as well as daily volume information, thus reducing transaction costs, contentious trade disputes, and the possibility of error arising from manual processing.

III

Recent Developments in Private Market Financing

Private market financial flows to developing countries increased significantly in 1992 and 1993 (Chart 4). Bond and equity flows accounted for much of the increase. The rapid expansion was mirrored in a broadening of the range of developing country borrowers attracting international investors, although portfolio flows continued to be concentrated in a few key countries in Asia and Latin America. In contrast, medium- and long-term bank lending to developing countries remained moderate; banks did demonstrate renewed interest in such lending, but on a highly selective basis.

In 1994, the situation changed dramatically. With higher U.S. interest rates, as well as unfavorable economic and political developments in some major borrowing countries, bond and equity issuance by developing countries plummeted between February and April 1994. A modest recovery came in the following months, but new flows remained vulnerable, especially because of the uncertain course of U.S. interest rates. Despite the market correction, however, portfolio flows to developing countries in the first half of 1994 were still significantly higher than levels recorded in the early 1990s.

Bonds

Bond placements by developing country borrowers reached $59.4 billion in 1993, more than twice the amount placed in 1992 (Tables 5 and A5).[11] There was a strong acceleration in bond issuance in the final quarter of 1993; bonds issued in that quarter amounted to $23.7 billion, almost equal to total issuance activity in 1992. This surge reflected a decline in U.S. interest rates combined with relatively high returns in emerging markets. Both factors encouraged a broader range of mainstream institutional investors to participate more actively in these markets. The continued implementation of prudent macroeconomic policies and structural adjustments in borrowing countries also improved investors' confidence. In relative terms, developing countries continued to increase their share of total international bond issuance from 7.1 percent in 1992 to 12.4 percent in 1993, and to 20.1 percent in the fourth quarter of 1993. The average size of developing

country bond placements also increased from $111 million in 1992 to $125 million in the first half of 1993, and to $135 million in the second half of the year. In particular, there were a number of sizable issues by borrowers in Latin America.

In the first half of 1994, volatile market conditions led to a sharp decline in the volume of international bond issuance by developing countries. Bonds worth $26.1 billion were issued, most in the beginning of the year and in June. Beginning in February, as bond yields rose throughout the world, both issuers and investors pulled back. For the first half of 1994 as a whole, the developing country share of total international bond issues fell to 12 percent. The decline was particularly notable for countries in Europe and Latin America.

The terms on new issues for many developing country borrowers improved throughout 1993 and into early 1994. The average yield spread fell from 288 basis points in the first quarter of 1993 to a low of 187 basis

Chart 4. Private Market Financing to Developing Countries
(In millions of U.S. dollars)

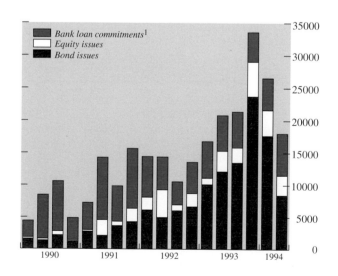

Sources: *International Financing Review;* OECD; and IMF staff estimates.
[1]Medium- and long-term bank loan commitments only.

---

[11]Includes reported private placements and notes issued under the Euro-medium-term note programs. The figures differ from OECD estimates, which have a narrower coverage.

Chart 5. Yield Spreads at Launch for Unenhanced Bond Issues by Developing Countries[1]
(In basis points)

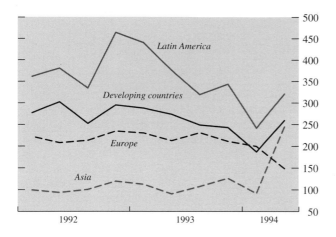

Sources: *International Financing Review;* and *Financial Times.*
[1]Reflect weighted averages.

Chart 6. Secondary Market Yield Spreads on U.S. Dollar Denominated Bonds by Selected Developing Countries
(In basis points)

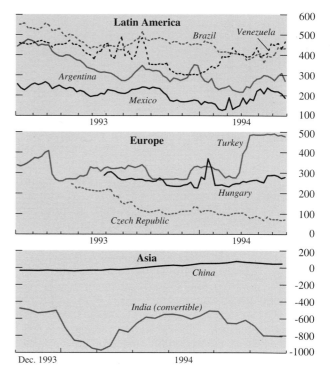

Source: Reuters.

points in the first quarter of 1994 (Chart 5).[12] The average spread widened sharply in the second quarter of 1994 to 259 basis points. This increase occurred despite the fact that bonds during this period were issued primarily by borrowers with higher credit ratings and carried shorter maturities. The weighted average maturity of bonds issued shortened to 6.3 years in the first half of 1994, after lengthening from 5.4 years in the first quarter of 1993 to 7.2 years in the final quarter of the year. Yield spreads in the secondary market for developing country bonds followed a similar pattern; notable increases were observed for bonds issued by Argentina, Brazil, Hungary, Mexico, Turkey, and Venezuela (Chart 6). A tightening of market conditions was also reflected in a sharp decline in secondary market prices for Brady bonds.

Yield spreads continued to vary considerably among countries. While borrowers without records of debt-servicing difficulties commanded lower spreads, market re-entrants were typically faced with spreads of over 200 basis points in 1993 and the first half of 1994. Moreover, the spread for public sector borrowers continued to be substantially lower than that for private sector borrowers (Table A6). Reflecting the uncertain path of U.S. interest rates, there was also renewed interest in new issues bearing floating rates. In the first

half of 1994, floating rate notes accounted for some 20 percent of total new issues, up from 8 percent in 1993.

Most of the recent bond issuance by developing countries represents net capital inflows. Maturing developing country bonds amounted to only $6.3 billion in the period from 1991 to 1993, compared with total bond issues worth $96 billion. As of the end of June 1994, the total outstanding stock of international bonds issued by developing countries is estimated to stand at $117.5 billion, 42 percent of which was accounted for by private sector borrowers. Amortization payments on this stock of debt will rise sharply in the next few years from an estimated $7.1 billion in 1994 to a peak of $21 billion in 1998, as bullet repayments on bonds placed in the early 1990s fall due (Table A7).[13] Payments are particularly concentrated in a few Western Hemisphere and Asian countries.

Although the range of borrowers continued to widen in 1993, developing country bond issuers remained concentrated in a few countries in Latin America, Asia,

---

[12]Throughout this chapter, yield spreads refer to the difference between the yield on a bond at the time of issuance and the yield on U.S. Treasury securities of comparable maturity or other comparable government securities if the bond is issued in other currencies. The U.S. Treasury security and other comparable government securities are used as a proxy for a risk-free return.

[13]These estimates can vary somewhat depending upon whether bondholders decide to take early redemption options for some bonds.

Table 5. International Bond Issues by Developing Countries and Regions[1]

(In millions of U.S. dollars)

	1991	1992	1993	1993 I	1993 II	1993 III	1993 IV	1994 I	1994 II
Developing countries	**12,838**	**23,780**	**59,437**	**10,109**	**12,117**	**13,492**	**23,719**	**17,668**	**8,443**
Africa	236	725	—	—	—	—	—	877	—
Congo	—	—	—	—	—	—	—	600	—
South Africa	236	725	—	—	—	—	—	—	—
Tunisia	—	—	—	—	—	—	—	277	—
Asia	3,000	5,917	20,401	2,230	3,200	3,481	11,391	7,645	5,465
China	115	1,359	3,047	406	651	1,209	681	1,500	872
Hong Kong	100	185	5,887	657	—	692	4,538	1,305	550
India	227	—	546	—	—	65	481	439	195
Indonesia	369	494	485	30	—	—	455	699	750
Korea	2,012	3,208	5,864	671	1,343	725	3,125	1,273	580
Macao	—	—	—	—	—	—	—	—	155
Malaysia	—	—	954	—	500	—	454	230	735
Pakistan	—	—	—	—	—	—	—	—	45
Philippines	—	—	1,293	170	175	190	758	154	555
Singapore	—	—	—	—	—	—	—	—	86
Taiwan Province of China	160	60	79	—	36	43	—	318	558
Thailand	17	610	2,247	296	495	557	899	1,728	384
Europe	1,960	4,561	9,638	2,863	1,257	1,988	3,530	875	439
Czech Republic	—	—	697	375	—	322	—	—	250
Czechoslovakia, former	277	129	—	—	—	—	—	—	—
Hungary	1,186	1,242	4,796	1,363	279	1,280	1,873	69	189
Slovak Republic	—	—	240	—	—	240	—	21	—
Turkey	497	3,190	3,905	1,125	978	145	1,657	785	—
Middle East	400	—	2,002	1,000	—	1,002	—	1,958	—
Israel	400	—	2,002	1,000	—	1,002	—	1,958	—
Western Hemisphere	7,242	12,577	27,396	4,017	7,559	7,022	8,798	6,313	2,539
Argentina	795	1,570	6,233	335	606	1,852	3,440	1,460	907
Barbados	—	—	—	—	—	—	—	—	20
Bolivia	—	—	—	—	—	—	—	10	—
Brazil	1,837	3,655	6,679	1,327	1,635	1,583	2,134	1,095	100
Chile	200	120	433	—	333	—	100	—	—
Colombia	—	—	566	—	325	50	191	250	83
Costa Rica	—	—	—	—	—	—	—	50	—
Guatemala	—	—	60	—	—	60	—	—	—
Mexico	3,782	6,100	10,783	2,205	4,136	1,851	2,591	3,307	1,390
Panama	50	—	—	—	—	—	—	—	—
Peru	—	—	30	—	—	—	30	40	40
Trinidad and Tobago	—	100	125	—	—	—	25	—	—
Uruguay		100	140	—	140	—	—	100	—
Venezuela	578	932	2,348	150	385	1,626	187	—	—
Memorandum items									
Issues under EMTN programs	375	1,215	3,713	607	393	1,439	1,274	384	695
Argentina	—	40	930	—	50	450	430	—	300
Bolivia	—	—	—	—	—	—	—	10	—
Brazil	—	110	422	62	110	100	150	35	—
Colombia	—	—	100	—	50	50	—	—	—
Korea	—	—	177	—	93	—	84	189	—
Mexico	375	665	1,741	545	90	646	460	150	395
Philippines	—	—	150	—	—	—	150	—	—
Thailand	—	—	194	—	—	194	—	—	—
Venezuela	—	400	—	—	—	—	—	—	—
Total bond issues in international bond markets	297,588	333,694	480,997	139,867	107,050	116,253	117,827	139,820	77,881
					(In percent)				
Shares of developing countries in global issuance	4.3	7.1	12.4	7.2	11.3	11.6	20.1	12.6	10.8

Sources: IMF staff estimates based on *Euroweek, Financial Times, International Financing Review, Financial Market Trends, Financial Statistics Monthly,* and *Organization for Economic Cooperation and Development.*

[1]Including note issues under Euro medium-term notes (EMTN) programs.

and Europe. Latin American borrowers had the largest share until they were surpassed by Asian borrowers in the final quarter of 1993. Bond issues by Latin American borrowers doubled to $27.4 billion in 1993, accounting for 46 percent of total issues by developing countries. That figure declined in the first half of 1994 to $8.9 billion, or 34 percent of total issues by developing countries.

Mexico continued to be the leading borrower, raising $10.8 billion in 1993 and $4.7 billion in the first half of 1994. An increasing number of companies placed bonds, including several private and public banks. Moreover, a few firms floated quite sizable individual issues during this period, including $1 billion issues by CEMEX (Mexico's largest cement producer) in May 1993 and BANCOMEXT in January 1994. Mexican entities also opened up new currency sectors, with Mexico's launching of Latin America's first "Samurai" issue since the debt crisis, BANAMEX issuing a Mexican peso-denominated Eurobond, and NAFINSA (a Mexican development bank) placing a "Dragon" bond, marking the first time that a Latin American noninvestment grade borrower has been able to issue in that market.

Borrowers in Argentina quadrupled their bond issues to $6.2 billion in 1993 and raised $2.4 billion in the first half of 1994. There were a number of new developments. A $1 billion global sovereign bond was issued in December 1993 at a spread of 280 basis points, the first global bond ever issued by a developing country borrower.[14] In addition, the first significant convertible bond by a private telephone company based in a developing country was placed in March 1994. *Brazil* also increased its bond issuance significantly in 1993, notwithstanding continued uncertainty about the course of its economic policies. All Brazilian bonds were issued by nonsovereign borrowers and included the first Euro-yen issue by a Latin American entity at a spread of 416 basis points. Venezuelan entities also increased their borrowing activity in 1993; among others, a $1 billion bond was issued by PDV America (a state oil company) at a spread of 210–218 basis points, and the first intraregional bond was issued simultaneously in Colombia and Luxembourg. Mainly reflecting the concerns of investors about the country's economic situation; however, no international bonds were placed by Venezuelan borrowers during the first half of 1994.

In general, the range of Latin American borrowers in the international bond market continued to broaden. Colombia, Guatemala, and Peru, and more recently Barbados, Bolivia, and Costa Rica, tapped the market for the first time in many years. Spreads ranged from 215 basis points for Colombia to over 700 basis points for Peru. At the same time, recent market re-entrants such as Chile, Trinidad and Tobago, and Uruguay maintained their presence in the market.

Asian borrowers tripled their international bond issues to $20.4 billion in 1993. They also raised $13 billion through this channel in the first half of 1994, despite overall market turbulence. As a result, their share in the total bond issues by developing countries rose from 34 percent in 1993 to 50 percent in the first half of 1994. The stock market booms in the region in 1993 also led to a strong increase in convertible bond issues; of total bonds issued, the share of convertibles rose from 18 percent in 1992 to 30 percent in 1993 before falling in the first half of 1994. Hong Kong emerged as the leading borrower in Asia, followed by Korea. Together, these two countries accounted for more than half of the bonds placed by Asian entities in 1993. The People's Republic of China also significantly increased its recourse to the international bond market. To facilitate market entry for Chinese enterprises, after a six-year absence, the Government entered the market directly in 1993 and placed three issues intended to establish a benchmark for China risk. In February 1994, the Government issued a 10-year, $1 billion global bond, which was priced at an 85 basis point spread; the issue was predominantly purchased by U.S. investors. In 1993, India, Malaysia, and the Philippines also tapped the international bond market for the first time in several years. Pakistan and Macao entered the market in the first half of 1994. Concerned about the country's overall debt profile, however, the Indian authorities moved in May 1994 to restrict convertible bond issues, except for companies using proceeds to restructure existing external debt.

European developing countries continued to step up their recourse to the international bond market in 1993, where they raised $9.6 billion. In the first half of 1994, however, bond issuance activity dropped dramatically, largely reflecting reduced placements by Hungary and Turkey. With increasing market concerns about economic conditions in these two countries, bond issues by Hungary fell from $4.8 billion in 1993 to less than $0.3 billion in the first half of 1994, while issues by Turkey declined from $3.9 billion to $0.8 billion. The Czech Republic and the Slovak Republic maintained access to the market in the first half of 1994.

In the rest of the developing countries, only a handful of borrowers have tapped the international bond market. Israel raised $2 billion in 1993 and another $2 billion in the first half of 1994 on exceptionally favorable terms because of guarantees provided by the U.S. Agency for International Development. In Africa, the Congo launched a $600 million ten-year bond, with interest payments secured by oil receivables and principal collateralized by U.S. Treasury bonds. In addi-

---

[14]Global bonds are issued simultaneously in several major international markets and allow issuers to tap into broader demand and obtain lower rates than those available in a single market. Some market participants estimated that Argentina was able to reduce the interest rate on the funds raised through the global issue by as much as 30 basis points.

tion, the Central Bank of Tunisia issued the first Samurai bond by an African country; the bond was launched with a spread of 221 basis points above the yield of a risk-free yen bond of comparable maturity.

Among developing country bond issuers, private sector borrowers scaled back their international issuance activity in the first half of 1994, following the doubling in volume that occurred in 1993. As a result, their share in total bonds issued by developing country borrowers declined from 45 percent in 1993 to 26 percent in the first half of 1994. The lower issuance activity was partly due to the sharp contraction in convertible bond issues by entities in Hong Kong, which were adversely affected by a decline in stock prices. Bond issues by sovereign borrowers, which tripled in 1993, declined in the first half of 1994, but their share of total bond issues rose from 27 percent to 50 percent. Lower issuance by sovereign borrowers was mainly accounted for by Hungary and Turkey.

Most bonds issued by developing countries continued to be denominated in U.S. dollars, yen, and deutsche mark. Bond issues in U.S. dollars accounted for 74 percent of the total in 1993 and 81 percent in the first half of 1994 (Table A8). This high share partly reflected both the greater appetite of U.S. investors for high-yielding, subinvestment grade securities and the impact of relatively low U.S. interest rates. Also facilitating bond issues in the U.S. market is Rule 144a, which exempts private placements from the disclosure requirements of the Securities and Exchange Commission (SEC) and permits qualified institutional buyers to trade privately placed securities without waiting the usually stipulated two-year holding period. In 1993, several borrowers in Hungary, Korea, and Mexico tapped the Yankee bond market for the first time.[15] While the yen sector remained the second largest currency sector for bonds issued by developing country borrowers, its share declined from 13 percent in 1993 to 10 percent in the first half of 1994. Deutsche mark bond issues, principally by European and Latin American borrowers, were subdued in 1993 and in the first half of 1994.

Following the market turbulence in early 1994, developing country borrowers increased the use of credit enhancement techniques, such as bond-equity conversion options, collateralization, and put options (Table A9). The most widely used enhancement technique was the bond-equity conversion option, especially in Asia where convertible bonds accounted for more than half of bond issues in the first half of 1994. Put options were the second most widely used technique; Latin American issuers were the principal users, possibly reflecting uncertainties about economic prospects in the region.

The expansion of the investor base was accompanied by an increase in the number of countries assigned credit ratings by major rating agencies (Table 6). During 1993 and the first half of 1994, Argentina, the Philippines, the Slovak Republic, Trinidad and Tobago, and Uruguay received initial subinvestment-grade ratings from the major U.S. credit rating agencies. Initial investment-grade ratings were also assigned to Colombia and Taiwan Province of China. In addition, Chile received an investment-grade rating from Moody's in February 1994, making it the only Latin American country to have received such a rating by the two major U.S. rating agencies. In March 1993, the Czech Republic became the only developing country in Europe with an investment-grade rating, and this rating subsequently was upgraded in May 1994. Other investment-grade countries receiving upgraded ratings during 1993 and the first half of 1994 included Chile, China, Israel, Malaysia, and Singapore. Owing to deteriorating economic conditions, conversely, Turkey was downgraded to a subinvestment grade rating in January 1994, and its rating was reduced further a few months later. The major rating agencies also downgraded Venezuela in March and April 1994.

Bond Pricing

The rapid increase in the prices of developing country bonds during 1993 raises some questions as to whether the markets were adequately pricing the risk of these securities. Moreover, the markets have at times appeared to react slowly to changes in economic conditions in a country.[16] In pricing bonds, the markets are reported to use two basic approaches. Risk may be priced on a relative basis, with bond yields set in relation to some benchmark issue or to the securities of other issuers judged to be of roughly comparable risk. Alternatively, market participants may attempt directly to assess risk using a scoring system based on a set of economic and political factors. Such scoring systems may vary widely in terms of their level of quantification, the factors considered, and the relative importance assigned to individual factors over time. All involve a high degree of judgment.

Observers suggest that Mexican bonds are frequently used as a benchmark, since Mexico is generally viewed as one of the best credit risks among those developing countries that previously rescheduled debts to private foreign creditors. To test this proposition, Granger causality tests were run on daily bond prices for sovereign issues by Argentina, Brazil, Hungary, Nigeria, the Philippines, Turkey, and Venezuela. The

---

[15]The Yankee bond market is the domestic U.S. market for U.S. dollar-denominated bonds issued by nonresident entities. Yankee issues are subject to SEC registration and disclosure requirements.

[16]Simple auto-regression tests of market efficiency were run on the prices of U.S. dollar-denominated sovereign bonds of Argentina, Brazil, Hungary, Mexico, Nigeria, the Philippines, Turkey, and Venezuela. In all cases, these tests suggest that the markets are inefficient.

Table 6. Credit Ratings of Developing Country Borrowers[1]

	Moody's Rating	S&P Rating	Recent Changes
Singapore	Aa2	AA+	Moody's upgraded rating from Aa3 in May 1994.
Taiwan Province of China	Aa3	AA+	Moody's assigned an Aa3 rating in March 1994.
Korea	A1	A+	
Thailand	A2	A–	
Malaysia	A2	A	Moody's upgraded rating from A3 in March 1993.
Hong Kong	A3	A	
China	A3	BBB	S&P (Standard & Poor's) assigned its BBB rating in February 1992, while Moody's assigned its rating A3 in September 1993.
Chile	Baa2	BBB+	Moody's assigned a Baa2 first-time investment rating in February 1994. S&P upgraded from BBB in December 1993.
Israel	NR	BBB+	S&P upgraded sovereign rating from BBB in September 1993.
Czech Republic	Baa2	NR	Moody's upgraded rating from Baa3 in May 1994.
Indonesia	Baa3	BBB–	S&P assigned first-time rating in July 1992.
India	Ba2	BB+	
Colombia	Ba1	BBB–	S&P and Moody's assigned first-time ratings in July and August 1993, respectively.
Hungary	Ba1	BB+	
Uruguay	Ba1	BB+	Moody's and S&P assigned ratings in October 1993 and February 1994, respectively.
Trinidad and Tobago	Ba2	NR	Moody's assigned first-time rating in February 1993.
Venezuela	Ba2	BB–	S&P downgraded its ratings in March 1994, while
(Conversion bonds)	Ba2	NR	Moody's downgraded its rating in April 1994.
(Par and discount bonds)	Ba3	NR	
Mexico	Ba2	BB+	S&P assigned first-time rating in July 1992.
(Par and discount bonds)	Ba3	BB+	
Slovak Republic	NR	BB–	S&P assigned its first-time rating in February 1994.
Philippines	Ba3	BB–	First-time ratings assigned in July 1993. S&P revised outlook to positive from stable in October 1994.
Turkey	Ba3	B+	S&P and Moody's downgraded the ratings below investment grade in January 1994 and March 1994, respectively, and downgraded several more times thereafter.
Argentina	B1	BB–	S&P assigned first-time rating in August 1993.
(Par discounts and bonds)		B2	
Brazil	B2	NR	

Sources: *Financial Times; International Financing Review;* and Salomon Brothers.

[1]Ranked in descending order according to rating. Ratings by Standard and Poor's and Moody's Investor Service. The ratings are ranked from highest to lowest as follows:

	Moody's	S&P
Investment grade	Aaa, Aa, A, Baa	AAA, AA+, AA, AA–, A+, A, A-, BBB+, BBB, BBB–
Noninvestment grade	Ba, B	BB+, BB, BB–, B+, B, B-
Default grade	Caa, Ca, C, D	CCC+, CCC, CCC–, CC, C

In addition, numbers from 1 (highest) to 3 are often attached to differentiate borrowers within a given grade.

tests used the price of the Mexican par bond as the benchmark for Brady bonds and the price of a Mexican new issue as the benchmark for Eurobonds. The results suggest that movements in the price of the Mexican par bond precede price movements in the par bonds of Argentina, Brazil, and the Philippines (Table A10). The price movements of the Mexican par bond, however, did not precede movements in either the prices of the Venezuelan or Nigerian par bonds, a result that could reflect country-specific factors.[17] Price movements in the Mexican Eurobonds were found to precede changes in the prices of most of the Eurobonds issued by the other countries sampled (Table A11).

The pricing of a bond should be in line with that of other bonds considered by the market as roughly comparable in terms of risk. The relationship between prices on U.S. corporate bonds and on bond issues from developing country sovereign borrowers with the same credit rating can provide some indication of how the markets view developing country risk (Chart 7). Deviations in the pricing of the two types of bonds, however, represent either mispricing of the riskiness of developing country bonds or market perceptions that such bonds are in fact riskier than their U.S. corporate counterparts (i.e., in the market's view, the rating agencies' ratings of developing country bonds are not accurate). IMF staff analysis indicates that Mexican and Philippine par bond prices and Hungarian and Turkish Eurobond prices do roughly track the prices of comparably rated U.S. corporate bonds, although prices for the latter two bonds are more volatile.[18] Argentina appears to have undergone a sharp reappraisal by the market of its creditworthiness in late 1992, and its yield steadily approached that of the comparable U.S. corporates, until early 1994. In the case of Venezuela, market perceptions of its creditworthiness may have adjusted much faster than the country's credit rating. The markets appear to have incorporated another downgrading into their pricing of Venezuelan bonds after the major credit rating agencies placed Venezuela on a credit watch. The market also appears to consider the unrated Brazilian and Nigerian par bonds as the equivalent of bonds rated below Caa.

The scoring systems used by market participants attempt more systematically to consider country-specific factors in bond pricing. Countries are ranked on the basis of a number of political and economic variables, and these rankings are used to assess the spread between the yield on a developing country bond and that on a "risk-free" bond. Factors often considered include (1) political conditions (e.g., the government's commitment to economic reform, its ability to implement policies, and popular support); (2) macroeconomic conditions (especially inflation, growth prospects, and fiscal policy); (3) structural reform; and (4) the country's balance of payments position and prospects. Data for the period 1989 to 1994 generally support the view that the market applies an ordinal ranking of developing country sovereign bonds in line with underlying economic fundamentals.[19] Among the Latin American Brady par bonds, Mexico carries the lowest spread, followed by Argentina, Venezuela, and Brazil (Chart 8). The markets considered Venezuela a better risk than Mexico prior to 1991, but since then Venezuela's spread has increased to approach that of Brazil. In contrast, the premium above Mexico paid by Argentina has declined steadily. The Philippines has also paid a spread higher than Mexico, and Nigeria's spread has been above that of the Philippines. Over time, though, the Philippine premium has narrowed, while Nigeria's spread has widened, reflecting differences in the relative economic performance of the two countries. Data from representative Eurobond issues present a more or less similar picture, taking into account the different duration and liquidity characteristics of the bonds.[20]

The movement in the secondary market spreads over time suggests a rough relationship with a country's rate of inflation and its level of foreign assets, perhaps because of the frequency of the availability of this information. For example, a very simple examination of the data reveals that the steady downward trend in the spread on Mexican bonds appears to have coincided with a period of declining inflation and rising foreign assets (Chart 9). The recent widening of the spread on Venezuela's bonds roughly coincided with a drop in net foreign assets and lagged a deterioration in inflation performance. The spread on Turkish bonds fell to less than 200 basis points by February 1994, before rising precipitously in March 1994; this turnaround took place five months after gross official

---

[17]In both countries, there was substantial deterioration in economic conditions and some political instability over the period tested.

[18]Since monthly price indices for subinvestment-grade U.S. corporates comprise only bonds with seven-year maturities, the analysis was conducted using Brady par bonds for the countries that have issued these securities. These bonds have remaining maturities of 25 years or more. A relatively constant differential between the prices of Brady bonds and U.S. corporate securities would largely represent a yield curve effect arising from the difference in the maturities of these two sets of bonds. For the Eurobonds analyzed, an adjustment had to be made to the prices of the developing sovereign bonds to factor in the effect of a declining yield curve as these securities moved closer to maturity.

[19]Unpublished work by William Cline at the Institute for International Economics has found on the basis of pooled cross-sectional data that countries that previously restructured bank debt and those with higher inflation and lower export or per capita GDP growth tend to have higher spreads on their new bonds. Preliminary regression analysis by IMF staff relating movements over time of country bond spreads to various indicators of economic fundamentals, however, did not produce significant results, in part owing to the limited time period for which data are available.

[20]A notable exception is the Venezuelan Eurobond. The lack of response in the yield spread for this bond to the deterioration in the country's recent economic performance may reflect the fact that the issuer of the bond is the state-owned oil company, which may be considered a better credit risk because of its external assets.

Chart 7. Comparison of Yields of Sovereign Bonds with Yields on U.S. Corporate Bonds

(In percentage points)

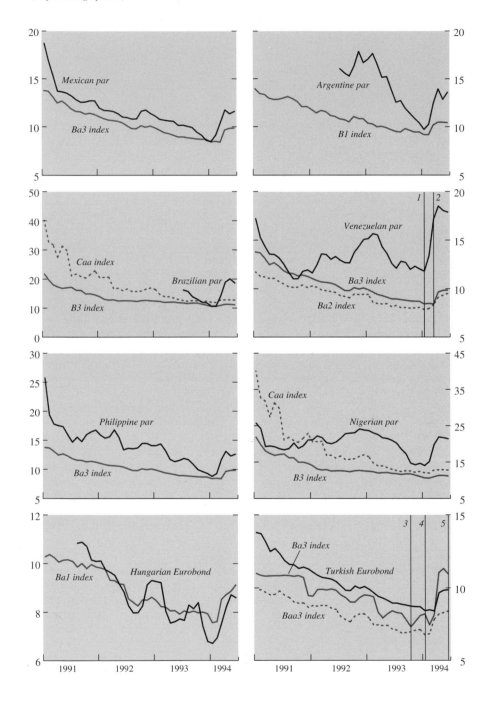

Sources: Moody's; Reuters; and Salomon Brothers.
[1]Venezuela placed on watch list by Moody's.
[2]Venezuela downgraded by Moody's to Ba3.
[3]Turkey placed on watch list.
[4]Turkey downgraded by Moody's to Ba1.
[5]Turkey downgraded by Moody's to Ba3.

reserves began to fall but roughly coincided with a reported surge in inflation (Chart 10). In the case of Hungary, the bond spread fell by roughly 200 basis points between September and December 1993; it then began to increase in early 1994, as foreign reserve assets declined and inflation turned up.

Equities

In contrast to bonds, the growth of equity placements in the international capital market moderated in 1993, after expanding sevenfold between 1990 and 1992 (Table 7). Issuance activity did pick up, however, in the final quarter of 1993, reflecting buoyant stock markets in Asia and Latin America. International equity placements by developing countries increased by 28 percent to $11.9 billion in 1993, but their share in total international equity placements declined to 23 percent from 41 percent in 1992. In the first half of 1994, developing country equity issues declined only moderately to $6.9 million from $7.7 billion in the second half of 1993. The lower issuance activity was accompanied by a general decline in share prices in major developing country stock markets.

Most international equity placements have been accounted for by Latin American and Asian companies. Latin American companies raised $5.7 billion in the international equity market in 1993 and $2.1 billion in the first half of 1994. Argentina emerged as the leading Latin American issuer, with issues increasing from $0.4 billion in 1992 to $2.8 billion in 1993. Issues occurred mainly through the vehicle of American depositary receipts (ADRs)[21] and were predominantly accounted for by the privatization of Yacimientos Petroliferos Fiscales (a state-owned oil and gas company) which raised $2.4 billion. Equity issues by Mexican companies declined from $3.1 billion in 1992 to $2.5 billion in 1993, partly because of uncertainty over approval of the North American Free Trade Agreement. Following approval, Mexican companies raised $1.7 billion in the final quarter of the year, mainly through ADR and global depositary receipt (GDR) programs;[22] this included an $822 million GDR offering by Grupo Televisa. Companies in Bolivia, Colombia, and Peru entered the market for the first time in 1993, together raising $127 million.

Asian companies raised $5.7 billion in 1993 and $3.8 billion in the first half of 1994. In 1993, companies from China were the leading issuers, raising $1.9 billion, or double the amount raised in 1992. In addition to "B" shares listed in Shanghai and Shenzhen and

[21]An ADR is a U.S. dollar-denominated equity-based instrument backed by shares in a foreign company held in trust. ADRs are traded like the underlying shares of stock on major U.S. exchanges or in the over-the-counter market.

[22]A GDR is similar to an ADR, but it is issued and traded internationally.

Chart 8. Comparison of Sovereign Bond Spreads

(In basis points)

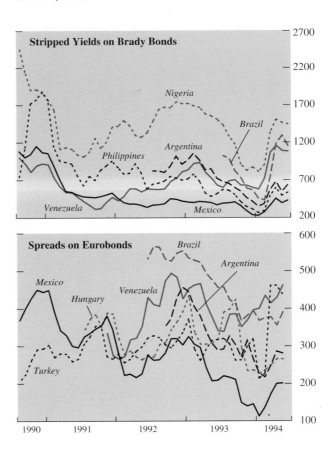

Sources: Reuters; Salomon Brothers; and IMF staff estimates.

reserved for foreign investors, Chinese companies in July 1993 began issuing shares listed on the Hong Kong Stock Exchange, so-called H shares. Other major developments included the first global equity placement by a Chinese company in July 1993 that combined ADRs and H shares, and the first equity placement in August 1993 by a private Chinese company on the Hong Kong Stock Exchange. Indian companies stepped up equity placements, raising over $1 billion in early 1994, compared with $0.3 billion in 1993, as they shifted away from convertible bonds to take advantage of the premium provided by a stock market boom. In light of the subsequent weakness in markets worldwide, however, Indian equity placements declined significantly. Indonesian entities, for their part, accelerated their equity issuance until March 1994, when the authorities moved to stem capital inflows. During the same period, a company in Sri Lanka entered the international equity market for the first time through GDRs, and entities from Bangladesh tapped the international equity market through small issues denominated in local currency.

Chart 9. Comparison of Movements in Spreads and Economic Variables for Mexico and Venezuela

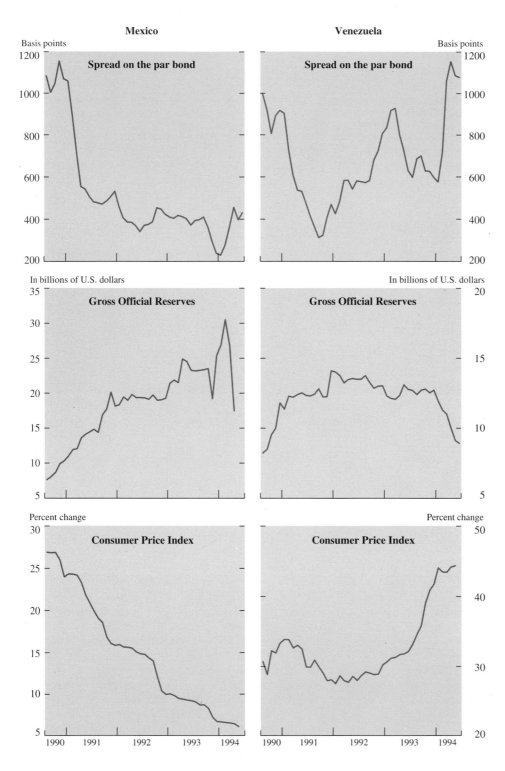

Sources: Reuters; Salomon Brothers; and IMF staff estimates.

Chart 10. Comparison of Movements in Spreads and Economic Variables for Hungary and Turkey

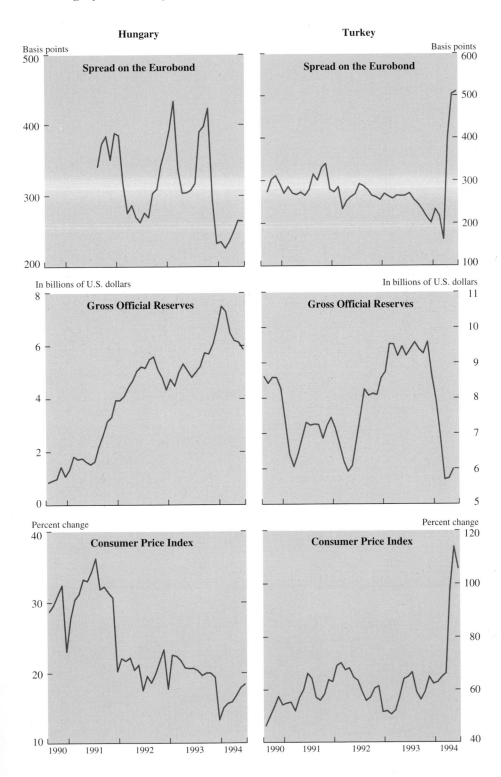

Sources: Reuters; Salomon Brothers; and IMF staff estimates.

Table 7. International Equity Issues by Developing Countries and Regions

(In millions of U.S. dollars)

| | 1991 | 1992 | 1993 | 1993 | | | | 1994 | |
				I	II	III	IV	I	II
Developing countries	**5,436**	**9,259**	**11,865**	**1,000**	**3,200**	**2,351**	**5,312**	**3,823**	**3,090**
Africa	143	270	8	—	—	—	8	—	466
Ghana	—	—	—	—	—	—	—	—	398
Morocco	—	—	8	—	—	—	8	—	—
South Africa	143	270	—	—	—	—	—	—	68
Asia	1,022	4,732	5,673	653	847	1,244	2,927	2,313	1,528
Bangladesh	—	—	19	3	15	—	—	—	3
China	11	1,049	1,908	115	343	550	900	364	247
Hong Kong	140	1,250	1,264	374	—	250	640	72	—
India	—	240	331	—	—	137	194	1,160	420
Indonesia	167	262	604	74	67	263	200	342	—
Korea	200	150	328	28	150	—	150	150	209
Malaysia	—	382	—	—	—	—	—	—	—
Pakistan	11	48	5	—	5	—	—	—	49
Philippines	159	392	64	—	—	44	19	2	—
Singapore	125	272	613	41	171	—	401	70	—
Sri Lanka	—	—	—	—	—	—	—	37	—
Taiwan Province of China	—	543	72	—	72	—	—	—	219
Thailand	209	145	466	18	24	—	424	116	380
Europe	91	67	202	2	28	—	172	330	150
Hungary	91	33	17	2	7	—	9	—	150
Poland	—	—	1	—	1	—	—	—	—
Turkey	—	34	184	—	20	—	164	330	—
Middle East	60	127	257	38	22	189	8	4	20
Israel	60	127	257	38	22	189	8	4	20
Western Hemisphere	4,120	4,063	5,725	307	2,304	917	2,197	1,176	927
Argentina	356	372	2,793	—	2,095	380	318	197	380
Bolivia	—	—	10	—	—	—	10	—	—
Brazil	—	133	—	—	—	—	—	300	—
Chile	—	129	271	—	114	94	63	96	71
Colombia	—	—	91	27	—	—	64	—	82
Mexico	3,764	3,058	2,493	280	95	443	1,674	583	346
Panama	—	88	—	—	—	—	—	—	—
Peru	—	—	26	—	—	—	26	—	48
Venezuela	—	283	42	—	—	—	42	—	—
Total equity issues in international equity market	15,548	22,632	51,654	4,300	8,554	15,863	22,937	12,900	15,600
				(In percent)					
Share of developing countries in global issuance	35.0	40.9	23.0	23.3	37.2	14.8	23.2	29.6	19.8

Sources: IMF staff estimates based on *Euroweek, Financial Times, International Financing Review (IFR),* and IFR Equibase.

International equity issues by companies in the rest of the developing world remained limited, with the exception of Turkey and Ghana. In the first half of 1994, a Turkish automobile company (TOFAS) raised $330 million through ADRs and GDRs. Ashanti Goldfields (a gold-mining company) in Ghana raised $398 million through GDRs. Companies from Morocco and Poland entered the market for the first time in 1993 with small issues.

Over the past few years, direct equity purchases by international investors on local exchanges have become another important source of equity inflows for several developing countries. Although comprehensive statistics are not available, fragmentary information suggests that the direct purchases of equities have been quite sizable. In addition, mutual funds have become increasingly important sources of equity flows to developing countries. The number of so-called emerging market mutual equity funds increased from 91 in 1988 to 465 in 1992 and 573 in 1993. Total net assets in these funds rose from about $6.0 billion in 1988 to $81.5 billion in 1993 (Chart 11 and Table A12).[23] The significant rise in the net asset position of emerging market mutual funds in 1993 largely reflected a sharp run-up in share prices in developing countries. The overall price index compiled by the International Finance Corporation (IFC) for developing country stocks that foreign investors are allowed to purchase (referred to as the investable index) rose by 75 percent in 1993 (Charts 12 and 13). Share prices in some Asian markets more than doubled during that year. Adjusting for these share-price increases, net purchases of developing country equities by emerging market mutual funds (including purchases of equities issued in international capital markets) can be approximated.[24] Mutual fund purchases of developing country equities are estimated to be $12.6 billion in 1993, compared with $8.4 billion in 1992 (Table A13). Issuance of closed end emerging market mutual funds accounted for $2.0 billion of the total in 1993 (Table A14).

Despite a sharp drop in stock prices, the number of emerging market mutual equity funds increased by more than 90 in the first quarter of 1994, probably reflecting the time lag involved in establishing these funds. The net asset value of all funds increased by about $9 billion, despite the large decline in share prices that occurred during that quarter. Data on open-end emerging market mutual funds domiciled outside the United States, however, suggest that the growth of emerging markets funds slowed considerably in the second quarter of the year. Issuance of shares in closed end emerging markets mutual funds also declined sharply from $4.2 billion in the first quarter of 1994 to $0.5 billion in the second quarter.

Mutual funds targeting Asian developing countries accounted for over 50 percent of total net assets in emerging market funds during 1993. Although global mutual funds have recently expanded considerably, it is reported that their investments have also been concentrated on Asian equities. Mutual funds designated for Latin American countries accounted for only 12

---

[23]Emerging market mutual funds' investment in developing country bonds has been limited. In 1993, net assets of fixed income funds amounted to only $8.5 billion. These figures are based on information provided by Emerging Market Funds Research, Inc., and Lipper Analytical Services, Inc. Since funds that have invested less than 60 percent of their portfolio in emerging markets are not included, developing country assets purchased by mutual funds may be understated. On the other hand, to the extent that emerging market mutual funds usually hold part of their assets in cash or developing country assets, the net asset value of these funds may overstate actual investment in emerging markets securities.

[24]Net equity purchases are estimated by deflating changes in net assets of each regional fund by the corresponding IFC investable share price index. The estimates are subject to a wide margin of error, especially because the country weights used for the IFC's regional and global indices may differ from the country composition of the equities held by the funds.

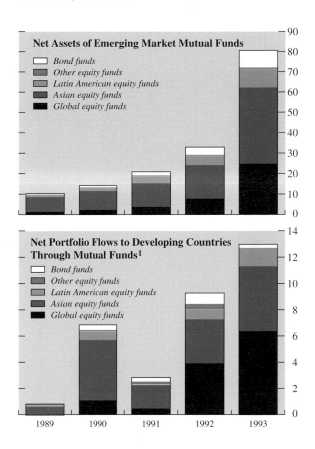

Chart 11. Emerging Market Mutual Funds

(In billions of U.S. dollars)

Sources: Emerging Market Funds Research, Inc; and Lipper Analytical Services, Inc.

[1]Net flows to developing countries are estimated by deflating changes in net assets of funds by IFC investable share price indices.

percent of the total net assets in emerging market funds.

Commercial Bank Lending

Banks began to show a renewed interest in lending to developing countries in 1993. In contrast to portfolio flows, however, the increase in medium- and long-term bank lending was modest. Medium- and long-term bank commitments to developing countries increased by 7 percent to $21 billion during the year (Table A15).[25] Banks in general, however, shortened maturities, raised spreads, and continued to use a variety of risk-reducing techniques like asset securitiza-

---

[25]As the total for 1992 was affected by a large credit to Saudi Arabia, the underlying growth was probably higher. The figure excludes loans guaranteed by export credit agencies.

Chart 12. Share Price Indices for Selected Markets In Latin America
(IFC Weekly Investable Price Indices, December 1988 = 100; in U.S. dollars)

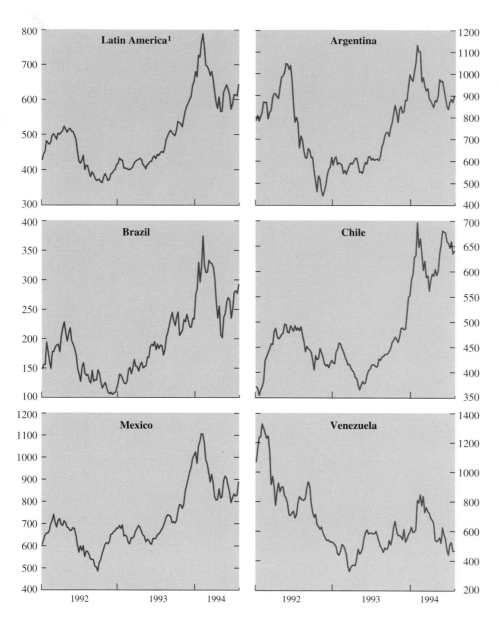

Source: IFC Emerging Markets Data Base.
[1]Argentina, Brazil, Chile, Colombia, Mexico, and Venezuela.

tion. The weighted average maturity of uninsured bank credits to developing countries declined from 6.7 years in 1992 to 5.5 years in 1993 (Table 8) and the weighted average spread over the LIBOR rose from 86 basis points in 1992 to 106 basis points in 1993. In the first half of 1994, the weighted average maturity increased to 6.8 years, and the spread narrowed to 99 basis points. But actual spreads varied considerably among developing countries ranging from 60 to 70 basis

points for borrowers in *Korea* and *Malaysia* to 300 basis points for borrowers in *India* and *Mexico* (Table A16). The U.S. dollar continued to be the most important currency of denomination, accounting for over 80 percent of total syndicated loans to developing countries in 1993.

The bulk of syndicated bank loans continued to be directed toward Asia, although lending to Latin America increased significantly in 1993. After having

Chart 13. Share Price Indices for Selected Markets In Asia
(IFC Weekly Investable Price Indices, December 1988 = 100; in U.S. dollars)

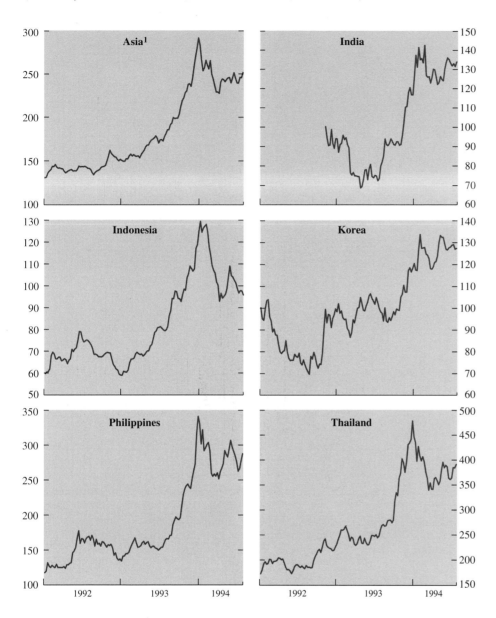

Source: IFC Emerging Markets Data Base.
[1]India, Indonesia, Korea, Malaysia, Pakistan, the Philippines, Taiwan Province of China, and Thailand.

declined in 1992, uninsured medium- and long-term bank loan commitments to Asian borrowers increased to $15.7 billion in 1993. China continued to be the largest Asian borrower, receiving loans totaling $3.6 billion in 1993. It was followed by Thailand ($3.4 billion), Hong Kong ($2.0 billion), Korea and Indonesia ($1.9 billion each), and Malaysia ($1.6 billion). In the first half of 1994, loan commitments to Asia amounted to $9.2 billion, including $3.7 billion to Thailand.

Other noteworthy developments included the first sovereign loan to Indonesia since 1991 ($400 million) and a $1.2 billion loan to a petroleum company in Thailand, the largest single borrowing in the Asian market in the past five years.

In Latin America, uninsured medium- and long-term bank loan commitments increased from $0.9 billion in 1992 to $2.2 billion in 1993. Venezuela increased bank borrowing to $0.8 billion in 1993, partly owing to

Table 8. Terms of Long-Term Bank Credit Commitments[1]

	1989	1990	1991	1992	1993	Jan.–June 1994
Average maturity *(in years)*	6.2	6.8	5.4	5.7	5.5	5.8
OECD countries	5.8	5.8	5.1	5.7	4.4	5.7
Eastern Europe	8.3	11.9	. . .	. . .	. . .	. . .
Developing countries	7.3	9.8	7.6	6.7	5.5	6.8
Other	8.8	7.7	3.5	6.9	5.3	5.0
Average spread *(basis points)*	56	54	79	85	81	82
OECD countries	54	51	80	86	77	79
Eastern Europe	49	50	. . .	. . .	. . .	. . .
Developing countries	68	66	75	86	106	99
Other	32	66	71	60	83	35
Memorandum items (in percent)						
Six-month Eurodollar interbank rate (average)	9.27	8.35	6.08	3.90	3.41	4.31
U.S. prime rate (average)	10.92	10.01	8.46	6.25	6.00	6.46

Sources: Organization for Economic Cooperation and Development (OECD), *Financial Market Trends;* and IMF, *International Financial Statistics* (for Eurodollar and prime rates).
[1]The country classification and loan coverage are those used by the OECD.

loans raised by public sector oil exporters. Argentina received $0.4 billion in commitments for the first time in the 1990s, while Brazil, Chile, and Mexico maintained access to bank credits on the order of $0.2–0.4 billion. In the first half of 1994, however, bank loan commitments to Latin American borrowers declined sharply to only $0.2 billion.

New commitments to developing countries in Europe remained subdued, amounting to $2.6 billion in 1993 and $0.6 billion in the first half of 1994. Those commitments were confined to a handful of countries. Turkey continued to be the major borrower, receiving new commitments of $1.9 billion in 1993; however, banks in 1994 became more cautious in light of the country's economic difficulties. Bank loan commitments to other European countries remained small, although several countries made their debut in the international credit markets, including the Czech Republic and Slovenia. A widely publicized DM 1.4 billion cofinancing facility for the Czech Republic's Skoda Automodilova was canceled in September 1993, as its German parent revised its international investment activity. New bank commitments to the Middle East increased to $1.3 billion in the first half of 1994, compared with $0.4 billion in 1993, while bank lending to Africa remained almost nonexistent.

Other Issues

The strong growth in demand for developing country securities in 1993 occurred even though these assets were generally riskier than their counterparts in developed financial markets. Returns on equities in some developing countries have been significantly more volatile than those in the United States. Similarly, returns on selected developing country bonds have tended to be more volatile than returns on comparable U.S. Treasury bonds (Chart 14). Despite the higher risk inherent in developing country equities, investors sought the significantly higher returns offered by these assets and increasingly perceived that these would offer good opportunities for risk diversification.

The evidence shows that equity returns in many developing countries have low or negative correlations with equity returns in the United States and other developed financial markets and that returns among many developing country equities are relatively uncorrelated.[26] This pattern of correlations suggests that the expected return of a portfolio can be increased for a given level of risk by adding developing country equities, even though these assets are riskier on average than equities in industrial country markets.[27] Total returns on developing country bonds (both Brady bonds and new issues) have also been relatively uncorrelated with the total return on comparable U.S. Treasury bonds and among themselves (Tables A17 and A18).

These historical correlations change over time and are not a certain guide to future relationships between returns on industrial and developing country securities.

---

[26]International Finance Corporation (1994b).

[27]Consider an example of two very risky assets with the same average return, but that always move in the opposite direction, that is, their returns are perfectly negatively correlated. A portfolio divided equally between these two assets would in principle involve no risk, as the movements in the two asset returns would always offset each other. Thus, a portfolio composed of both assets would yield the same expected return, while involving less risk than a portfolio consisting entirely of either one of the assets. These points have been applied to portfolios with emerging markets assets in a number of research papers, such as Campbell (1993).

Chart 14. Weekly Volatility of Total Returns on Bonds and Equities for Selected Countries[1]
(In percent)

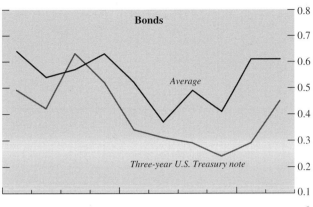

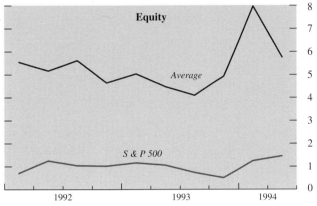

Sources: International Finance Corporation; and Reuters.
[1]Simple volatility averages of representative bond issues and IFC investable equity indices for Argentina, Brazil, Hungary, Korea, Mexico, Thailand, Turkey, and Venezuela.

The correlation between prices on Brady bonds and U.S. Treasury securities rose substantially in 1993 and the first half of 1994. Returns on new developing country bond issues also became more highly correlated with U.S. bond returns and among each other in the first half of 1994. Correlations among equity returns appear to have been more stable, although for some countries correlations rose significantly in the first half of 1994 (Table A19). This evidence suggests that the benefits to be gained by diversifying into developing country securities may be weaker in periods of significant market disturbances.

The volatility of returns on many developing country securities has not tended to diminish over time, and for many countries it increased in the first half of 1994. Strong movements in 1994 followed a period of rapid expansion in the investor base, which raises questions about the relationship between market volatility and the stability of that base. In the traditional analytical

view, growth in the number of investors should diminish volatility over time as new investors add liquidity and more diversity of risk preferences. This implies that a market could be cleared with smaller movements in prices.[28] Such a view, however, is based on the assumption that differences in expectations, risk preferences, and liquidity needs among investors are purely random, which means that new investors are essentially drawn from the same population as existing investors. If, instead, new investors differ systematically from existing investors with respect to such considerations, an expansion of the investor base could contribute to higher volatility. For example, if new investors have much poorer information, their expectations will be more variable, and their entry into the market could add to price volatility.

The traditional framework also assumes that no individual investor is able to influence the price of assets traded in the market. Recent analytical work, however, has focused on the implications of a less-competitive structure in financial markets.[29] In such a context, the investor base in a market can be assumed to consist of small, risk-averse investors, arbitragers, and a few large investors with inside information and an ability to influence market prices. To maintain the value of their inside information, large investors might try to conceal their trades from other market participants, suggesting that the price of the asset will not necessarily reflect all available information. In this situation, an increase in the number of large investors could at least initially add to volatility.[30]

The experiences of developing countries that have opened their stock markets to foreign investors do not provide a clear picture as to the relationship between market volatility and the investor base. The volatility of equity returns in 17 developing countries was compared before and after the opening of their equity markets to foreign investors; the results show that price volatility increased in eight cases (Table 9).[31] The volatility of equity purchases was also examined for 14 of these countries using U.S. balance of payments data that provide country details on purchases by U.S. residents.[32] In all cases, these data show that both the volume and volatility of equity purchases by U.S. investors increased substantially after these countries opened their stock markets to foreign investors (Table 10).

---

[28]This view of the structure of a financial market is reviewed in Grossman and Stiglitz (1980).
[29]This approach is developed in Kyle (1985) and Campbell and Kyle (1993).
[30]The ability of large traders to conceal their trades would be expected to diminish over time as the number of large traders increased.
[31]The indices of equity prices were drawn from the Emerging Markets data base of the International Finance Corporation.
[32]U.S. Department of Treasury, *Treasury Bulletin.*

Table 9. Total Returns on Equity in Selected Emerging Market Countries:
Before and After Opening to Foreign Investors[1]

(In percent at annual rate)

	Before		After	
	Mean	Volatility[2]	Mean	Volatility[2]
Greece	1.7	28.3	29.4	45.6
Portugal	107.1	72.8	5.6	24.9
Turkey	52.4	79.5	47.6	71.7
Jordan	10.6	16.4	11.6	18.6
Argentina	63.9	102.6	61.8	63.6
Brazil	13.9	56.5	75.1	59.8
Chile	33.5	41.9	42.3	25.8
Colombia	32.1	21.9	67.2	42.4
Mexico	24.0	47.0	45.2	27.3
Venezuela	6.3	40.6	52.8	49.2
India	19.2	25.9	21.8	34.6
Korea	20.8	30.6	8.8	28.5
Malaysia	12.1	31.6	25.1	23.9
Pakistan	12.3	10.5	46.4	35.8
Philippines	76.9	38.3	23.0	36.5
Taiwan Province of China	52.9	54.3	14.4	50.4
Thailand	20.6	23.9	29.0	31.5

Source: IFC Emerging Markets data base.

[1]Time period is 1976, quarter I to 1994, quarter II. The actual dates of opening to foreign investors are as follows: Greece—December 1988; Portugal—December 1988; Turkey—August 1989; Jordan—December 1988; Argentina—October 1991; Brazil—May 1991; Chile—December 1988; Colombia—February 1991; Mexico—May 1989; Venezuela—January 1990; India—November 1992; Korea—January 1992; Malaysia—December 1988; Pakistan—February 1991; Philippines—October 1989; Taiwan Province of China—January 1991; Thailand—December 1988. For analytical purposes, and to capture the fluctuations in the market caused by changes in investor expectations, the opening date was taken to be four months prior to the actual date.

[2]Volatility is measured by the standard deviation of the percent change in the IFC total return indices.

Table 10. U.S. Net Purchases of Foreign Equity in Selected Countries:
Before and After Opening to Foreign Investors

(In millions of U.S. dollars)

	Before		After	
	Mean	Volatility[1]	Mean	Volatility[1]
Greece	−0.4	4.5	41.3	20.0
Portugal	1.8	3.2	58.6	44.8
Argentina	−1.2	12.2	1,037.8	496.6
Brazil	50.7	71.9	1,165.9	403.4
Chile	2.6	9.9	114.3	73.8
Mexico	24.4	26.5	2,283.5	1,331.2
Venezuela	−0.5	3.0	1.5	66.2
India	0.8	2.1	149.7	99.8
Korea	2.7	16.3	817.9	502.9
Malaysia	13.1	16.3	275.8	162.7
Philippines	3.8	14.4	94.3	57.3
Taiwan Province of China	−4.2	12.6	27.7	34.4
Thailand	15.6	13.7	29.1	48.9

Source: U.S. Treasury, *Treasury Bulletin.*

[1]Measured by the standard deviation.

IV

Institutional and Regulatory Framework for Developing Country Financing

Efforts by many developing countries to establish reliable domestic capital markets have played an important role in attracting foreign capital. This section reviews recent measures adopted to improve the institutional setting of those markets, to harmonize regulations, and to broaden investor bases at home and abroad. It also reviews recent changes in regulations in creditor countries affecting the access of developing countries to international capital markets.

Reform of Regulatory Structures

Over the last year, many emerging market countries have taken steps to improve the quality of regulation in their capital markets. Mexico introduced thoroughgoing reforms in 1993. New measures strengthened the supervisory authority of the Comisión Nacional de Valores, improved the institutional structure of the stock market, and formalized automated trading. Uruguay is taking similar steps to regulate its capital markets and create an independent securities regulator, which will take over functions currently exercised by the central bank. In February 1994, Poland introduced a new securities law to govern the over-the-counter securities market.

Russia has some 80 small stock exchanges dispersed throughout the country, and most trading is conducted over the counter. In a recent survey, about half of the country's privatized enterprises envisaged raising capital with new share issues in 1994 (and from July 1, 1994, all shares are to be sold for cash rather than vouchers). The country's recently formed Commission on Securities and Stock Exchanges is now responsible for unifying all state agencies under a single entity and developing regulations. The Commission is currently drafting legislation to create a single independent regulatory body that will have jurisdiction over such matters as disclosure requirements and clearing and settlement systems.

Following an overhaul of China's regulatory framework in early 1993, a number of further revisions were made over the last year. A permanent National Securities Law, however, has yet to be ratified by the People's Congress.[33] In an effort to restrict the rising incidence of informal curb markets, the authorities have made it mandatory for all shares to be issued and traded through state-run securities firms. Following the closure of a large black market exchange, Chengdu, in southwestern China's Sichuan province, is currently seeking to establish China's third stock exchange after Shenzhen and Shanghai. Efforts to increase the listings and quality of "B" shares, and thereby to attract more foreign investors, are being taken across the exchanges. The Shenzhen Stock Exchange, for example, recently introduced a number of measures aimed at improving disclosure, regulation, and accounting standards applying to "B" shares.

Many countries over the last year have taken actions to improve disclosure, listing, and accounting standards, which make local capital markets more transparent and promote investor confidence. Introduced in December 1993, Venezuela's Comisión Nacional de Valores issued regulations to harmonize the financial statements of companies listed on the country's stock exchanges and to clarify the responsibilities of auditors in the preparation of financial reports. Peru's Bolsa de Valores de Lima now requires that all listed companies disclose complete financial information for parent companies. In Malaysia, all listed companies now have to establish audit committees, which review internal accounting controls, supervise external financial reporting, and assure accurate financial disclosure.

Deficiencies in investor protection can seriously undermine investor confidence in emerging markets.[34] As markets mature and develop in sophistication, countries have increasingly recognized the need, in particular, to improve the enforcement of measures to limit and oversee insider trading. From the beginning of 1994, for example, the Securities Board of India (SEBI) has introduced a series of legislative measures specifically aimed at tightening investor protection. These include regulating all transactions between clients and brokers and permitting the SEBI to inspect

---

[33]Early in 1993, the State Council Securities Policy Commission assumed chief responsibility for regulation and surveillance for China's securities markets. Temporary regulations were introduced governing the domestic market ("A" shares and bonds) and Hong Kong flotations ("H" shares). As yet, China's "B" shares for foreign investors, listed on the Shanghai and Shenzhen exchanges, do not necessarily receive the same level of protection. For further information of developments of China's capital markets, see Goldstein and others (1994).

[34]According to the IFC, of 22 emerging markets, only 6 have investor protection laws of internationally acceptable quality. See International Finance Corporation (1994b).

the books of debenture trusts. The SEBI has also been empowered to prosecute companies whose prospectuses misrepresent the facts. Further plans include requiring disclosure on a continuous basis and improving transparency through screen-based trading and internationally acceptable custodial and depository services. In Malaysia, the Kuala Lumpur Stock Exchange recently introduced new minimum standards of conduct for member brokerage firms to ensure equal opportunities and information for all clients. Peru introduced a new insider trading law at the end of 1993 that specifically forbade the use of preferential information. In Chile, insider trading was more clearly defined and made punishable by law in January 1994. Plans by Chile's Superintendencia de Valores y Seguros to improve market surveillance, including the expansion of electronic monitoring capacity, will strengthen enforcement. Similar changes to Mexico's National Securities Law late in 1993 included much stricter legislative criteria and penalties on the misuse of insider information. Finally, Poland's new securities law, among other things, establishes strict penalties for securities offenses, including the falsifying of information in prospectuses.

Steps also continue to be taken to improve clearance and settlement procedures in emerging markets as well as to enhance overall trading systems. The efficiency of such systems can help to promote rapid market development, and several countries are moving toward fully electronic systems. Well-developed procedures help to ensure effective surveillance and regulatory control, promote investor confidence, and facilitate cross-border securities transactions. Chile, for example, has recently established a centralized clearing house and depository, which was expected to be fully operational for equity-fixed income and money market trading by the end of 1994. Venezuela is presently formulating plans for a similar depository. Currently, the custodial function is decentralized, with asset titles held by the transfer agent, brokerage house, custodian bank, or final investors. Over the last year, Mexico's national securities depository (S.D. INDEVAL) has been authorized to provide simultaneous payment and securities delivery, as well as direct securities clearance services in ADR-related operations. These modifications are specifically aimed at providing efficient trading and liquidation, and overcoming differences in settlement periods across international markets. Having commenced electronic trading in 1991, Singapore's stock exchange is expected to have a completely electronic settlement system this year. As part of Indonesia's plans to improve settlement procedures and strengthen enforcement capabilities, Jakarta's stock exchange intends to replace manual trading with computerized trading in mid-1994. During 1994, Hungary established a fully operational clearing house and share depository, which has reduced settlement time.

Expanding the Investor Base

Several countries have established new securities markets where none previously existed. At the beginning of 1994, Zambia formalized a securities regulatory regime, with oversight power invested in a Securities and Exchange Commission. This permitted the opening of the country's first stock exchange, which commenced operations in Lusaka in February. Nepal also opened its first stock exchange in January 1994, and 62 firms listed their shares. Nicaragua is expected to open a securities exchange, which will be the prime vehicle for the privatization of state assets.

In an effort to provide smaller companies with easier access to investable funds, a number of countries have recently established second-tier markets characterized by less stringent listing and disclosure requirements. This has the benefit of providing a phased movement to full public listing; it also assists in longer-term efforts to deepen markets. Recent changes to Mexico's Securities Law, for example, defined a second market with more lenient regulatory and disclosure requirements. Similarly, Brazil released draft regulations in February 1994 for a special over-the-counter market to handle smaller companies. In the Czech Republic, while listed companies on the Prague Stock Exchange must provide quarterly as well as annual financial reports and are required to promptly report substantive events affecting the value of their shares, unlisted but tradable companies face more lenient disclosure requirements.

Many developing countries with advancing capital markets have also expanded their efforts to widen the product range of assets available and to liberalize investors' access. Colombia recently modified rules to allow small and medium-sized investors access to securitized bond issues. In tandem, new legislation permitted both the state oil company and other public sector entities to issue securitized debt related to infrastructure projects; securitization of real estate assets has also been allowed. Under Venezuela's new banking law, banks can now diversify into securities other than traditional instruments like certificates of deposit. Thailand recently relaxed its restrictions on provident funds to enable them to invest in unsecured instruments. Similarly, Chile has permitted pension funds to invest in nonrated company shares, derivatives, and foreign securities; securitized paper has also been expanded to include home mortgages.

The creation of credit rating agencies can also help to expand the investor base by standardizing and improving the quality of available information. Several countries, therefore, allow foreign credit agencies to participate in joint ventures in their domestic markets to help develop credit criteria that conform to international standards. Over the last year, a number of countries have also introduced domestic rating agencies. Chile recently modified the role of the National Ratings Commission (NRC) to preclude it from making its own evaluations but to extend its authority to oversee the work of private agencies. Peru recently set up a risk classification commission to develop a credit rating system in line with international standards. Under the current stock market code and new legislation relating to recently formed pension funds, the Peruvian authorities have specified that all institutional investors must operate within such a system. In early 1994, Venezuela's CNV established regulations for new credit risk agencies, the first of which opened in March. Colombia also opened its first risk-rating agency (under foreign ownership) in late 1993.

Several countries have made it easier for foreign brokers to operate in domestic markets, often in partnership with domestic companies. Such measures potentially have the virtues of facilitating the transfer of valuable information technology and of providing a useful degree of comfort for new foreign investors. In an effort to enhance market competition, the Security and Exchange Commission in Taiwan Province of China reduced capital requirements for foreign brokerage firms and brought them into line with domestic houses.[35] In April 1994, Thailand allowed foreign brokerage firms to purchase up to 49 percent of the shares of Thai securities firms. In March 1994, Russia granted the first securities license to a foreign-owned investment institution. Similarly, Poland is scheduled to allow foreign brokers to set up offices.

In the course of market development, a greater variety of instruments become available to investors. This allows them to diversify their portfolio and hedge possible risks more effectively. Derivative instruments, including futures, options, and warrants, greatly enhance flexibility. To make effective use of such instruments, however, markets need adequate liquidity in underlying assets. Well-functioning regulatory structures and clearing-and-settlement systems also are essential. Without adequate liquidity and regulatory oversight, the premature introduction of such instruments can increase the risk of destabilizing fledgling domestic securities markets and undermining the local banking system. With such factors in mind, Taiwan Province of China is currently in the final phase of a three-stage program to establish a domestic futures market; operations are scheduled to begin in late 1994. Thailand recently commissioned a feasibility study on the establishment of a similar market; the study is aimed particularly at specifying necessary regulatory structures, capital adequacy requirements, and product ranges. Hong Kong is expected to open an options market in late 1994 in line with continuing efforts to expand the availability of financial derivatives. Likewise, in October 1993, Mexico approved the trading of inflation-linked options based on government securities linked to the consumer price index. Finally, in February 1994, Venezuela issued regulations to govern new markets for options and futures.

Regulatory Harmonization

During the past few years, countries have been cooperating more intensively on capital market regulatory issues. Such efforts tend to accelerate as domestic markets become more mature. Countries with relatively advanced markets commonly see greater integration as a way of improving their global competitive positions. Regulatory harmonization, however, can also strengthen emerging markets.[36]

A recent study by the Development Committee of the International Organization of Securities Commission surveyed securities regulatory commissions of 23 developing countries and found that nearly all were moving toward harmonizing procedures, regulatory requirements, and accounting standards.[37] Many are also removing restrictions on the sale of local securities abroad and foreign securities in local markets. On the basis of this survey, three goals were set: (1) to promote the provision of reliable information on changes and improvements in international regulatory procedures and accounting standards; (2) to stimulate the interest of members in lifting restrictions on the placement of local securities in foreign markets and foreign securities in local markets; and (3) to organize regional associations that will help overcome difficulties commonly faced in emerging markets.

Consistent with the latter goal, a number of countries in Latin America passed legislation over the last year providing for the approval of cross-border listings with nearby countries. The MERCOSUR group of countries (Argentina, Brazil, Paraguay, and Uruguay), for example, had passed legislation by early 1994 to allow the trading of stocks and bonds across one another's markets. Colombia recently approved the listing of foreign companies on its domestic market, provided certain listing and disclosure requirements were met. It also broadened the scope for domestic companies to make public offerings abroad. Separately, Argentina is considering granting Mexican companies access to its local capital market. Mexico's new National Securities Market Law established an international trading section on the Mexican exchange and allowed a recently created central depository institute (INDEVAL) to serve as custodian for foreign securities. This enables local brokers to complete transactions in foreign securities for their clients. In an analogous effort to promote interregional investment as well as to facilitate privati-

---

[35]Foreign brokers have been allowed to operate in Taiwan Province of China since early 1993, but only one full branch has in fact opened.

[36]For further information on the integration of capital markets in developing countries with those in the rest of the world, see Goldstein and others (1993).

[37]International Organization of Securities Commissions (1993).

zation, the stock exchanges of Bahrain, Jordan, Kuwait, Oman, Morocco, and Tunisia were expected to be linked by September 1994; the Arab Monetary Fund was providing assistance. Similarly, the Hong Kong Stock Exchange announced its intention to focus on attracting equity placements by foreign countries (particularly China).

In order to promote information sharing and advance toward market integration, a number of countries have recently negotiated memoranda of understanding with one another. In Latin America, all countries have signed memoranda with at least one other country, often a regional partner. In March 1994, for example, the Venezuelan and Colombian securities commissions signed a memorandum of understanding to formalize cooperation on the exchange of information about changes in regulatory and judicial issues, technical assistance, and investor protection. One purpose of the agreement is to combat money laundering. In early 1994, the London Stock Exchange and the Shanghai Securities Exchange also signed a memorandum of understanding to promote technical cooperation and lay foundations for the joint listing and trading of securities. In addition, Brazil's Bolsa de Mercadorias and Futuros and the New York Mercantile Exchange signed a memorandum of understanding to share information on regulatory and technical issues.

Regulatory Changes in Creditor Countries

Securities Markets

In November 1993, the U.S. Securities and Exchange Commission (SEC) adopted measures to simplify the listing of foreign companies in U.S. markets. The new measures include recognition of international accounting standards, easier registration procedures, and reducing the required reporting history from three years to 12 months. They also narrow the size requirement for a public flotation from $300 million to $75 million. Over the last year, the SEC has also assigned "recognized custodian status" to a number of emerging markets. This allows the foreign custodian to handle securities deposited by American investors, which simplifies clearance and settlement procedures. To a large extent, this recognition reflects improvements in the institutional environment in several developing countries, including Mexico and Thailand. In a similar vein, during the last year, the SEC accorded "ready market status" to Mexican Government debt instruments denominated in pesos, including treasury certificates

(CETES), inflation-adjusted bonds (ADJUSTABONOS), and long-term instruments (BONDES). This modification allows U.S. securities firms to assign only a 7 percent capital charge against the asset, in contrast to the 100 percent charge required previously.

In analogous moves, the Australian Stock Exchange recently proposed to establish a separate "Asian market" trading board in order to attract listings from China and other Asian countries. At present, around 14 Chinese companies have expressed an interest along with a number of firms from Korea, Malaysia, and Singapore. It is expected that by the end of 1994 up to 10 companies could be listed. Asian companies intending to list would have to comply with the same requirements that apply to domestic firms, including abiding by international auditing standards and submitting semiannual reports.

Provisioning Standards

Over the past several years, nearly all creditor countries have modified their provisioning requirements for commercial banks in light of the improving prospects of many developing countries.[38] Although this trend in part reflects the stronger capitalization of creditor banks, it is also based on the enhanced creditworthiness of certain indebted countries. Sound macroeconomic policies, the effective restructuring of existing commercial bank debt, and the restoration of access to the international capital markets, all underlay the trend.

Provisioning requirements now tend to be much more responsive to variations in creditworthiness. For example, changes introduced by Belgium and Switzerland in 1993 replaced flat cover ratios of 60 percent and 65 percent, respectively, with a graded system that assesses debt-servicing capacity and a range of macroeconomic and political factors. In most countries, average provisioning to cover exposure to developing countries has declined. In Japan, however, where bank provisioning is relatively low by international standards, a reduction in developing country exposure has helped to raise the average level of provisioning. In addition, an increase in provisioning by German banks over the last few years reflects proportionately higher exposure to Eastern Europe and the countries of the former Soviet Union (Table A20).

---

[38]For further information on regulatory practices in creditor countries as well as procedures by which developing countries may "graduate" from the need for creditor banks to make provisions, see Collyns and others (1992 and 1993).

V

Foreign Direct Investment

Along with the rise in portfolio capital inflows, developing countries have experienced a surge in foreign direct investment inflows during the 1990s. Like portfolio capital, these inflows have gone to a relatively small number of countries in Latin America and Asia. Their sharp rise is in part explained by factors that are likely to exert an influence over a limited period of time, such as the privatization of government assets or the rebalancing of asset holdings in response to economic reforms in developing countries. Although foreign direct investment is often perceived as a relatively stable source of financing, a review of experience in the 1980s of a sample of highly indebted developing countries suggests a more cautious view. When balance of payments difficulties are encountered, the net impact of all transactions associated with foreign direct investment (including both current and capital account transactions) may serve to exacerbate external imbalances.

Recent Trends in Direct Investment

Since the mid-1970s, when only modest flows were recorded, net inflows of foreign direct investment to developing countries have risen rapidly.[39] Nevertheless, there have been substantial fluctuations around this upward trend (Table A21 and Chart 15). For example, a surge in inflows has occurred since 1990. Over the period 1991–93, cumulative net inflows amounted to $134 billion. In real terms, net foreign direct investment flows to developing countries in the early 1990s were almost two and a half times their average level in the 1980s.

The surge in foreign direct investment is notable not only for its size, but also for its coincidence with the growth of other private capital flows. The rate of increase in net foreign direct investment in developing countries since 1990 has been comparable with that of portfolio flows. This simultaneous upturn in both direct and portfolio inflows contrasts sharply with previous experiences of private capital surges to developing countries. For example, bond financing was dominant in the 1920s and 1930s, but defaults during the interwar period led in the first twenty years of the postwar period to foreign direct investment replacing bonds as the primary form of capital inflow. A new surge in portfolio flows, specifically in the form of bank lending, began in the 1960s and peaked in the early 1980s, but it was accompanied by a steep decline in foreign direct investment flows.[40]

Although many countries have experienced increases in direct investment inflows, as was the case with previous surges, the latest upturn has been concentrated in only a few countries. Three countries—Brazil, Indonesia, and Mexico—accounted for over 60 percent of all foreign direct investment flows to developing countries between 1971 and 1981.[41] At the end of the 1980s, 63 percent of the total stock of foreign direct investment in developing countries was held in five countries—Brazil, China, Egypt, Malaysia, and Mexico. In contrast, the five developing countries with the most external debt—Argentina, Brazil, India, Indonesia, and Mexico—accounted for only 33 percent of the total stock of debt.[42] Between 1990 and 1993, the bulk of foreign direct investment flows went to two regions: Latin America and Asia.

In Latin America, the total inflow doubled after 1990. It reached $14 billion in 1992 before declining modestly to around $13 billion in 1993. Over this period, average annual inflows were two to three times higher than in the 1980s. Two thirds of the total foreign direct investment inflow to Latin America during the period went to Mexico and Argentina, with Chile, Venezuela, Brazil, and Colombia accounting for a large share of the remainder. Developing countries in Asia received an estimated $66 billion in foreign direct investment inflows in 1991–93, roughly half of the total flow to developing countries. China was by far the largest recipient, accounting for more than 40 percent of the inflows to Asia. Malaysia and Singapore were also major recipients of foreign direct investment, but at less than half of the level of flows to China. In the case of Malaysia, this represented a substantial pickup in inflows, while for Singapore it represented a relatively steady inflow of investment. Thailand and Indonesia also saw sizable foreign direct investment inflows over the period. Inflows to the economies in transition in Central and Eastern Europe also rose sharply over the period 1991–93, amounting to

---

[39]Net foreign direct investment inflows are defined as foreign direct investment capital inflows less capital outflows for direct investments abroad by domestic residents.

[40]See Cardoso and Dornbusch (1988).
[41]Edwards (1990).
[42]Claessens (1993).

Chart 15. Net Foreign Direct Investment to Developing Countries
(In billions of U.S. dollars)

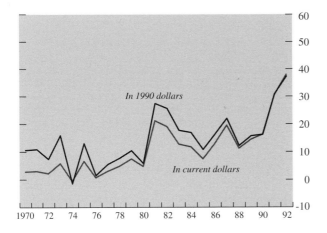

Source: World Economic Outlook data base.

approximately 10 percent of total foreign direct investment inflows to developing countries. Finally, annual flows to Africa were largely unchanged in 1991–93, with almost all of the funds going to Nigeria and South Africa.

The nature of and motivation for foreign direct investment suggest that longer-term considerations play a role in explaining these flows. As a result, direct investment might be expected to exhibit greater stability than other types of private capital flows.[43] Moreover, there are factors at work in the global economy, such as growing trade, greater market homogeneity, and improved communications technology, that should provide long-term impetus for increased flows of foreign direct investment.[44] While all of this may be true in general, the recent experience of developing countries may be explained by a number of factors that can be expected to have an impact over a more limited period of time.

Far-reaching economic reforms—including the removal of legal restrictions on capital movements and on nonresident holdings of domestic assets—have eliminated many of the barriers that formerly acted to deter foreign direct investment. At the same time, the alleviation of debt burdens has sharply lessened risks for all would-be investors.[45] Thus, the response of foreign direct investment to these changes may to an extent represent a stock adjustment—implying a one-time rebalancing of the pattern of corporate asset holdings in response to policy changes in host countries.

Foreign direct investment related to privatization has also been an important factor in the recent upturn, particularly in flows to Latin America. The potential for further foreign direct investment inflows from new privatizations, however, will inevitably depend on the size of the remaining stock of public sector assets that can be earmarked for sale. In general, the pace of this type of inflow can be expected to slow as countries near the end of their privatization programs. There may be further inflows related to the restructuring of newly privatized enterprises, but these are not likely to continue on the scale of the initial inflows associated with the sale of the enterprises.

Beyond such specific factors, general economic expansion in the largest recipient countries also contributed to the recent surge in foreign direct investment. Domestic growth not only provides foreign firms with enhanced investment opportunities, it also provides a pool of funds for reinvestment. In part because enterprises typically view such internally generated resources as cheaper than funds raised in the capital market, reinvested earnings now account for a large proportion of total foreign direct investment capital flows. Reinvested earnings, nonetheless, appear to move procyclically; a slowdown in economic growth has a dampening effect.

Behavior of Foreign Direct Investment Transactions in a Crisis

Foreign direct investment capital flows have been viewed as potentially providing a more stable form of financing for economic development, as well as a substitute for reduced flows of commercial bank financing.[46] An important question remains, however, about the behavior of such flows when a country encounters balance of payments difficulties.[47] It is widely argued that the longer-term motivations for foreign direct investment, together with the substantial costs usually entailed in liquidating fixed assets, would result in these flows being less responsive to adverse short-run macroeconomic developments.

The stability of foreign direct investment capital flows during crisis periods would, indeed, appear to be largely confirmed by a review of balance of payments data reported to the IMF.[48] Chart 16 shows the compo-

---

[43]See Lizondo (1991).
[44]See Graham and Krugman (1993).
[45]Dooley (1986).

[46]See, for example, Goldsbrough (1986) and Cardoso and Dornbusch (1988) for discussion of these issues.
[47]See Claessens, Dooley, and Warner (1993); the authors find that broadly speaking foreign investment is no less volatile on a year-on-year basis for a given country than other capital flows.
[48]These data conceptually include reinvested earnings of domestic affiliates of foreign firms. In practice, however, the recording of reinvested earnings is incomplete in many developing countries. Foreign direct investment statistics are usually compiled by the central bank using actual cross-border flows and generally fail to adequately capture the reinvested portion of domestic affiliates' earnings.

sition of total net private capital flows to six heavily indebted countries that experienced external payments difficulties during the 1980s.[49] The data are expressed in real terms, deflating U.S. dollar values by an index of the unit price of exports for industrial countries. While small in magnitude compared with other private short- and long-term flows, net foreign direct investment capital flows were relatively stable throughout the debt crisis. Moreover, after rising substantially in the late 1970s, those flows returned to previous levels in the 1980s. Throughout the period, inflows of foreign direct investment were recorded, while sizable outflows of other forms of investment occurred in the mid-1980s.

Focusing solely on recorded capital flows, however, may not fully capture the influence of foreign direct investment on a country's external position. Whether foreign direct investment contributes to or alleviates a balance of payments "shock" depends on the behavior of the net flow resulting from both current and capital account transactions between a domestic affiliate and its foreign parent. Conceptually, all earnings from affiliated companies are assumed to accrue to their foreign parents and are included in current account transactions; the portion of earnings that is reinvested by the foreign parents in their affiliates is recorded as an inflow in the host country's capital account. Thus, the net impact of foreign direct investment transactions is measured by associated capital inflows (comprising both reinvested earnings and "new" investment flows) less total earnings of foreign-owned companies. There is an a priori reason to expect that, in addition to the stability of inflows through the capital account, foreign direct investment may also exert a stabilizing influence during a crisis through its effects on the current account. Current account outflows in the form of repatriated earnings may be expected to decline during a crisis, since the crisis is likely to reduce the total earnings of foreign-owned companies.

To capture fully the influence of foreign direct investment transactions on a country's external position, it is important that the data accurately record total earnings and total capital flows (i.e., reinvested earnings are fully accounted for). Given uncertainties about the coverage of balance of payments data in many countries, U.S. data on U.S. direct investment abroad have been used to examine the overall balance of payments effects of foreign direct investment transactions for the six heavily indebted countries discussed above.[50] While the U.S. data capture only the activity of U.S. firms, they have the advantage of including all

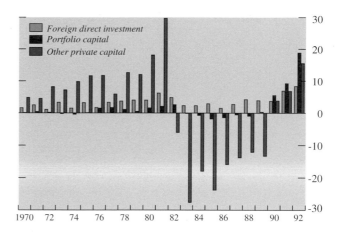

Chart 16. Composition of Net Private Capital Flows[1]
(In billions of 1985 U.S. dollars)

Sources: IMF, *International Financial Statistics*; World Economic Outlook; and IMF staff estimates.
[1]Argentina, Brazil, Chile, Mexico, the Philippines, and Venezuela. Excludes errors and omissions.

components of direct investment and, thus, may better capture short-run changes in the behavior of foreign investors. The data are also likely to be broadly representative, owing to the fact that U.S. companies account for roughly half of the foreign investment in the group of six heavily indebted developing countries.

For U.S. affiliates, total earnings fell when external payments difficulties of the host countries became more severe. These affiliates, however, responded to the crisis by reducing reinvested earnings by more than the decline in total earnings. Repatriated earnings, thus, remained relatively stable, and actually increased throughout the period. In 1983, repatriated earnings exceeded income, generating negative reinvested earnings (i.e., a reduction in the assets of the U.S. affiliates in these countries).

The sharp drop in reinvested earnings during the crisis was accompanied by a decline in flows of other foreign direct investment capital to the six countries. With the more complete coverage of reinvested earnings in the U.S. data, it appears that there was substantially more volatility in foreign direct investment inflows during the debt crisis than is suggested by the balance of payments data for the six countries. Moreover, the foreign direct investment capital inflows shown in the U.S. data appear to have behaved in a manner generally consistent with domestic investment as a whole in the host countries. For the group of countries surveyed,

---

[49]Argentina, Brazil, Chile, Mexico, the Philippines, and Venezuela.

[50]U.S. Department of Commerce, *Survey of Current Business,* various issues. All data have been converted into 1985 U.S. dollars using an index of the unit value of industrial country exports. Earnings data and repatriated earnings data are expressed net of with-

holding taxes and include interest received from loans. Beginning in 1981, earnings and reinvested earnings data exclude increases in the dollar value of stocks either through exchange rate changes or through capital gains or losses.

domestic investment fell from 24 percent of GDP in 1981 to 18 percent of GDP in 1985, reflecting poor output performance, low profitability, and an unstable financial environment. Net resource transfers back to the parents increased sharply beginning in 1983 and continued until 1991. Over the period 1983–89, these transfers averaged around 7 percent per year of the total stock of U.S. direct investment in the six countries.

This analysis contrasts with the perception that direct investment flows may help stabilize the balance of payments during a crisis. The persistence of large net resource transfers associated with foreign direct investment out of the six countries sampled here may be related to the balance of payments difficulties these countries encountered. In common with all other external creditors, foreign investors faced the risk that the unallocated loss implied by these debt-service difficulties could fall on them, and they appear to have been reluctant to commit to new investment until expected losses to creditors declined, as signaled by increases in the secondary market value of debt.[51] The recent surge in direct investment inflows into these countries has largely corresponded with a return to creditworthiness and renewed access to foreign capital markets in general.

_____
[51]Dooley (1986).

Statistical Appendix

Table A1. Chronology of Bank Debt Restructurings and Bank Financial Packages, 1984–July 1994

Agreement classified by month of signature[1]

1984
Brazil: January[2]
Chile: January, June, and November
Sierra Leone: January
Guyana: January, July (deferment)
Nicaragua: February (deferment)
Peru: February[3]
Senegal: February
Niger: March
Mexico: April (new financing only)
Sudan: April (modification of 1981 agreement)
Yugoslavia: May
Jamaica: June
Zaïre: June (deferment)
Poland: July[2]
Madagascar: October
Liberia: December[3]
Zambia: December[3]

1985
Côte d'Ivoire: March[2]
Mexico: March, August
Costa Rica: May[2]
Senegal: May
Philippines: May[2]
Zaïre: May (deferment)
Guyana: July (deferment)
Argentina: August[2]
Jamaica: September
Panama: October[2]
Sudan: October (modification of 1981 agreement)
Chile: November[2]
Colombia: December[4]
Ecuador: December[2]
Madagascar: December (modification of 1984 agreement)
Yugoslavia: December

1986
Dominican Republic: February
Morocco: February
Venezuela: February
South Africa: March (standstill)
Niger: April
Zaïre: May (deferment)
Brazil: July

Uruguay: July
Poland: September[2]
Romania: September
Congo: October[2, 3]
Côte d'Ivoire: December

1987
South Africa: March
Mexico: March (public sector debt)[2], August (private sector debt)
Jamaica: May
Mozambique: May[3]
Zaïre: May (deferment)
Chile: June
Honduras: June[3]
Madagascar: June (modification of 1985 agreement)
Argentina: August[2]
Morocco: September
Romania: September (modification of 1986 agreement)
Bolivia: November (amendment to 1981 agreement)
Nigeria: November[2, 3]
Venezuela: November
Gabon: December[5]
Philippines: December

1988
Gambia, The: February
Chile: August (amendment to 1987 agreement)[3]
Uruguay: March (modification of 1986 agreement)
Côte d'Ivoire: April[2, 3]
Guinea: April
Togo: May
Poland: July
Yugoslavia: September[2]
Malawi: October
Brazil: November[2]

1989
Nigeria: April
Zaïre: June (deferment)
Poland: June (deferment)[3]
South Africa: October
Honduras: August[3]

Niger: October[3]
Trinidad and Tobago: December

1990
Philippines: February[2]
Mexico: February[2]
Madagascar: April
Bulgaria: April (standstill)[3]
Costa Rica: May
Jamaica: June
Morocco: September
Senegal: September
Chile: December (amendments to previous agreements)
Venezuela: December[2]

1991
Colombia: April [5]
Niger: April
Uruguay: January[2]
Brazil: May[6]
U.S.S.R., former: December (deferment)
Mozambique: December
Nigeria: December

1992
Algeria: March
Gabon: May
Philippines: July[2]
Guyana: November
Argentina: December

1993
Uganda: February
Bolivia: March
Russia: July[3]
South Africa: September
Brazil: November[2]
Jordan: December

1994
Dominican Republic: February
Gabon: May
Bulgaria: June
Zambia: July
Poland: September[2]
Ecuador: October

Under negotiation

Albania	Nicaragua	Russia
Congo	Panama	Sao Tome and Principe
Côte d'Ivoire	Peru	Sierra Leone
		Tanzania

Sources: Restructuring agreements.
Note: "Restructuring" covers rescheduling and also certain refinancing operations.
[1]Agreement either signed or reached in principle (if signature has not yet taken place); not all signed agreements have become effective.
[2]The restructuring agreement includes new financing.
[3]Agreed in principle or tentative agreement with banks' Steering Committees.
[4]Refinancing agreement.
[5]A separate club deal for new financing was arranged at the same time.
[6] Preliminary agreement on interest arrears.

Table A2. Amounts of Medium- and Long-Term Bank Debt Restructured[1]

(In millions of U.S. dollars; by year of agreement in principle)

	1986	1987	1988	1989	1990	1991	1992	1993	First Half 1994
Argentina	—	29,500[2]	—	—	—	—	27,980[3]	—	—
Bolivia	—	473[3,4]	—	—	—	—	170[3,4]	—	—
Brazil	6,671[5]	—	61,000[2]	—	—	7,100	46,600[3]	—	—
Bulgaria	—	—	—	—	—	—	—	8,666	—
Chile	—	5,902[2]	—	—	1,800[6]	—	—	—	—
Congo	217	—	—	—	—	—	—	—	—
Costa Rica	—	—	—	1,570[3]	—	—	—	—	—
Côte d'Ivoire	691[2]	—	2,211[2]	—	—	—	—	—	—
Dominican Republic	—	—	—	—	—	—	—	1,100[3,7]	—
Ecuador	—	—	—	—	—	—	—	—	7,117[7]
Gabon	—	39	—	—	—	157	—	—	150[7]
Gambia, The	—	19	—	—	—	—	—	—	—
Guinea	—	43	—	—	—	—	—	—	—
Guyana	(57)[8]	—	—	—	—	—	—	93[9]	—
Honduras	—	248[2]	—	132[2]	—	—	—	—	—
Jamaica	—	285[2]	—	—	332	—	—	—	—
Jordan	—	—	—	—	—	—	—	857[3]	—
Madagascar	—	. . .[10]	—	—	21	—	—	—	—
Malawi	—	—	35[2]	—	—	—	—	—	—
Mexico	43,700[2]	—	3,671[3]	48,231[3]	—	—	—	—	—
Morocco	2,174	—	—	—	3,150	—	—	—	—
Mozambique	—	253[2]	—	—	—	124[4,9]	—	—	—
Nicaragua	—	—	—	—	—	—	—	—	—
Niger	52	—	—	—	—	111[4,9]	—	—	—
Nigeria	4,250	—	5,824[2]	—	—	5,811[9]	—	—	—
Panama	—	—	—	—	—	—	—	—	—
Peru	—	—	—	—	—	—	—	—	—
Philippines	—	9,010[2]	—	781	1,339[9]	4,473[3]	—	—	—
Poland	1,970	8,411[2]	—	(351)[8]	—	—	—	—	12,669[7]
Romania	800	—	—	—	—	—	—	—	—
Russia	—	—	—	—	—	—	—	24,000[7]	—
Senegal	—	—	—	—	37	—	—	—	—
Sierra Leone	—	—	—	—	—	—	—	—	—
South Africa	(13,600)[8]	11,900[2]	—	8,000	—	—	—	5,000	—
Sudan	—	—	—	—	—	—	—	—	—
Togo	—	—	49[2]	—	—	—	—	—	—
Trinidad and Tobago	—	—	470[2]	—	—	—	—	—	—
Uganda	—	—	—	—	—	—	—	153[4,9]	—
Uruguay	—	1,770[2]	—	—	1,608[3]	—	—	—	—
Venezuela	—	20,338[2]	—	—	19,700[3]	—	—	—	—
Yugoslavia	—	—	6,895[2]	—	—	—	—	—	—
Zaïre	(65)[8]	(61)[8]	—	(61)[8]	—	—	—	—	—
Zambia	—	—	—	—	—	—	—	—	414[7]
Total[9]	60,525	87,221	80,155	50,714	27,987	17,776	74,843	40,276	20,350

Sources: Restructuring agreements; and IMF staff estimates.

[1]Including short-term debt converted into long-term debt and debt exchanges involving interest or principal reduction. Amounts represent face value of old claims restructured; includes past due interest where applicable.

[2]Multiyear rescheduling agreement (MYRA) entailing the restructuring of all eligible debt outstanding as of a certain date.

[3]Financing packages involving debt and debt-service reduction.

[4]Excludes past due interest.

[5]Excluding $9.6 billion in deferments corresponding to maturities due in 1986.

[6]Amendments to previous restructuring agreements.

[7]Estimates of eligible debt.

[8]Deferment agreement.

[9]Face value of debt extinguished in buy-back.

[10]Agreements in 1985 and 1987 modified debt-service profiles on debt rescheduled under the 1984 agreements; the amounts involved are not shown because repayments made during 1985–87 have not been identified.

Table A3. Terms and Conditions of Bank Debt Restructurings and Financial Packages, 1989–July 1994[1]

Country, Date of Agreement, and Type of Debt Rescheduled	Basis	Amount Provided (In millions of U.S. dollars)	Grace Period (In years, unless otherwise noted)	Maturity	Interest Rate (In percent spread over LIBOR/U.S. prime, unless otherwise noted)
Argentina Preliminary agreement on April 7, 1992; term sheet June 23, 1992; final agreement December 6, 1992 and closing of agreement for principal on April 7, 1993					
Collateralized debt exchange	Debt reduction (see Table A4)				
Bolivia Agreement in principle of April 1992; term sheet July 10, 1992; final agreement March 30, 1993 and closing of agreement on May 19, 1993					
Waiver to allow debt buy-back and exchanges	Debt reduction (see Table A4)				
Brazil Preliminary agreement on July 8, 1992; term sheet September 22, 1992; final agreement November 29, 1993 and closing of agreement April 15, 1994	Old debt (equal to 5.5 times the new money provided) to be exchanged at par for new noncollateralized bonds.	...	7	15	$\frac{7}{8}$
New money bonds					
Restructuring loan	Difference between interest rate in years 1–6 and LIBOR plus $\frac{13}{16}$ to be capitalized.	...	10	20	Years 1–2: 4 percent Years 3–4: 4.5 percent Years 5–6: 5 percent Years 7–20: $\frac{13}{16}$
Capitalization bond	Difference between interest rate in years 1–6 and 8 percent to be capitalized. Back-loaded amortization schedule.	...	10	20	Years 1–2: 4 percent Years 3–4: 4.5 percent Years 5–6: 5 percent Years 7–20: 8 percent
Collateralized debt exchanges	Debt reduction (see Table A4)				

Table A3 (continued)

Country, Date of Agreement, and Type of Debt Rescheduled	Basis	Amount Provided (In millions of U.S. dollars)	Grace Period (In years, unless otherwise noted)	Maturity	Interest Rate (In percent spread over LIBOR/U.S. prime, unless otherwise noted)
Bulgaria Agreement in principle on November 24, 1993; term sheet March 11, 1994; final agreement on June 29, 1994					
Collateralized debt exchange	Debt reduction (see Table A4)				
Costa Rica Preliminary agreement on November 16, 1989; final agreement on May 21, 1990	Debt reduction (see Table A4)				
Dominican Republic Preliminary agreement on May 3, 1993; term sheet August 6, 1993; final agreement on February 14, 1994					
Collateralized debt exchange	Debt reduction (Table A4)				
Ecuador Agreement in principle on May 2, 1994; term sheet June 14, 1994					
Collateralized debt exchange	Debt reduction (see Table A4)				
Gabon Agreement in principle on December 11, 1991; final agreement on May 12, 1992					
Rescheduling of principal due January 1, 1989–December 31, 1992	100 percent of principal	157	3	13	⅞
Guyana Agreement on term sheet on August 27, 1992; final agreement on November 24, 1992	Debt reduction (see Table A4)				

			Grace	Maturity	Interest rate
Honduras					
Agreements of August 17, 1989					
Bilateral concessional rescheduling of debt to Lloyds Bank					
Principal outstanding at end of October 1989	100 percent	46[2]	7	20	6.25 percent fixed rate[3]
Interest arrears at end of October 1989	100 percent	22[2,4]	7	20	6.25 percent fixed rate[3]
Bilateral concessional rescheduling of debt to Bank of America					
Principal outstanding	100 percent	47[2]	10	20	6.5 percent
Interest arrears as of end of October 1989	100 percent	17[4]	⅔	20	4 percent fixed rate
Jamaica					
Agreement on June 26, 1990					
Refinancing of debt previously rescheduled in 1987					
Tranche A	100 percent of principal	144	—	10½	¹³⁄₁₆
Tranche B	100 percent of principal	188	8	14½	¹³⁄₁₆
Jordan					
Agreement in principle on November 20, 1989					
Restructuring of medium-term loans maturing between January 1, 1989–June 30, 1991	100 percent of principal	580	5	11½	¹³⁄₁₆
New medium-term money facility	New money	50	3	3	¹³⁄₁₆
Preliminary agreement on June 30, 1993; term sheet August 20, 1993; final agreement December 10, 1993 and closing of agreement December 23, 1993					
Collateralized debt exchange	Debt reduction (see Table A4)				
Madagascar					
Agreement in principle in October 1989 and signed on April 10, 1990					
Rescheduling	100 percent of principal falling due on December 15, 1989 and 50 percent of principal falling due in 1990–93	21.1	3½	9	⅞–1

Table A3 *(continued)*

Country, Date of Agreement, and Type of Debt Rescheduled	Basis	Amount Provided	Grace Period	Maturity	Interest Rate
		(In millions of U.S. dollars)	*(In years, unless otherwise noted)*	*(In years, unless otherwise noted)*	*(In percent spread over LIBOR/U.S. prime, unless otherwise noted)*
Mexico					
Agreement on February 4, 1990					
New money	New money	1,090[5]	7	15	13⁄16
Collateralized debt exchanges	Debt reduction (see Table A4)				
Restructuring of maturities of eligible debt not subject to debt and debt-service reduction	100 percent of principal	6,400	7	15	13⁄16
Morocco					
Agreement in principle of April 1990; final agreement of September 1990					
Restructuring of the entire debt outstanding at end of 1989	100 percent of pre-cutoff debt	3,150	7–10	15–20	13⁄16
Debt buy-backs authorized					
Mozambique					
Agreement in principle on November 1, 1991; operation completed December 27, 1991					
Waivers to allow debt buy-back	Debt reduction (see Table A4)				
Niger					
Agreement in principle on January 14, 1991; operation completed March 8, 1991					
Waivers to allow debt buy-back	Debt reduction (see Table A4)				
Nigeria					
Agreement in principle of September 1988; final agreement of April 1989					
Restructuring of debt outstanding at end of 1987					
Not previously rescheduled medium-term debt	100 percent of principal	1,256	3	20	7⁄8

Item	Terms	Amount			
Nigeria (*continued*)					
Debt covered by the November 1987 rescheduling agreement	100 percent of principal	1,635	3	20	7/8
Debt (letters of credit) covered by the November 1987 refinancing agreement	Arrears on interest, fees, and commissions on letters of credit	2,448	3	15	13/16
	100 percent	490[6]	—	3	Non-interest-bearing
Agreement in principle of March 1991; final agreement December 20, 1991 and closing of agreement on January 21, 1992					
New money bond exchange	Banks would provide new money in an amount equivalent to 20 percent of debts exchanged for noncollateralized new bonds.	—			
Buy-back and debt exchange	Debt reduction (see Table A4)	—	7	15	1
Philippines					
Agreement in principle of October 1989; final agreement of February 1990:					
New money bonds or loans[7]	New money	710	8	15	13/16
Rescheduling of maturities falling due in 1990–93	100 percent of principal	781	8	15	13/16
Change in spread on previously restructured debt	—		13/16		
Waivers to allow debt buy-backs and exchanges	Debt reduction (see Table A4)	Unchanged			
Preliminary agreement of August 1991; term sheet February 1992, final agreement July 24, 1992 and closing of agreement on December 1, 1992					
New money bonds	Old debt (equal to four times the new money provided) to be exchanged at par bond for new noncollateralized bonds.	139[8]	5	17	13/16
Collateralized debt exchanges	Debt reduction (see Table A4)				
Poland					
Agreement in principle of June 16, 1989					
Deferment of amortization payments falling due between May 1989 and December 1990[9]	100 percent	206	...	...	Unchanged

Table A3 (*continued*)

Country, Date of Agreement, and Type of Debt Rescheduled	Basis	Amount Provided (*In millions of U.S. dollars*)	Grace Period	Maturity (*In years, unless otherwise noted*)	Interest Rate (*In percent spread over LIBOR/U.S. prime, unless otherwise noted*)
Poland (*continued*)					
Agreement in principle of October 1989 Rescheduling of interest falling due in the fourth quarter of 1989[10]	85 percent	145	...	...	
Agreement in principle on March 10, 1994; term sheet May 23, 1994 New money bonds	New money bonds to be provided corresponding to 35 percent of debt allocated to debt conversion bonds (see Table A4)	...	10	15	13/16
Collateralized debt exchange	Debt reduction (see Table A4)				
Russia					
Agreement in principle of July 30, 1993 Rescheduling of existing stock of debt and interest arrears	100 percent of principal	24,000	5	15	...
	100 percent of interest arrears after cash payments of $500 million	3,000	5	10	...
Senegal					
Agreement of September 1990	100 percent of principal	37	—	9	7/8
South Africa					
Debt arrangement of September 27, 1993 Rescheduling of short and medium-term debt subject to September 1985 standstill and falling due at expiration of third interim arrangement	100 percent of principal	5,000	1/2	8	1 1/8
Trinidad and Tobago					
Agreement in principle of November 1988; final agreement December 1989 Medium- and long-term maturities falling due September 1, 1988–August 31, 1992	100 percent of principal	446	4 1/2	12 1/2	15/16
Uganda					
Final agreement: February 26, 1993	Debt reduction (Table A4)				

Uruguay

Agreement in principle of November 1990; final agreement January 1991

New Money Bond Exchange

20 percent increase in exposure via purchase of new bonds would entitle banks to exchange at par old debt for noncollateralized "debt-conversion notes."   89   7   15

Buy-back and debt exchange

Debt reduction (see Table A4)   1.0

Venezuela

Agreement in principle on March 20, 1990; final term sheet of June 25, 1990; final agreement on December 5, 1990

New money bond exchange

Old debt (equal to five times the new money provided) to be exchanged at par for new, noncollateralized bonds.   1,197   7   15   1 and ⅞[11]

Collateralized debt exchanges

Debt reduction (see Table A4)

Zambia

Agreement in principle, July 1, 1994

Debt reduction (see Table A4)

Sources: Restructuring agreements; and IMF staff estimates.

[1] Arrangements approved in principle before January 1, 1989 are reported in previous background papers.

[2] Voluntary amortization payments made during the grace period would be matched on a 1:1 basis by debt forgiveness (equivalent to a buy-back option at 50 cents on the dollar).

[3] Interest rate would be increased by a maximum of 3 percentage points if GDP growth exceeds a threshold rate.

[4] Seventy percent of these arrears were forgiven in 1990 upon down-payment equal to 5 percent of these arrears. Beginning at the end of 1990 and provided that Honduras remained current on interest due on all rescheduled amounts under the agreement, the creditor bank would further forgive interest arrears by a yearly amount equal to 5 percent of the arrears outstanding at the end of October 1989.

[5] New money options include medium-term loan, new money bonds, on-lending facility, and medium-term trade facility. As of the end of March 1992, $952 million had been disbursed.

[6] Includes $112 million of previously capitalized interest arrears on letters of credit.

[7] Allowance for re-lending for up to 366 days of up to 20 percent of the new money on a revolving basis, of which one half would be available in any one calendar year and one half would be available to the private sector.

[8] Committed to the new money option at the end of June 1992, with 95 percent of eligible debt tendered under the package.

[9] Payment was to be deferred until December 30, 1991. Alternatively, banks would receive payments according to the original schedule in return for an equal increase in the short-term revolving trade facility.

[10] Payment was deferred until the second quarter of 1990.

[11] The interest rate of LIBOR plus ⅞ applies to the new money bonds issued by the central bank (as opposed to bonds issued by Venezuela).

49

Table A4. Debt and Debt-Service Reduction in Commercial Bank Agreements, 1987–July 1994

(By year of agreement in principle)

(In millions of U.S. dollars)

	Face Value of Debt to Commercial Banks		Resources Used	Terms	Enhancements for New Instruments	Special Features
	Retired	Issued				
Argentina (1987) Noncollateralized debt exchange with interest reduction	15	15	—	Old claims exchanged at par for new exit bonds with a 25-year maturity (12 years' grace) and 4 percent fixed rate.	—	New bonds excluded from future new money base.
Argentina (1992) Principal reduction	6,663	4,331	3,059[1] (including resources from IMF, World Bank, Inter-American Development Bank, Eximbank Japan, and Argentina's own resources)	Old claims exchanged for new bonds, with a 30-year bullet maturity and interest at LIBOR plus 13/16, at prenegotiated exchange ratio of 1:0.65.	Principal fully collateralized and 12-month rolling interest guarantee based on 8 percent rate.	Part of past due interest settled at closing date (through cash payments of $700 million). The balance refinanced (3 years' grace) bearing interest of LIBOR plus 13/16 and all semiannual amortization payments rising from 1 percent of the original face value in payments 1–7, 5 percent in payment 8, and 8 percent in payments 9–19.
Interest reduction	12,734	12,734		Old claims exchanged at par for new bonds with a 30-year bullet maturity and interest increasing gradually from 4 percent in year one, to 6 percent in year seven, and remaining at that level until maturity.	Principal fully collateralized and 12-month rolling interest guarantee based on 6 percent rate.	Interest due reduced to respective monthly LIBOR through end of 1991, and to 4 percent thereafter. Bonds eligible for debt conversion.
Bolivia (1987) Cash buy-back	253	—	28 (bilateral donations)	At preannounced price of 11 cents on the dollar.	—	—
Collateralized debt exchange with principal reduction	204	22	7 (bilateral donations)	Old claims exchanged for new zero-coupon 25-year bond carrying 9.25 percent yield at a preannounced exchange ratio of 1:0.11.	Principal and interest fully collateralized.	Past due interest canceled under all options. New bonds eligible for debt conversion.
Debt forgiveness	16	—	—	—	—	Includes $0.6 million of debt-for-nature swap.

Bolivia (1992)					
Cash buy-back	78	—	At preannounced price of 16 cents on the dollar.	—	Past due interest canceled under all options.
Interest reduction	33	27 (including resources from IDA debt-reduction facility and grants from the United States, Sweden, Switzerland, and the Netherlands)	33	Old claims exchanged at par for non-interest-bearing new bonds with a 30-year bullet maturity.	Principal fully collateralized.	Value recovery clause based on the world price of tin. Upon maturity, bonds exchanged into assets denominated in domestic currency at prenegotiated ratio of 1:1.5 for approved investment in special projects.
Principal reduction	60		10	Old claims exchanged for new short-term bonds at prenegotiated exchange ratio of 1:0.16	—	—
Brazil (1988)					
Noncollateralized debt exchange with interest reduction	1,100	—	1,100	Old claims exchanged at par for new exit bonds with a 25-year maturity (10 years' grace) and 6 percent fixed rate.	—	New bonds excluded from future new money base. Eligible for debt-equity conversion program.
Brazil (1992)					
Principal reduction	14,210		9,237	Old claims exchanged for new bonds with a 30-year bullet maturity and interest at LIBOR plus 13/16, at prenegotiated exchange ratio of 1:0.65.	Principal fully collateralized and 12-month rolling interest guarantee.	Cash payment of $2.0 billion paid during May–December 1991. The past due interest remaining at end of 1990 converted into a 10-year bond (3 years' grace) at LIBOR plus 13/16. Interest due in 1992–93 reduced to 4 percent.
Interest reduction	12,992	2,800 (own resources and about 400 of new money). Additional 900 are to be delivered in the next two years.	12,992	Old claim exchanged at par for new bonds with a 30-year bullet maturity and interest increasing gradually from 4 percent in year one, to 6 percent in year seven, and remaining at that level until maturity.	Principal fully collateralized and 12-month rolling interest guarantee.	
Temporary interest reduction	2,030		2,030	Old claim exchanged at par for new bonds with a 15-year maturity (9 years' grace) and an interest rate of 4 percent in the years 1–2, 4.5 percent in years 3–4, 5 percent in years 5–6, and LIBOR plus 13/16 from years 7 to 15.	Twelve-month rolling interest guarantee for the first six years.	Remaining past due interest accumulated in 1991 and 1992 is converted into 12-year bonds (3 years' grace) at LIBOR plus 13/16; semiannual amortization payments of 1 percent of original principal for payments 1–7, 5 percent for payment 8, and 8 percent bonds eligible for debt conversions for payments 9–19.

Table A4 (*continued*)

(In millions of U.S. dollars)

	Face Value of Debt to Commercial Banks		Resources Used	Terms	Enhancements for New Instruments	Special Features
	Retired	Issued				
Bulgaria (1993)						
Cash buy-back	798	—		At preannounced price of 25.1875 cents on the dollar.	—	Buy-back price applies to principal and interest arrears separately.
Principal reduction	3,730	1,865		Old claims exchanged for new bonds, with a 30-year bullet maturity and interest at LIBOR plus $^{13}/_{16}$, at prenegotiated exchange ratio of 1:0.50.	Principal fully collateralized and 12-month rolling interest.	At closing, 3 percent of past due interest will be settled through cash payments. The balance will be refinanced as an uncollateralized 17-year bond (7 years' grace) bearing interest of LIBOR plus $^{13}/_{16}$ and semiannual amortization payments rising from 1 percent of the original face value in payments 1–6 to 3 percent in payments 7–11, to 6 percent in payments 12–16 and to 9.8 percent in payments 17–21. Value recovery clause based on GDP performance. Package includes short-term debt. A special issue of discount and temporary interest reduction bonds will be made for 30 percent of the short-term debt allocated to these options at an interest rate $\frac{1}{2}$ of 1 percent higher. The package includes a currency option for deutsche mark. Agreement limits allocation for temporary interest reduction bonds to 30 percent.
Temporary interest reduction	1,658	1,658	652[2] (expected to come from IMF, World Bank, and own resources).	Old claims exchanged at par for new bonds with an 18-year maturity (7 years' grace) and an interest rate of 2 percent in years 1–2, 2.25 percent in years 3–4, 2.5 percent in year 5, 2.75 percent in year 6, 3 percent in year 7, and LIBOR plus $^{13}/_{16}$ from years 8 to 18.	Twelve-month rolling interest guarantee for the first seven years.	
Chile (1988)						
Cash buy-back	439	—	248 (own resources)	$299 million bought back in November 1988 at average price of 56 cents on the dollar; $140 million bought back in November 1989 at average price of 58 cents on the dollar. Price determined in Dutch auction.	—	Resources used for buy-backs subject to aggregate limit of $500 million; debt to be extinguished subject to aggregate ceiling of $2 billion.

Operation	Amount	Amount	Funding	Terms	Guarantees	Memorandum items
Costa Rica (1989)						
Cash buy-back	991	—		At preannounced price of 16 cents on the dollar.	—	Includes $223 million of past due interest.
Collateralized debt exchange with interest reduction	290	290	196[3] (from bilateral and multilateral sources and Costa Rica's own reserves)	(a) Old debt exchanged at par for new 20-year bond (10 years' grace) carrying 6.25 percent fixed, negotiated rate. (b) Past due interest, after 20 percent cash downpayment, exchanged at par for a new claim with a 15-year maturity (no grace period) and LIBOR plus 13/16.	(a) Eighteen-month interest guarantee (excess enhancement funds to be applied to increase coverage up to 18 months). (b) Thirty-six month interest guarantee.	(a) and (b) available only to banks tendering at least 60 percent of their exposure to the buy-back option. Value recovery clause linked to GDP growth. Converted past due interest equaled $53 million. (c) and (d) optional to banks tendering less than 60 percent of their exposure (including past due interest) to the buy-back option. Converted past due interest equaled $61 million.
Noncollateralized debt exchange with interest reduction	289	289		(c) Old claims (including past due interest) exchanged at par for a new 25-year bond (15 years' grace) carrying 6.25 percent fixed, negotiated rate. (d) Past due interest, after a 20 percent cash downpayment, exchanged at par for a new claim with a 15-year maturity (no grace period) and LIBOR plus 13/16.	—	(a), (b), (c), and (d): new bonds eligible for debt-equity conversion program. Value recovery clause activated if GDP exceeds 1989 GDP by 120 percent in real terms.
Dominican Republic (1993)						
Cash buy-back	272	—		At preannounced price of 25 cents on the dollar.	—	Buy-back price applies to principal and interest arrears separately.
Principal reduction	505	328	149 (own resources)	Old claims exchanged for new bonds with 30-year bullet maturity and interest at LIBOR plus 13/16 at prenegotiated exchange rate of 1:0.65.	Principal fully collateralized and 9-month rolling interest guarantee (to be capitalized until 12 months).	At closing, 12.5 percent of remaining past due interest will be settled through cash payments. The balance will be refinanced as uncollateralized 15-year bonds (3 years' grace) bearing interest of LIBOR plus 13/16 and semiannual amortization payments rising from 1 percent of the original face value in payments 1–7 and equal installments thereafter.
Temporary interest reduction	—			Old claims exchanged at par for new bonds with an 18-year maturity (9 years' grace) with equal semiannual installments after grace and an interest rate of 3 percent in years 1–2, 3.5 percent in years 3–4, 4 percent in years 5–6, and LIBOR plus 13/16 from years 7 to 18.	—	Agreement included a "pull-back" clause if banks' allocation does not yield at least 50 percent debt reduction.

53

Table A4 (continued)

(In millions of U.S. dollars)

	Face Value of Debt to Commercial Banks		Resources Used	Terms	Enhancements for New Instruments	Special Features
	Retired	Issued				
Ecuador (1994)						
Principal reduction	2,621	1,442		Old claims exchanged for new bonds with 30-year bullet maturity and interest at LIBOR plus ¹³⁄₁₆ at prenegotiated exchange ratio of 1:0.55.	Principal fully collateralized and 12-month rolling interest guarantee based on 7 percent.	Part of past due interest settled before closing (through cash payment of $75 million). The balance will be refinanced as an uncollateralized 20-year bond (10 years' grace) bearing interest of LIBOR plus ¹³⁄₁₆ and semiannual amortization payments rising from 2.5 percent of the original face value in payments 1–6 to 4 percent in payments 7–12, to 6.78 percent in payments 13–21. The past due interest bond will have the option to capitalize interest due in excess of the following rates during the first 6 years of the bond: 3 percent in years 1–2, 3.25 percent in years 3–4, and 3.75 percent in years 5–6. An uncollateralized 10-year interest equalization bond for $191 million will be issued to regularize presently discriminatory payments to creditors.
Interest reduction	1,898	1,898	583[4] expected to come from IMF, World Bank, official sources, and own resources	Old claims exchanged at par for new bonds with 30-year bullet maturity and interest increasing gradually from 3 percent in year 1 to 5 percent in year 11, and remaining at that level until maturity.	Principal fully collateralized and 12-month rolling interest guarantee at 3.75 percent (to be capitalized until it reaches 5 percent).	
Guyana (1992)						
Cash buy-back	69	—	10 (fully financed by IDA debt-reduction facility)	At preannounced price of 14.5 cents on the dollar.	—	Excludes export credit debt. Buy-back price applied to principal, past due interest ($23.5 million) canceled.
Jordan (1993)						
Cash buy-back	—	—		At preannounced price of 39 cents on the dollar.	—	Buy-back price applies to principal and interest arrears separately.
Principal reduction	243	158	118[5] (own resources)	Old claims exchanged for new bonds with a 30-year bullet maturity and interest at LIBOR plus ¹³⁄₁₆ at prenegotiated exchange ratio of 1:0.65.	Principal fully collateralized and 6-month rolling interest guarantee based on 8 percent.	At closing, 50 percent of past due interest associated with the discount exchange and 10 percent of past due interest associated with the par exchange will be settled through cash payments. The balance will be refinanced as uncollateralized 12-year bond (3 years' grace) bearing interest of LIBOR plus ¹³⁄₁₆ and equal semiannual installments after grace.

Interest reduction	493	493		Old claims exchanged at par for new bonds with a 30-year bullet maturity and interest increasing gradually starting at 4 percent in years 1–4, 5 percent in year 5, 5.5 percent in year 6 and 6 percent from years 7 to 30.	Principal fully collateralized and 6-month rolling interest guarantee based on 6 percent.	Interest due after March 1991 and until the closing date reduced to an interest rate of 4 percent.
Mexico (1988) Collateralized debt exchange with principal reduction	3,671	2,556	555 (own resources)	Old claims exchanged for new bond with 20-year bullet maturity and LIBOR plus 1⅜; average exchange ratio 1:0.7 (determined in Dutch auction).	Principal fully collateralized.	New bonds excluded from future new money base.
Mexico (1989) Collateralized debt exchange with principal reduction	20,546	13,354[6]	7,122 (including resources from IMF and World Bank)	Old claims exchanged for new bond with 30-year bullet maturity and LIBOR plus ¹³⁄₁₆; exchange ratio 1:0.65 (negotiated).	Principal fully collateralized and 18-month rolling interest guarantee	Recovery clause in case real oil prices exceed threshold real price of $14 a barrel. New bonds excluded from future new money base and eligible for debt-equity conversion.
Interest reduction	22,427	22,427		Old claims exchanged at par for new bond with 30-year bullet maturity and 6.25 percent fixed, negotiated interest rate.	Same as above	
Mozambique (1991) Cash buy-back	124	—	12 (including resources from IDA debt-reduction facility and French, Swiss, Swedish, and Dutch grants)	At a preannounced price of 10 cents on the dollar.	—	Buy-back price applied to principal, past due interest canceled.
Niger (1991) Principal reduction	111	—	23 (including resources from IDA debt-reduction facility and French and Swiss grants)	Old claims exchanged for new 60-day notes with face value equivalent to 18 percent of outstanding face value of principal.	Principal fully guaranteed by BCEAO.	Buy-back price applied to principal, past due interest canceled. Operation has been structured as a novation, that is, the exchange of a new obligation for an old obligation to avoid seeking waivers from certain provisions in existing loan contracts.
Interest reduction	...	...		Old claims exchanged at par for 21-year non-interest-bearing notes.	Principal fully collateralized by zero coupon bonds purchased by the BCEAO.	—

Table A4 (continued)

(In millions of U.S. dollars)

	Face Value of Debt to Commercial Banks		Resources Used	Terms	Enhancements for New Instruments	Special Features
	Retired	Issued				
Nigeria (1991)						
Cash buy-back	3,390	1,356	1,708[7] (own resources)	At preannounced price of 40 cents on the dollar.		All past due interest cleared prior to closing date. Recovery clause in the event that oil prices exceed threshold of $28 a barrel in 1996, adjusted for inflation thereafter. New bonds eligible for debt conversions.
Interest reduction	2,048	2,048		Old claims exchanged at par for new registered bonds with a 30-year bullet maturity and a fixed interest rate of 5.5 percent for 3 years and 6.25 percent thereafter.	Principal fully collateralized by U.S. Treasury bonds with a 12-month rolling interest guarantee, based on rate of 6.25 percent.	
Philippines (1989)						
Cash buy-back	1,339	—	670 (including resources from IMF and World Bank).	At preannounced price of 50 cents on the dollar.	—	Included waiver for second round of buy-backs.
Philippines (1992)						
Cash buy-back	1,263	—	1,125 (including resources from IMF, World Bank, Eximbank Japan, and the Philippines' own resources)	At a preannounced price of 52 cents on the dollar.	—	—
Temporary interest reduction	757	757		Old claims exchanged at par for new bonds with 15-year maturity (7 years' grace) and an interest rate of 4 percent in the first two years, 5 percent in years 3–5, 6 percent in year 6, and LIBOR plus 13/16 from year 7 onward.	Twelve-month rolling interest guarantee based on a 6 percent annual rate for the first six years.	—
Principal collateralized interest reduction	1,894	1,894		Old claims exchanged at par for new bonds with a 25-year bullet maturity and an interest rate that gradually rises from 4.25 percent in the first year to 6.5 percent in the sixth year and remains at that level until maturity.	Principal fully collateralized and 14 months' rolling interest guarantee based on a rate of 6.5 percent.	

Poland (1994) Cash buy-back	2,454	—		At preannounced price of 41 cents on the dollar for medium- and long-term debt and 38 cents on the dollar for short-term debt.	—	—
Principal reduction	5,336	2,935	1,866[8] (expected to come from IMF, World Bank, official sources, and own resources)	Old claims exchanged for new bonds with a 30-year bullet maturity and interest at LIBOR plus 13/16 at prenegotiated exchange ratio of 1:0.55.	Principal fully collateralized; no interest collateral.	
Interest reduction	1,743	1,743		Old claims exchanged at par for new bonds with a 30-year bullet maturity and interest increasing gradually from 2.75 percent in year 1 to 5 percent from year 21 onward.	Principal fully collateralized; no interest collateral.	Separate par bonds with slightly different interest profile for medium- and long-term and short-term debt. Payment of 85 percent of interest due in December 1989 and 30 percent of interest due accruing from May 1993 expected before closing. The balance will be subject to debt-service reduction through an uncollateralized 20-year bond (7-years' grace) bearing an interest rate gradually increasing from 3.25 percent in year 1 to 7 percent in year 9 and remaining at that level until maturity. Amortization payments are semiannual rising from 1 percent of the original face value in payments 1–3 to 2 percent in payments 4–6, to 3 percent in payments 7–17, to 5 percent in payments 18–23, to 7 percent in payments 24–27.
Noncollateralized debt exchange with interest reduction	386	386		Old claims exchanged at par for debt conversion bonds with 25-year maturity (20 years' grace) and interest increasing gradually from 4.5 percent in year 1 to 7.5 percent from year 11 and remaining at that level until maturity.	—	
Uganda (1993) Cash buy-back	153	—	18 (including resources from IDA debt-reduction facility and grants from the Netherlands, Switzerland, Germany, and the EC)	At preannounced price of 12 cents on the dollar.		Buy-back price applied to principal, past due interest canceled.

Table A4 (*continued*)

(In millions of U.S. dollars)

	Face Value of Debt to Commercial Banks		Resources Used	Terms	Enhancements for New Instruments	Special Features
	Retired	Issued				
Uruguay (1991)						
Cash buy-back	633	—	463 (including resources from the IDB)	At preannounced price of 56 cents on the dollar.		
Interest reduction	530	530		Old claims exchanged at par for new bonds with a 30-year bullet maturity and a fixed interest rate of 6.75 percent.	Principal fully collateralized and an 18-month rolling interest guarantee.	Value recovery clause allowing for larger payments in the event of a favorable performance of an index of Uruguay's terms of trade.
Venezuela (1990)						
Collateralized debt exchanges						
Principal reduction	1,411	647		Old claims exchanged for new three-month notes with present value equal to 45 percent of face value of old claims.	Face value of notes fully collateralized by short-term U.S. Treasury securities.	
Principal reduction	1,808	1,265	2,585 (including resources from IMF and World Bank)	Old claims exchanged for new bond with 30-year maturity and LIBOR plus $^{13}\!/_{16}$ at prenegotiated exchange ratio of 1:0.70.	Principal fully collateralized and 14-month rolling interest guarantee.	Eligible for debt-equity conversion. Includes warrants to be triggered in case oil prices exceed threshold price of $26 a barrel in 1996, adjusted for inflation thereafter through 2020.
Interest reduction	7,450	7,450		Old claims exchanged at par for new bond with 30-year maturity and fixed interest rate of 6.75 percent.	Principal fully collateralized and 14-month rolling interest guarantee.	
Temporary interest reduction	3,018	3,018		Old claims exchanged for new bond with 17-year maturity and interest rate of 5 percent in years 1–2, 6 percent in years 3–4, 7 percent in year five, and LIBOR plus $^7\!/_8$ of 1 percent thereafter.	Twelve-month rolling-interest guarantee for the first five years.	Eligible for debt-equity conversion.
Zambia (1994)	200	—	22 (including resources from IDA debt-reduction facility and grants from Germany, the Netherlands, Sweden, and Switzerland)	At a preannounced price of 11 cents on the dollar.		Buy-back price applied to principal, past due interest canceled.

Sources: Debt-restructuring agreements; and IMF staff estimates.

Note: BCEAO = Banque Centrale des Etats de L'Afrique de L'Ouest; IDA = International Development Association; IDB = Inter-American Development Bank.

[1]Excludes $700 million in downpayment on past due interest.

[2]Excludes $64 million in downpayment on past due interest.

[3]Excludes $29 million in downpayment on past due interest.

[4]Excludes $75 million in interest equalization payments.

[5]Excludes $29 million in downpayment on past due interest.

[6]Includes $2,447 million of debt of domestic commercial banks, for which no enhancements were provided (the Gurria bonds).

[7]Excludes $373 million of cash payments to clear all interest arrears.

[8]Excludes $158 million in catch-up and downpayment on past due interest.

Table A5. International Bond Issues by Developing Countries and Regions, by Type of Borrower

(In millions of U.S. dollars)

	1990	1991	1992	1993	First Half 1993	First Half 1994
Sovereign borrowers	1,520	4,189	5,490	16,378	6,502	6,852
Argentina	—	500	425	2,111	256	657
Barbados	—	—	—	—	—	20
Chile	—	200	120	—	—	—
China	—	—	—	582	—	1,823
Colombia	—	—	—	216	125	250
Congo	—	—	—	—	—	—
Czech Republic	—	—	—	697	375	—
Czechoslovakia, former	—	277	—	216	—	—
Hungary	887	1,186	1,242	4,733	1,580	258
Israel	—	400	—	2,002	1,000	1,958
Mexico	40	620	377	352	259	—
Philippines	—	—	—	150	150	—
Slovak Republic	—	—	—	240	—	—
South Africa	—	236	318	—	—	—
Thailand	—	—	300	343	149	189
Trinidad and Tobago	—	—	100	125	—	—
Tunisia	—	—	—	—	—	277
Turkey	593	497	2,508	3,725	2,053	720
Uruguay	—	—	100	100	100	100
Venezuela	—	273	—	1,003	455	—
Other public sector	3,551	3,827	8,054	16,441	7,186	6,185
Algeria	89	—	—	—	—	—
Argentina	—	—	—	350	150	100
Brazil	—	1,341	1,320	1,837	940	350
China	—	115	1,359	2,443	1,157	548
Colombia	—	—	—	250	150	—
Costa Rica	—	—	—	—	—	50
Czech Republic	—	—	—	—	—	250
Czechoslovakia, former	375	—	114	—	—	—
Guatemala	—	—	—	60	—	—
Hong Kong	—	—	—	102	—	—
Hungary	—	—	—	63	63	—
India	273	227	—	—	—	100
Indonesia	80	—	250	—	—	179
Korea	755	705	1,742	3,987	1,340	437
Macao	—	—	—	—	—	155
Malaysia	—	—	—	954	500	600
Mexico	1,851	1,192	1,432	4,401	2,462	3,240
Philippines	—	—	—	615	175	154
Slovak Republic	—	—	—	—	—	21
South Africa	—	—	408	—	—	—
Thailand	—	17	—	250	250	—
Turkey	—	—	572	130	—	—
Venezuela	127	230	857	1,000	—	—

Table A5 *(concluded)*

	1990	1991	1992	1993	First Half 1993	First Half 1994
Private sector	1,263	4,823	10,238	26,618	8,538	13,074
Argentina	21	295	1,145	3,772	535	1,610
Bolivia	—	—	—	—	—	10
Brazil	—	496	2,335	4,842	2,022	845
Chile	—	—	—	433	333	—
China	—	—	—	23	—	—
Colombia	—	—	—	100	50	83
Czechoslovakia, former	—	—	—	—	—	—
Hong Kong	66	100	185	5,785	657	1,855
India	—	—	—	546	—	534
Indonesia	—	369	243	485	30	1,270
Korea	350	1,307	1,466	1,877	674	1,415
Malaysia	—	—	—	—	—	365
Mexico	586	1,971	4,292	6,030	3,620	1,457
Pakistan	—	—	—	—	—	45
Panama	—	50	—	—	—	—
Peru	—	—	—	30	—	80
Philippines	—	—	—	528	20	555
Singapore	105	—	—	—	—	86
Taiwan Province of China	—	160	60	79	36	876
Thailand	—	—	312	1,654	392	1,923
Turkey	—	—	111	50	50	65
Uruguay	—	—	—	40	40	—
Venezuela	135	75	75	345	80	—
Total	**6,335**	**12,838**	**23,780**	**59,437**	**22,226**	**26,111**
Memorandum items						
Share in total issues by developing countries and regions *(in percent)*						
Sovereign issues	24.0	32.6	23.1	27.6	29.3	26.2
Other public issues	56.1	29.8	33.9	27.7	32.3	23.7
Private sector issues	19.9	37.6	43.1	44.8	38.4	50.1

Sources: IMF staff estimates based on *International Financing Review, Euroweek,* and *Financial Times.*

Table A6. Yield Spread at Launch for Unenhanced Bond Issues by Developing Countries and Regions[1]

(In basis points)

	1990	1991	1992	1993	1993 I	1993 II	1993 III	1993 IV	1994 I	1994 II
Sovereign borrower	151	261	222	230	236	248	223	223	134	180
Argentina	—	456	294	269	—	—	255	280	120	220
Barbados	—	—	—	—	—	—	—	—	—	450
Chile	—	150	150	—	—	—	—	—	—	—
China	—	—	—	88	—	—	89	88	94	98
Colombia	—	—	—	178	270	215	184	126	148	—
Czech Republic	—	—	—	230	—	—	—	—	—	—
Czechoslovakia, former	133	281	—	—	—	—	—	—	—	—
Hungary	—	249	240	235	240	255	223	238	200	226
Mexico	—	201	215	189	208	—	149	—	—	—
Philippines	—	—	—	320	320	—	—	—	—	—
Slovak Republic	—	—	—	344	—	—	344	—	—	—
South Africa	—	190	198	—	—	—	—	—	—	—
Thailand	—	—	100	67	57	—	74	—	54	—
Trinidad and Tobago	—	—	565	480	—	—	—	480	—	—
Tunisia	166	—	—	193	205	196	—	—	221	—
Turkey	—	234	207	228	—	228	221	179	196	—
Uruguay	—	—	275	—	—	—	—	—	158	—
Venezuela	260	230	—	355	482	428	284	245	—	—
Other public sector	250	373	232	179	199	187	200	148	177	162
Algeria	100	—	—	—	—	—	—	—	—	—
Argentina	—	—	—	440	440	—	—	—	407	333
Brazil	—	540	446	465	518	528	390	413	—	—
China	—	—	110	82	57	64	98	108	—	145
Colombia	—	—	—	217	—	218	—	215	—	—
Costa Rica	—	—	—	—	—	—	—	—	395	—
Czech Republic	—	—	—	—	—	—	—	—	—	—
Czechoslovakia, former	96	—	—	—	—	—	—	—	—	—
Guatemala	—	—	—	605	—	—	605	—	—	—
Hungary	127	—	—	324	—	324	—	—	—	—
India	—	140	—	—	—	—	—	—	158	—
Indonesia	—	—	129	83	82	86	—	81	—	—
Korea	—	—	89	96	—	100	89	91	67	120
Malaysia	—	247	—	192	—	—	—	—	154	—
Mexico	366	—	205	250	190	182	213	187	178	126
Philippines	—	—	—	—	—	310	265	217	325	250
Slovak Republic	—	—	—	—	—	—	—	—	—	—
South Africa	—	—	159	—	—	—	—	—	—	—
Thailand	—	—	242	40	43	38	—	—	—	—
Turkey	—	—	—	205	—	—	—	—	—	—
Venezuela	260	275	263	212	—	—	212	—	—	—

Private sector	650	493	376	348	424	370	339	315	256	337
Argentina	730	447	419	397	623	533	371	371	310	411
Bolivia	—	—	—	—	—	—	—	—	428	—
Brazil	530	516	505	642	563	473	425	—	386	465
Chile	—	—	194	—	210	—	170	—	—	—
Colombia	—	—	310	—	320	300	—	—	—	641
Czechoslovakia, former	—	300	118	133	—	83	126	—	—	115
Hong Kong	—	180	110	—	—	110	—	—	—	—
India	—	—	—	500	—	—	—	—	—	—
Indonesia	—	—	410	500	—	405	405	—	—	467
Korea	—	116	87	86	90	92	76	68	—	69
Mexico	613	377	358	413	365	331	347	253	—	430
Panama	24	—	—	—	—	—	—	—	—	—
Peru	—	—	706	—	—	—	706	706	680	—
Philippines	—	—	375	—	375	375	375	75	127	340
Thailand	—	43	60	250	58	—	75	—	—	94
Turkey	—	250	—	—	—	—	—	—	—	—
Uruguay	—	—	300	—	—	—	—	—	—	—
Venezuela	362	375	469	450	516	468	—	468	—	—
Total	245	346	282	259	288	274	249	243	187	259

Sources: IMF staff estimates based on *International Financing Review*, *Euroweek*, and *Financial Times*.

[1]Yield spread measured as the difference between the bond yield at issue and the prevailing yield for industrial country government bonds in the same currency and of comparable maturity. All figures are weighted averages.

Table A7. Maturing Bonds of Developing Countries and Regions

(In millions of U.S. dollars)

	1993	1994	1995	1996	1997	1998	1999	2000	2001	2002	2003	2004	2005–2007
Africa	—	159	89	236	602	—	123	—	—	—	—	877	—
Asia	123	578	1,674	3,451	4,021	6,887	4,267	4,064	2,845	1,325	6,192	2,629	1,021
China	—	—	249	398	808	1,658	915	198	143	—	820	1,000	—
Hong Kong	—	—	259	710	80	1,893	227	2,194	908	50	1,150	—	—
Korea	80	378	947	1,535	1,447	2,219	1,517	818	155	750	1,550	364	786
Thailand	—	—	—	79	405	574	479	149	519	340	1,322	935	—
Europe	66	200	1,490	2,629	2,236	2,875	3,458	2,916	903	875	3,062	402	—
Hungary	—	—	318	1,138	355	1,097	1,837	1,399	300	443	1,974	—	—
Turkey	66	—	782	1,015	1,783	1,658	1,371	1,075	602	432	1,089	288	—
Middle East	879	1,160	—	160	—	352	122	340	—	—	—	117	—
Western Hemisphere	2,995	4,947	7,588	9,421	7,060	10,590	3,062	3,058	1,760	1,035	3,756	2,035	—
Argentina	812	435	1,082	1,730	885	2,100	425	960	—	—	1,450	350	—
Brazil	1,026	2,381	3,037	2,559	820	1,566	157	100	590	350	400	—	—
Mexico	1,122	1,986	2,555	3,451	4,523	5,753	2,355	1,437	1,070	485	1,123	1,435	—
Total	4,063	7,045	10,841	15,897	13,919	20,704	11,032	10,378	5,508	3,235	13,282	6,060	1,021

Sources: *International Financing Review; Euroweek;* and IMF staff estimates.

Table A8. International Bond Issues by Developing Countries by Currency of Denomination

(In millions of U.S. dollars)

	1990	1991	1992	1993	First Half 1993	First Half 1994
U.S. dollar	3,890	8,755	16,991	44,192	16,796	21,207
African borrowers	—	—	—	—	—	600
Asian borrowers	960	1,683	4,143	16,700	4,301	9,943
European borrowers	550	300	1,014	1,395	575	336
Latin American borrowers	2,380	6,372	11,834	24,095	10,920	8,370
Middle Eastern borrowers	—	400	—	2,002	1,000	1,958
Deutsche mark	1,693	1,618	2,013	4,521	1,699	688
African borrowers	89	236	408	—	—	—
Asian borrowers	283	96	125	—	—	206
European borrowers	983	961	1,063	3,285	1,370	—
Latin American borrowers	337	326	417	1,236	329	482
Yen	450	1,458	3,554	7,965	3,118	2,692
African borrowers	—	—	—	—	—	277
Asian borrowers	259	1,001	1,306	3,099	1,009	1,694
European borrowers	190	457	2,247	4,078	2,108	720
Latin American borrowers	—	—	—	787	—	—
European currency unit (ECU)	127	423	630	—	—	—
African borrowers	—	—	630	—	—	—
Asian borrowers	127	—	—	—	—	—
European borrowers	—	242	186	—	—	—
Latin American borrowers	—	181	126	—	—	—
Other currencies	175	585	593	2,759	614	1,524
Asian borrowers	127	—	—	—	220	1,266
European borrowers	—	242	186	—	67	258
Latin American borrowers	—	181	126	—	328	—
Total	**6,335**	**12,838**	**23,780**	**59,437**	**22,226**	**26,111**

Memorandum items — *(In percent)*

Share in total issues by developing countries

	1990	1991	1992	1993	1993	1994
U.S. dollars	61	68	71	74	75	81
Deutsche mark	27	13	8	8	8	3
Yen	7	11	15	13	14	10
ECU	2	3	3	3	—	—
Other	3	5	2	5	3	6

Share in total issues in global bond market

	1990	1991	1992	1993	1993	1994
U.S. dollars	32	30	39	36	35	37
Deutsche mark	8	7	11	13	13	7
Yen	14	14	13	12	12	13
ECU	9	11	7	11	1	2
Other	38	40	34	38	40	41

Sources: IMF staff estimates based on *International Financing Review, Euroweek,* and *Financial Times.*

Table A9. Enhancements of International Bond Issues by Developing Countries[1]

(Number of issues featuring enhancements in percent of total issues by region)

	1990	1991	1992	1993	First Half 1993	First Half 1994
Africa	—	—	—	—	—	50
Secured	—	—	—	—	—	50
Asia	18	56	38	48	36	65
Convertible	18	56	25	41	23	56
Put option	—	4	25	20	23	34
Warrant	—	—	6	1	—	—
Europe	7	—	14	3	7	13
Guaranteed	7	—	—	—	—	—
Secured	—	—	5	3	7	13
Put option	—	—	9	—	—	—
Middle East	—	100	—	100	100	100
Guaranteed	—	100	—	100	100	100
Western Hemisphere	41	22	18	12	12	16
Convertible	3	—	1	1	2	8
Guaranteed	—	—	1	—	—	—
Secured	28	8	10	4	4	3
Put option	13	14	8	7	6	5
Warrant	—	—	—	1	1	—
All developing countries	27	33	22	25	20	48
Convertible	6	20	7	14	7	36
Guaranteed	2	1	1	2	3	3
Secured	14	4	7	3	3	3
Put option	6	9	12	11	10	22
Warrant	—	—	1	1	1	—

Memorandum items
Amount raised through enhanced instruments
(in percent of total)

	1990	1991	1992	1993	First Half 1993	First Half 1994
All developing countries	31	31	20	21	16	43
Africa	—	—	—	—	—	68
Asia 7	39	18	35	19	50	
Europe	11	—	8	1	1	5
Middle East	—	100	—	100	100	100
Western Hemisphere	59	34	26	12	13	23

Sources: IMF staff estimates based on *International Financing Review, Euroweek,* and *Financial Times.*
[1]Totals by region may be smaller than the sum of their components because some issues feature multiple enhancements.

Table A10. Granger Causality Tests on Daily Data of Brady Par Bond Prices[1]

Dependent Variable	Independent Variable	Coefficient for Independent Variable (β_i)	T-Value		Sample Period
Argentina	Mexico	0.0276	2.2250	(*)	01/02/91–06/20/94
Brazil	Mexico	0.0499	2.2753	(*)	07/30/93–06/20/94
Venezuela	Mexico	−0.0022	−0.6335		01/02/91–06/20/94
Philippines	Mexico	0.0173	3.7506	(**)	01/02/91–06/20/94
Nigeria	Mexico	0.0056	1.6855		01/02/91–06/20/94
Mexico	Argentina	−0.0088	−1.4816		01/02/91–06/20/94
	Brazil	−0.0053	−0.8010		07/30/93–06/20/94
	Venezuela	0.0034	0.9191		01/02/91–06/20/94
	Philippines	−0.0047	−1.1291		01/02/91–06/20/94
	Nigeria	0.0021	0.4741		01/02/91–06/20/94

Source: Reuters Data Base.

Note: * denotes that coefficients are statistically significant at a 5 percent level; ** denotes that coefficients are statistically significant at a 1 percent level.

[1]The following regression was tried for different lags (i.e., different values of k). If Granger causality was found for $k > 1$, only the value for $k = 1$ is reported here:

$$y_t = \sum_{i=1}^{k} \alpha_i y_{(t-i)} + \sum_{i=1}^{k} \beta_i x_{t-i} + u_t,$$

where if $\beta_i = 0$ ($i = 1,2,3, \ldots, k$), x_t fails to cause y_t.

Table A11. Granger Causality Tests on Daily Data of Sovereign Eurobond Prices[1]

Dependent Variable	Independent Variable	Coefficient for Independent Variable (β_i)	T-Value		Sample Period
Argentina (1)	Mexico (1)	−0.0042	−1.4189		09/13/91–10/06/93
(2)		0.0118	1.8193		09/30/92–06/24/94
Brazil (1)	Mexico (1)	0.0041	1.5429		05/22/92–06/24/94
(2)		0.0107	3.1970	(**)	09/18/91–06/24/94
Venezuela (1)	Mexico (1)	0.0339	3.3307	(**)	03/09/93–06/24/94
(2)		0.0279	3.3978	(**)	08/23/91–06/24/94
(3)		0.1271	2.1626	(*)	11/14/91–06/24/94
Philippines (1)	Mexico (1)	0.0129	2.5320	(*)	02/23/93–06/24/94
(2)		0.0808	3.7377	(**)	07/22/93–06/24/94
Turkey (1)	Mexico (1)	0.0234	3.6438	(**)	07/31/90–06/24/94
Hungary (1)	Mexico (1)	0.0653	5.3052	(**)	06/21/91–06/24/94
Mexico (1)	Argentina (1)	0.0121	2.8046	(**)	09/13/91–10/06/93
	(2)	−0.0016	−0.6937		09/30/92–06/24/94
	Brazil (1)	−0.0023	−1.2590		05/22/92–06/24/94
	(2)	−0.0035	−0.7198		09/18/91–06/24/94
	Venezuela (1)	−0.0009	−0.1339		03/09/93–06/24/94
	(2)	0.0013	0.5037		08/23/91–06/24/94
	(3)	0.0016	0.6114		11/14/91–06/24/94
	Philippines (1)	−0.0065	−1.3571		02/23/93–06/24/94
	(2)	−0.0028	−0.3609		07/22/93–06/24/94
	Turkey (1)	0.0059	1.6003		07/31/90–06/24/94
	Hungary (1)	−0.0039	−1.4616		06/21/91–06/24/94

Source: Reuters Data Base.

Note: * denotes that coefficients are statistically significant at a 5 percent level; ** denotes that coefficients are statistically significant at a 1 percent level.

[1]The following regression was tried for different lags (i.e., different values of k). If Granger causality was found for $k > 1$, only the value for $k = 1$ is reported here:

$$y_t = \sum_{i=1}^{k} \alpha_i y_{(t-i)} + \sum_{i=1}^{k} \beta_i x_{t-i} + u_t,$$

where if $\beta_i = 0$ ($i = 1,2,3, \ldots, k$), x_t fails to cause y_t.

Table A12. Emerging Markets Mutual Funds
(Net assets in millions of U.S. dollars)

	1988 Net assets	1988 Number of funds	1989 Net assets	1989 Number of funds	1990 Net assets	1990 Number of funds	1991 Net assets	1991 Number of funds	1992 Net assets	1992 Number of funds	1993 Net assets	1993 Number of funds
Equities	**5,857**	**91**	**9,975**	**142**	**13,320**	**225**	**19,180**	**290**	**29,535**	**465**	**73,043**	**573**
Global	900	15	1,350	18	2,300	29	3,750	39	7,750	78	24,750	108
Asia	4,437	72	7,435	112	9,240	174	11,575	211	16,823	312	38,465	372
Regional	1,750	35	3,100	50	4,000	75	5,350	92	8,000	115	21,500	130
China	47	2	50	2	60	3	110	4	1,300	34	3,220	48
Hong Kong	...	...	...	...	...	...	...	...	348	19	591	20
India	270	3	300	4	830	6	970	6	1,090	7	2,055	13
Indonesia	35	1	260	7	525	18	400	18	440	21	860	22
Korea	990	10	1,215	13	1,205	17	1,310	24	1,710	38	3,420	56
Malaysia and Singapore	75	3	240	7	505	17	600	17	645	23	1,039	21
Pakistan	—	—	—	—	—	—	65	2	65	3	310	6
Philippines	45	3	280	7	240	8	290	8	350	9	670	10
Sri Lanka	—	—	—	—	—	—	—	—	—	—	30	1
Taiwan Province of China	80	4	600	4	475	5	890	13	925	15	1,860	16
Thailand	845	11	1,390	18	1,400	25	1,580	26	1,920	26	2,860	26
Viet Nam	—	—	—	—	—	—	10	1	30	2	50	3
Latin America	520	4	985	9	1,455	16	3,525	33	4,517	64	9,068	78
Regional	—	—	175	2	380	5	1,510	18	2,000	40	5,200	53
Argentina	—	—	—	—	—	—	115	2	105	2	170	3
Brazil	220	3	320	3	165	3	380	4	485	8	625	8
Chile	—	—	160	2	380	4	740	4	850	4	1,115	4
Colombia	—	—	—	—	—	—	—	—	17	1	63	1
Mexico	300	1	330	2	530	4	780	5	1,040	8	1,865	8
Peru	—	—	—	—	—	—	—	—	20	1	30	1
Europe	—	—	205	3	325	6	330	7	430	10	715	13
Regional	—	—	90	2	210	4	240	5	350	8	570	11
Turkey	—	—	115	1	115	2	90	2	80	2	145	2
Africa	—	—	—	—	—	—	—	—	15	1	45	2
Bonds	**275**	...	**500**	...	**900**	...	**1,700**	...	**3,750**	...	**8,500**	...
Total funds	6,132	...	10,475	...	14,220	...	20,880	...	33,285	...	81,543	...

Sources: Emerging Market Funds Research, Inc; and Lipper Analytical Services, Inc.

69

Table A13. Net Bond and Equity Purchases by Emerging Markets Mutual Funds[1]

(In millions of U.S. dollars)

	1989	1990	1991	1992	1993
Equities	**784**	**6,464**	**2,511**	**8,448**	**12,615**
Global	−32	1,076	457	3,908	6,372
Asia	620	4,632	1,798	3,385	4,949
Regional	317	1,976	876	1,577	3,075
China	−14	26	40	1,016	857
Hong Kong	—	—	—	271	−74
India	24	412	2	−77	563
Indonesia	132	285	146	30	−35
Korea	160	407	352	342	1,131
Malaysia and Singapore	92	331	54	−64	−140
Pakistan	—	—	25	34	95
Philippines	131	302	−69	3	−84
Sri Lanka	—	—	—	—	17
Taiwan Province of China	−78	368	427	388	90
Thailand	−145	525	−64	−150	−540
Viet Nam	—	—	9	16	−4
Latin America	120	652	57	738	1,403
Regional	106	185	267	446	1,320
Argentina	—	—	21	28	−6
Brazil	50	244	−60	108	−149
Chile	118	124	−13	7	−4
Colombia	—	—	—	12	25
Mexico	−154	99	−158	117	213
Peru	—	—	—	20	5
Europe	75	103	199	393	−115
Regional	53	102	141	313	−81
Turkey	22	1	58	80	−33
Africa	—	—	—	24	6
Bonds	...	**400**	**323**	**827**	**248**
Total funds	784	6,864	2,834	9,275	12,864

Sources: Emerging Market Funds Research, Inc.; Lipper Analytical Services, Inc.; and IMF staff estimates.

[1]Estimated by deflating changes in the stock of fund net assets by IFC investable share prices indices for equities and by the J.P. Morgan Eurobond price index for bonds.

Table A14. Issues of Closed End Funds Targeting Emerging Markets in Developing Countries and Regions

(In millions of U.S. dollars)

	1989	1990	1991	1992	1993	1994 I	1994 II
Developing countries	**1,859**	**3,482**	**1,193**	**1,421**	**4,151**	**4,246**	**510**
Global funds	76	36	253	137	2,669	1,042	106
Africa	—	—	—	—	16	369	—
Multicountry	—	—	—	—	—	302	—
Specific country	—	—	—	—	—	66	—
Mauritius	—	—	—	—	16	—	—
South Africa	—	—	—	—	—	66	—
Asia	1,417	1,895	213	870	1,373	2,095	122
Multicountry	487	602	—	22	566	651	—
Specific country or region	930	1,294	213	848	806	1,444	122
China	—	—	—	646	456	192	—
India	168	105	—	—	—	1,138	122
Indonesia	199	312	—	—	—	—	—
Korea	—	478	140	170	110	—	—
Malaysia	150	292	—	—	—	—	—
Pakistan	—	—	23	6	178	—	—
Philippines	253	—	—	—	—	—	—
Singapore	—	—	—	—	—	—	—
Sri Lanka	—	—	—	—	—	50	—
Taiwan Province of China	56	—	40	26	—	64	—
Thailand	105	107	—	—	—	—	—
Viet Nam	—	—	10	—	62	—	—
Europe	136	976	—	122	32	312	—
Multicountry	45	841	—	—	32	312	—
Specific country	136	135	—	122	—	—	—
Bulgaria	—	—	—	—	—	—	—
Czechoslovakia	—	—	—	31	. . .	. . .	. . .
Hungary	80	100	—	22	—	—	—
Poland	—	—	—	69	—	—	—
Turkey	56	35	—	—	—	—	—
Middle East	—	—	—	—	50	146	—
Egypt	—	—	—	—	50	—	—
Israel	—	—	—	—	—	146	—
Western Hemisphere	230	575	727	293	10	283	282
Multicountry	178	203	440	181	10	283	282
Specific country	230	372	288	112	—	—	—
Argentina	—	—	56	—	—	—	—
Brazil	—	—	—	112	—	—	—
Chile	230	180	—	—	—	—	—
Mexico	—	192	132	—	—	—	—
Venezuela	—	—	100	—	—	—	—
Memorandum items							
Equity funds	. . .	. . .	. . .	. . .	2,075	4,098	381
Fixed income funds	. . .	. . .	. . .	. . .	2,076	148	129

Source: Lipper Analytical Services, Inc.

Table A15. Bank Credit Commitments by Country or Region of Destination[1]

(In billions of U.S. dollars)

					First Half	
	1990	1991	1992	1993	1993	1994
Developing countries	**24.6**	**28.5**	**18.5**	**21.2**	**11.2**	**11.4**
Africa	0.6	0.2	0.6	0.2	0.1	0.1
Algeria	—	0.1	—	—	—	—
Angola	—	—	0.3	—	—	—
Côte d'Ivoire	—	—	—	—	—	—
Ghana	0.1	0.1	0.1	—	—	0.1
Morocco	0.1	—	—	—	—	—
Nigeria	—	—	—	—	—	—
South Africa	—	—	—	—	—	—
Tunisia	—	—	0.1	0.1	0.1	0.1
Zimbabwe	—	0.1	—	0.1	—	—
Other	0.4	—	0.1	—	—	—
Asia	13.4	14.6	11.9	15.7	8.7	9.2
China	1.5	2.3	2.7	3.6	2.6	1.9
Hong Kong	1.1	0.7	1.0	2.0	1.2	0.6
India	0.7	—	0.2	—	—	0.1
Indonesia	3.9	5.0	1.8	1.9	0.7	1.6
Korea	2.0	3.5	1.8	1.9	1.2	0.8
Malaysia	0.5	0.2	1.2	1.6	0.8	1.7
Pakistan	0.4	0.1	—	—	—	—
Philippines	0.7	—	—	—	—	—
Singapore	0.3	0.4	0.4	0.4	0.4	—
Taiwan Province of China	0.8	0.7	0.8	0.9	0.3	—
Thailand	1.3	1.6	2.0	3.4	1.4	2.3
Viet Nam	—	—	—	—	—	—
Other	0.2	0.3	—	—	0.1	0.2
Europe	4.9	1.9	2.1	2.6	1.4	0.6
Bulgaria	—	—	—	—	—	—
Czech Republic	...	...	...	0.2	0.2	—
Hungary	—	0.1	0.2	0.3	0.1	0.2
Slovak Republic	—	—	—	0.1	—	—
Turkey	1.8	1.6	1.8	1.9	1.0	0.2
U.S.S.R., former	3.0	—	—	—	—	—
Other	0.1	0.2	0.1	—	0.1	0.2
Middle East	1.7	10.7	3.0	0.4	0.3	1.3
Bahrain	1.6	0.4	0.1	0.1	0.1	0.5
Egypt	—	—	—	—	—	—
Kuwait	—	5.5	—	—	—	—
Jordan	—	—	—	—	—	—
Saudi Arabia	0.1	4.5	2.9	0.2	0.2	0.2
Other	0.1	0.3	—	0.1	—	0.6
Western Hemisphere	4.0	1.0	0.9	2.2	0.7	0.2
Argentina	—	—	—	0.4	—	—
Brazil	—	—	0.2	0.2	—	—
Chile	0.3	—	0.4	0.3	—	0.1
Colombia	—	0.2	—	0.1	0.1	—
Mexico	1.6	0.6	0.2	0.4	0.4	0.1
Uruguay	—	0.1	—	—	—	—
Venezuela	1.4	—	0.2	0.8	0.2	—
Banking centers (Cayman and Bahamas)	—	—	—	0.1	—	—
Other	0.7	0.1	—	—	—	—
Memorandum items						
Total bank credit commitments	124.5	116.0	117.9	136.7	74.1	54.8
Share of bank credit commitments to developing countries in total *(in percent)*	19.8	24.6	15.7	15.5	15.2	20.7

Source: Organization for Economic Cooperation and Development, *Financial Statistics Monthly.*
[1]Covers only medium- and long-term loans that are not insured by export credit agencies and includes offshore banking centers.

Table A16. Terms on Syndicated Bank Credits for Selected Developing Countries and Regions[1]

	1990 Maturity (In years)	1990 Spread (In basis points)	1991 Maturity (In years)	1991 Spread (In basis points)	1992 Maturity (In years)	1992 Spread (In basis points)	1993 Maturity (In years)	1993 Spread (In basis points)	Jan.–June 1993 Maturity (In years)	Jan.–June 1993 Spread (In basis points)	Jan.–June 1994 Maturity (In years)	Jan.–June 1994 Spread (In basis points)
Africa												
Algeria	...	...	7.0	75	...	...	...	...	...	...	...	...
Tunisia	...	...	...	...	4.0	101	6.0	126	6.0	126	...	...
Zimbabwe	...	...	1.0	85	1.0	85	1.0	95	...	...	...	...
Asia												
China	10.8	61	9.3	114	7.5	111	7.9	96	7.5	99	7.7	98
Hong Kong	5.3	52	7.8	66	6.5	96	7.8	69	9.2	53	6.4	58
India	9.1	32	...	...	4.6	100	5.0	260	...	...	2.2	140
Indonesia	10.5	76	9.9	99	5.7	134	3.0	157	3.7	155	4.2	126
Korea	10.2	48	8.8	67	5.5	68	4.0	66	4.8	64	6.0	78
Malaysia	13.3	58	9.5	102	9.9	78	8.8	57	7.8	60	10.9	93
Pakistan	13.0	100	1.0	90	...	...	...	...	...	...	...	...
Singapore	9.3	34	3.8	134	...	...	6.4	110	5.3	125	3.0	125
Taiwan Province of China	...	...	2.3	93	2.4	104	3.6	104	4.3	101	5.0	100
Thailand	8.8	54	7.8	78	5.3	82	5.1	102	4.8	99	4.7	98
Europe												
Hungary[2]	8.0	82	6.0	138	6.1	134	8.3	200	9.9	266	5.3	172
Turkey[2]	2.2	65	2.4	85	2.9	133	2.7	94	2.8	90	2.0	65
Middle East												
Bahrain	8.6	43	4.8	67	2.0	75	...	...	...	...	5.8	99
Kuwait	...	...	5.0	50	...	...	...	...	...	...	...	...
Saudi Arabia	...	...	3.0	38	...	...	...	...	...	...	3.0	100
Western Hemisphere												
Chile	...	...	...	...	9.0	38	4.2	125	...	...	...	...
Colombia	...	...	12.8	150	...	...	...	...	...	...	...	...
Mexico	14.4	89	...	...	...	...	6.7	300	6.7	300	6.0	250
Uruguay	...	...	13.0	98	1.0	75	...	...	...	...	...	...
Venezuela	...	...	...	...	1.2	134	6.5	223	8.8	174	...	...

Sources: Organization for Economic Cooperation and Development (OECD); and Euromoney Loanware.

[1]Excludes concerted commitments.

[2]Based on Euromoney Loanware for 1992–June 1994.

Table A17. Correlation Among Total Returns on Bonds for Selected Countries

	United States	Hungary	Turkey	Venezuela	Brazil	Argentina	Mexico	Thailand
	April 1992–December 1993							
United States	1.00	. . .	. . .	. . .	. . .	. . .	. . .	. . .
Hungary	0.25	1.00	. . .	. . .	. . .	. . .	. . .	. . .
Turkey	0.65	0.16	1.00	. . .	. . .	. . .	. . .	. . .
Venezuela	0.48	0.32	−0.03	1.00	. . .	. . .	. . .	. . .
Brazil	0.19	0.27	−0.29	0.35	1.00	. . .	. . .	. . .
Argentina	—	−0.06	0.16	−0.03	−0.24	1.00	. . .	. . .
Mexico	0.66	0.65	0.44	0.71	0.33	0.09	1.00	. . .
Thailand	0.94	0.33	0.65	0.48	0.16	0.01	0.72	1.00
	January–June 1994							
United States	1.00	. . .	. . .	. . .	. . .	. . .	. . .	. . .
Hungary	0.96	1.00	. . .	. . .	. . .	. . .	. . .	. . .
Turkey	0.95	0.88	1.00	. . .	. . .	. . .	. . .	. . .
Venezuela	0.74	0.67	0.60	1.00	. . .	. . .	. . .	. . .
Brazil	0.51	0.61	0.24	0.59	1.00	. . .	. . .	. . .
Argentina	0.80	0.92	0.67	0.46	0.75	1.00	. . .	. . .
Mexico	0.88	0.98	0.78	0.60	0.68	0.96	1.00	. . .
Thailand	0.98	0.96	0.92	0.64	0.56	0.88	0.90	1.00

Sources: Reuters News Service; and Bloomberg Business News.

Table A18. Correlation Among Secondary Market Prices of Brady Bonds

February–December 1992

	Argentina	Brazil	Bulgaria	Ecuador	Mexico	Morocco	Nigeria	Panama	Peru	Philippines	Poland	Russia	Venezuela
Argentina	1.00	...	...	...	...	...	...	...	...	...	...	...	...
Brazil	0.47	1.00	...	...	...	...	...	...	...	...	...	...	...
Bulgaria	0.27	1.65	1.00	...	...	...	...	...	...	...	...	...	...
Ecuador	0.60	−0.14	−0.05	1.00	...	...	...	...	...	...	...	...	...
Mexico	0.50	−0.24	−0.12	0.80	1.00	...	...	...	...	...	...	...	...
Morocco	0.70	−0.07	−0.20	0.86	0.75	1.00	...	...	...	...	...	...	...
Nigeria	0.72	0.72	0.51	0.14	0.10	0.22	1.00	...	...	...	...	...	...
Panama	0.77	0.20	0.17	0.64	0.51	0.76	0.35	1.00	...	...	...	...	...
Peru	0.14	−0.26	−0.43	0.50	0.28	0.53	−0.13	0.14	1.00	...	...	...	...
Philippines	0.30	−0.52	−0.36	0.82	0.79	0.74	−0.21	0.45	0.62	1.00	...	...	...
Poland	0.61	−0.15	−0.20	0.73	0.73	0.85	0.03	0.78	0.23	0.64	1.00	...	...
Russia	0.07	0.74	0.54	−0.48	−0.53	−0.48	0.55	−0.26	−0.31	−0.66	−0.63	1.00	...
Venezuela	0.31	0.12	0.50	0.41	0.53	0.18	0.34	0.28	−0.28	0.25	0.16	−0.01	1.00
Thirty-year U.S. Treasury bond	0.06	−0.68	−0.45	0.53	0.73	0.55	−0.40	0.35	0.27	0.75	0.67	−0.88	0.21

January–December 1993

	Argentina	Brazil	Bulgaria	Ecuador	Mexico	Morocco	Nigeria	Panama	Peru	Philippines	Poland	Russia	Venezuela
Argentina	1.00	...	...	...	...	...	...	...	...	...	...	...	...
Brazil	0.97	1.00	...	...	...	...	...	...	...	...	...	...	...
Bulgaria	0.92	0.91	1.00	...	...	...	...	...	...	...	...	...	...
Ecuador	0.87	0.82	0.94	1.00	...	...	...	...	...	...	...	...	...
Mexico	0.98	0.93	0.93	0.89	1.00	...	...	...	...	...	...	...	...
Morocco	0.98	0.98	0.91	0.82	0.95	1.00	...	...	...	...	...	...	...
Nigeria	0.96	0.92	0.88	0.85	0.95	0.93	1.00	...	...	...	...	...	...
Panama	0.90	0.82	0.92	0.96	0.92	0.83	0.89	1.00	...	...	...	...	...
Peru	0.96	0.92	0.97	0.96	0.96	0.93	0.93	0.96	1.00	...	...	...	...
Philippines	0.97	0.91	0.90	0.86	0.94	0.93	0.94	0.89	0.94	1.00	...	...	...
Poland	0.94	0.90	0.98	0.93	0.95	0.91	0.89	0.94	0.98	0.91	1.00	...	...
Russia	0.95	0.93	0.94	0.90	0.95	0.94	0.94	0.91	0.96	0.89	0.94	1.00	...
Venezuela	0.94	0.95	0.85	0.76	0.89	0.96	0.87	0.75	0.86	0.91	0.85	0.86	1.00
Thirty-year U.S. Treasury bond	0.88	0.87	0.73	0.58	0.85	0.90	0.85	0.63	0.75	0.84	0.76	0.81	0.87

Table A18 (*concluded*)

	Argentina	Brazil	Bulgaria	Ecuador	Mexico	Morocco	Nigeria	Panama	Peru	Philippines	Poland	Russia	Venezuela
							February–December 1992						
Argentina	1.00	...	...	...	...	...	...	...	...	...	...	...	...
Brazil	0.87	1.00	...	...	...	...	...	...	...	...	...	...	...
Bulgaria	0.84	0.95	1.00	...	...	...	...	...	...	...	...	...	...
Ecuador	0.90	0.86	0.76	1.00	...	...	...	...	...	...	...	...	...
Mexico	0.98	0.91	0.87	0.91	1.00	...	...	...	...	...	...	...	...
Morocco	0.90	0.64	0.58	0.87	0.84	1.00	...	...	...	...	...	...	...
Nigeria	0.98	0.89	0.83	0.92	0.97	0.86	1.00	...	...	...	...	...	...
Panama	0.85	0.86	0.77	0.93	0.85	0.82	0.83	1.00	...	...	...	...	...
Peru	0.94	0.91	0.82	0.95	0.95	0.86	0.95	0.94	1.00	...	...	...	...
Philippines	0.98	0.88	0.83	0.89	0.96	0.88	0.97	0.86	0.95	1.00	...	...	...
Poland	0.97	0.83	0.77	0.92	0.95	0.92	0.96	0.86	0.94	0.95	1.00	...	...
Russia	0.11	0.68	0.65	0.75	0.86	0.77	0.86	0.60	0.79	0.83	0.87	1.00	...
Venezuela	0.97	0.85	0.80	0.89	0.97	0.86	0.92	0.78	0.92	0.96	0.96	–0.01	1.00
Thirty-year U.S. Treasury bond	0.95	0.94	0.89	0.86	0.97	0.76	0.96	0.83	0.93	0.95	0.90	0.80	0.94

Source: Salomon Brothers.

Table A19. Correlation Among Total Returns on Equity for Selected Countries

	Brazil	Mexico	Argentina	Venezuela	Thailand	Malaysia	Turkey	United States	United Kingdom	Japan
					January 1992–December 1993					
Brazil	1.00	...	...	...	...	...	...	...	...	...
Mexico	0.17	1.00	...	...	...	...	...	...	...	...
Argentina	0.39	0.42	1.00	...	...	...	...	...	...	...
Venezuela	0.27	−0.06	−0.03	1.00	...	...	...	...	...	...
Thailand	−0.12	0.30	0.23	0.04	1.00	...	...	...	...	...
Malaysia	−0.08	0.40	0.14	0.26	0.52	1.00	...	...	...	...
Turkey	0.10	−0.42	−0.07	0.28	0.05	0.15	1.00	...	...	...
United States	0.64	0.29	0.27	0.22	−0.10	−0.13	−0.07	1.00	...	...
United Kingdom	0.14	0.56	0.49	−0.24	0.27	0.33	−0.21	0.35	1.00	...
Japan	0.20	−0.11	—	−0.10	−0.04	0.20	0.17	0.14	0.19	1.00
					January–June 1994					
Brazil	1.00	...	...	...	...	...	...	...	...	...
Mexico	0.43	1.00	...	...	...	...	...	...	...	...
Argentina	0.31	0.96	1.00	...	...	...	...	...	...	...
Venezuela	0.37	0.18	0.35	1.00	...	...	...	...	...	...
Thailand	−0.64	0.40	0.46	−0.23	1.00	...	...	...	...	...
Malaysia	−0.74	−0.34	−0.18	−0.07	0.43	1.00	...	...	...	...
Turkey	0.06	0.07	−0.08	−0.32	0.18	−0.03	1.00	...	...	...
United States	0.76	0.40	0.29	0.34	−0.30	−0.45	0.62	1.00	...	...
United Kingdom	0.69	0.74	0.73	0.39	−0.12	−0.18	−0.07	0.54	1.00	...
Japan	0.88	0.17	0.12	0.51	−0.72	−0.37	0.13	0.78	0.67	1.00

Source: IFC Emerging Markets data base.

Table A20. Provisioning Regulations Against Claims on Developing Countries

Country	Provisioning Regulations	Process for Graduation	Actual Range of Provisioning[1] (End of 1992)	Trade/Interbank Claims Guaranteed OECD Export Credit Agency	Collateralized Claims[2]	Subparticipation of Official Agency/ IFIs	Country Discrimination[3]
Belgium	Mandatory: 20, 30, 50, and 60 percent on 4 groups of countries.	Provisioning levels reviewed semi-annually.	55–60 percent	Trade credits to limit of 12 months' exposure base (provisioning required on nonperforming trade credits with arrears of more than six months).	That part of the claim which is legally secured by a cash deposit, or securities issued, is exempted.	Participation in "B" loans of the IFC and in cofinancing transactions of the EBRD is exempted.	Yes
Canada	Mandatory: Minimum 35 percent to 46 countries.	Country removed after lapse of 5 years since previous rescheduling.[4]	50–63 percent[5]	No specific guidance on allocation of provisioning by type of credit.	Exclusion for OECD government securities used as collateral on principal.[6]	No specific guidance.	No
France	Mandatory: Average 55 percent to about 80 countries.[7]	Country considered for removal from basket if banks consistently reduce provisioning for the country.	37–68 percent	Exposure base includes short-term interbank claims but excludes short-term trade credits and those guaranteed by OECD export credit agencies.	For collateralized principal, provisioning considered unwarranted.	On a selective basis, some loans with subparticipation are excluded for provisioning purposes.	No
Germany	Voluntary.[8]	Not applicable.	73–90 percent	Case by case.[9]	Case by case.[9]	Case by case.[9]	Yes[9]
Japan	Indicative: 30 percent to undisclosed basket of countries.[10]	Country removed from basket after 5 years have lapsed since previous rescheduling.	30–35 percent	No specific guidance on allocation of provisioning by type of credit.	Present value of collateral on interest or principal taken into consideration.	No specific guidance.	No
Netherlands	Mandatory: 10–90 percent against approximately 45 countries.	Provisioning levels reviewed semi-annually.	60 percent	Exposure base excludes claims for which a guarantee has been obtained.	Certain collateralized credit is excluded.	Some cofinancing claims with certain multilateral and regional development banks excluded.	Yes
Switzerland	Indicative: 5–100 percent against approximately 90 countries.	...	60–90 percent	Banks may individually decide on the level of provisions for short-term credit.	For collateralized principal, provisioning considered unwarranted.	Case by case.	Yes

United Kingdom	Indicative: Bank of England guideline; 5–100 percent on approximately 55 countries.[11]	The matrix allows for regular re-assessment, which can lead to lower recommended provisioning range.	49–80 percent	If a credit is considered to have a higher probability of repayment, notably in the case of short-term credits and interbank claims, these are treated more favorably or can be excluded altogether from the calculated exposure base.	Case by case.	Some loans with subparticipation are excluded for provisioning purposes.	Yes
United States	Indicative/Mandatory: On loans that are evaluated value impaired.	The ICERC meets three times a year to review country rankings and status of value-impaired countries.	24–60 percent	Provisioning is required on all loans except performing trade and interbank credits.	Collateralized principal is factored into calculation for reserve requirement.	Considered on a case-by-case basis.	Yes

Sources: National Authorities; press reports; and World Bank Technical Paper No. 158.

Note: ICERC = Interagency Country Exposure Review Committee; IFC = International Finance Corporation; EBRD = European Bank for Reconstruction and Development.

[1] In percent of relevant exposure; numbers indicate range for major banks.
[2] Indicates under what circumstances the assessment of exposure is adjusted for collateralized claims for provisioning purposes.
[3] Indicates which regulatory authorities assess the exposure base by individual country performance.
[4] The time period can be reduced to two years if the country can demonstrate an ability to raise new funds on a voluntary unsecured basis on the international capital markets.
[5] Based on end-of-1993 data.
[6] A one-for-one adjustment is made (i.e., if collateral only partially covers asset, the uncovered portion is factored into the calculation for total exposure requiring provisioning).
[7] Mandatory target is set by industry average of previous fiscal year.
[8] Adequacy judged against industry average.
[9] Banks individually determine the requirement for provisions in liaison with their external auditors. In this context, allowance can be made by credit type and by country risk.
[10] Until March 1991, the 25 percent level represented a *maximum* statutory cap. Although this is no longer the case, the level is set to provide an indicative guideline.
[11] The Bank of England does not instruct provisioning against a set list of countries; this is left up to individual banks to determine using the Bank's matrix criteria.

Table A21. Net Foreign Direct Investment Flows to Developing Countries

(In billions of U.S. dollars)

	1988	1989	1990	1991	1992	Est. 1993	Est. 1991–93
Developing countries[1]	**19.2**	**21.5**	**23.5**	**33.8**	**44.4**	**55.5**	**134.0**
Africa	1.1	2.8	1.2	1.2	1.1	1.5	3.8
Algeria	—	—	—	−0.1	—	0.1	—
Botswana	—	0.1	0.1	—	0.1	0.1	0.2
Cameroon	—	—	—	—	0.1	0.1	0.2
Gabon	0.4	—	−0.1	−0.2	—	−0.3	−0.5
Morocco	0.1	0.2	0.2	0.4	0.5	0.5	1.4
Nigeria	0.4	2.4	0.6	0.6	0.8	0.6	2.0
South Africa	0.1	−0.4	−0.1	—	−0.9	—	−0.9
Tunisia	0.1	0.1	0.2	0.2	0.2	0.2	0.6
Other	—	0.2	0.3	0.3	0.2	0.2	0.7
Asia	10.5	10.7	13.8	15.4	20.6	30.3	66.3
China	2.3	2.6	2.7	3.7	7.1	17.0	27.8
India	0.3	0.3	0.4	0.2	0.3	0.6	1.1
Indonesia	0.6	0.7	1.2	1.5	1.7	2.0	5.2
Korea	0.7	0.5	−0.1	−0.2	−0.3	−0.3	−0.8
Malaysia	0.7	1.7	2.3	4.0	4.5	4.3	12.8
Myanmar	—	—	0.2	0.2	0.1	0.3	0.6
Pakistan	0.2	0.2	0.2	0.3	0.3	0.3	0.9
Papua New Guinea	0.1	0.2	0.1	0.2	0.2	0.1	0.5
Philippines	1.0	0.8	0.5	0.7	0.7	0.6	2.0
Singapore	3.5	1.9	3.9	3.2	4.3	4.0	11.5
Sri Lanka	—	—	—	—	—	0.1	0.1
Thailand	1.0	1.7	2.2	1.4	1.5	1.2	4.1
Other	—	0.1	0.1	0.1	0.1	0.1	0.3
Europe	0.9	0.9	0.8	3.2	5.1	6.7	15.0
U.S.S.R., former	0.5	−0.3	−0.7	—	1.1	1.8	2.9
Czechoslovakia, former	—	0.3	0.2	0.6	1.1	0.9	2.6
Hungary	—	0.2	0.3	1.5	1.5	2.3	5.3
Poland	—	—	—	0.1	0.3	0.6	1.0
Romania	—	—	—	—	0.1	0.1	0.2
Turkey	0.4	0.7	0.7	0.8	0.8	0.9	2.5
Other	—	0.1	0.3	0.2	0.2	0.1	0.5
Latin America	6.9	6.4	7.1	10.9	14.2	12.8	37.9
Argentina	1.1	1.0	1.9	2.4	4.2	3.3	9.9
Bolivia	—	—	—	0.1	0.1	0.1	0.3
Brazil	2.9	0.7	0.2	—	1.3	—	1.3
Chile	0.1	0.3	0.6	0.5	0.6	1.4	2.5
Colombia	0.2	0.5	0.5	0.4	0.7	0.8	1.9
Costa Rica	0.1	0.1	0.1	0.2	0.2	0.1	0.5
Dominican Republic	0.1	0.2	0.1	0.1	0.2	0.1	0.4
Ecuador	0.1	0.1	0.1	0.1	0.1	0.5	0.7
Guatemala	0.1	0.1	0.1	0.1	0.1	0.1	0.3
Jamaica	—	0.1	0.1	0.1	0.1	0.1	0.3
Mexico	1.7	2.6	2.5	4.8	5.4	4.9	15.1
Paraguay	—	—	0.1	0.1	0.1	0.1	0.3
Peru	—	0.1	—	0.1	0.1	0.5	0.7
Trinidad and Tobago	0.1	0.1	0.1	0.2	0.2	0.3	0.7
Venezuela	0.1	0.2	0.5	1.6	0.5	0.1	2.2
Other	0.2	0.3	0.2	0.3	0.3	0.3	0.9
Middle East	−0.2	0.7	0.6	3.1	3.4	4.5	11.0
Egypt	1.1	1.2	0.7	0.3	0.4	0.5	1.2
United Arab Emirates	0.2	0.2	0.2	0.2	0.2	0.2	0.6
Yemen, Republic of	−0.3	−0.2	−0.2	0.3	0.7	0.7	1.7
Other	−1.2	−0.5	−0.1	2.3	2.1	3.0	7.4

Source: IMF, *World Economic Outlook.*

[1]Taiwan Province of China is excluded from this group because it has become a significant provider of foreign direct investment in recent years.

Bibliography

Campbell, H., "Portfolio Enhancement Using Emerging Markets as Conditioning Information," paper presented at World Bank Symposium on Portfolio Investment in Developing Countries, Washington, D.C., September 1993.

Campbell, J.Y., and A.S. Kyle, "Smart Money, Noise Trading, and Stock Price Behavior," *Review of Economic Studies,* Vol. 60 (January 1993), pp. 1–34.

Cardoso, E., and R. Dornbusch, "Foreign Private Capital Flows" in *Handbook of Development Economics,* Vol. 2, ed. by Hollis Chenery and T.N. Srinivasan (Amsterdam; New York: North-Holland, 1988).

Claessens, S, "Alternative Forms of External Finance: A Survey," *World Bank Research Observer,* Vol. 8 (January 1993), pp. 91–117.

____, M. Dooley, and A. Warner, "Portfolio Capital Flows: Hot or Cool?" World Bank Discussion Paper, August 27, 1993.

Collyns, Charles, and others, *Private Market Financing for Developing Countries* (Washington: International Monetary Fund, 1993, 1992, and 1991).

Dooley, Michael, "An Analysis of the Debt Crisis," IMF Working Paper, WP/86/14 (Washington: International Monetary Fund, 1986).

Edwards, Sebastian, "Capital Flows, Foreign Direct Investment, and Debt-Equity Swaps in Developing Countries," National Bureau of Economic Research Working Paper, No. 3497 (October 1990).

Goldsbrough, David J., "Investment Trends and Prospects: The Link with Bank Lending" in *Investing in Development: New Roles for Private Capital,* ed. by Theodore T. Moran and others (New Brunswick, Connecticut: Transaction Books, 1986)

Goldstein, Morris, and M. Mussa, "The Integration of World Capital Markets," IMF Working Paper, WP/93/95 (Washington: International Monetary Fund, 1993).

Goldstein, Morris, and others, *International Capital Markets Part II, Systemic Issues in International Finance* (Washington: International Monetary Fund, August 1993).

____, *International Capital Markets: Developments, Prospects, and Key Policy Issues* (Washington: International Monetary Fund, 1994).

Graham, Edward M., and Paul R. Krugman, "The Surge in Foreign Direct Investment in the 1980s" in *Foreign Direct Investment,* ed. by Kenneth Froot (Chicago: University of Chicago Press, 1993).

Grossman, S. J., and J.E. Stiglitz, "On the Impossibility of Informationally Efficient Markets," *American Economic Review,* Vol. 70 (1980).

International Finance Corporation (1994a), *Emerging Markets Factbook* (Washington: IFC, 1994).

____(1994b), *Quarterly Review of Emerging Markets,* (First Quarter 1994).

International Organization of Securities Commissions (IOSCO), *Report of the Development Committee on Internationalization* (Montreal: IOSCO, October 1993).

Kuhn, Michael G., and others, *Official Financing for Developing Countries* (Washington: International Monetary Fund, April 1994).

Kyle, Albert S., "Continuous Auctions and Insider Trading," *Econometrica,* Vol. 53 (November 1985), pp. 1315–35.

Lizondo, Saul, "Foreign Direct Investment," in *Determinants and Systemic Consequences of International Capital Flows,* IMF Occasional Paper, No. 77 (Washington: International Monetary Fund, 1991), pp. 68–82.

U.S. Department of Commerce, *Survey of Current Business,* Bureau of Economic Analysis (Washington, various issues).

U.S. Treasury Department, *Treasury Bulletin* (Washington, various issues.)

World Economic and Financial Surveys

This series (ISSN 0258-7440) contains biannual, annual, and periodic studies covering monetary and financial issues of importance to the global economy. The core elements of the series are the *World Economic Outlook* report, usually published in May and October, and the annual report on *International Capital Markets*. Other studies assess international trade policy, private market and official financing for developing countries, exchange and payments systems, export credit policies, and issues raised in the *World Economic Outlook*.

World Economic Outlook: A Survey by the Staff of the International Monetary Fund

The *World Economic Outlook*, published twice a year in English, French, Spanish, and Arabic, presents IMF staff economists' analyses of global economic developments during the near and medium term. Chapters give an overview of the world economy; consider issues affecting industrial countries, developing countries, and economies in transition to the market; and address topics of pressing current interest.

ISSN 0256-6877.
$34.00 (academic rate: $23.00; paper).
1994 (May). ISBN 1-55775-381-4. **Stock #WEO-194.**
1994 (Oct.). ISBN 1-55775-385-7. **Stock #WEO-294.**

International Capital Markets: Developments, Prospects, and Policy Issues
by an IMF Staff Team led by Morris Goldstein and David Folkerts-Landau

This annual report reviews developments in international capital markets, including recent bond market turbulence and the role of hedge funds, supervision of banks and nonbanks and the regulation of derivatives, structural changes in government securities markets, recent developments in private market financing for developing countries, and the role of capital markets in financing Chinese enterprises.

$20.00 (academic rate: $12.00; paper).
1994. ISBN 1-55775-426-8. **Stock #WEO-694.**

1993. *Part I: Exchange Rate Management and International Capital Flows*, by Morris Goldstein, David Folkerts-Landau, Peter Garber, Liliana Rojas-Suarez, and Michael Spencer.
ISBN 1-55775-290-7. **Stock #WEO-693.**

1993. *Part II: Systemic Issues in International Finance*, by an IMF Staff Team led by Morris Goldstein and David Folkerts-Landau.
ISBN 1-55775-335-0. **Stock #WEO-1293.**

Staff Studies for the World Economic Outlook
by the IMF's Research Department

These studies, supporting analyses and scenarios of the *World Economic Outlook*, provide a detailed examination of theory and evidence on major issues currently affecting the global economy.

$20.00 (academic rate: $12.00; paper).
1993. ISBN 1-55775-337-7. **Stock #WEO-393.**

Developments in International Exchange and Payments Systems
by a Staff Team from the IMF's Exchange and Trade Relations Department

The global trend toward liberalization in countries' international payments and transfer systems has been most dramatic in central and Eastern Europe. But developing countries in general have brought their exchange systems more in line with market principles and moved toward more flexible exchange rate arrangements, while industrial countries have moved toward more pegged arrangements.
$20.00 (academic rate: $12.00; paper).
1992. ISBN 1-55775-233-8. **Stock #WEO-892.**

Private Market Financing for Developing Countries
by a Staff Team from the IMF's Policy Development and Review Department

This study surveys recent trends in private market financing for developing countries, including flows to developing countries through banking and securities markets; the restoration of access to voluntary market financing for some developing countries; and the status of commercial bank debt in low-income countries.
$20.00 (academic rate: $12.00; paper).
1995. ISBN 1-55775-456-X. **Stock #WEO-995.**
1993. ISBN 1-55775-361-X. **Stock #WEO-993.**

International Trade Policies
by a Staff Team led by Naheed Kirmani

The study reviews major issues and developments in trade and their implications for the work of the IMF. Volume I, *The Uruguay Round and Beyond: Principal Issues*, gives and overview of the principal issues and developments in the world trading system. Volume II, *The Uruguay Round and Beyond: Background Papers*, presents detailed background papers on selected trade and trade-related issues. This study updates previous studies published under the title *Issues and Developments in International Trade Policy*.
$20.00 (academic rate: $12.00; paper).
1994. *Volume I. The Uruguay Round and Beyond: Principal Issues*
ISBN 1-55775-469-1. **Stock #WEO-1094.**
1994. *Volume II. The Uruguay Round and Beyond: Background Papers*
ISBN 1-55775-457-8. **Stock #WEO-1494.**
1992. ISBN 1-55775-311-1. **Stock #WEO-1092.**

Official Financing for Developing Countries
by a Staff Team from the IMF's Policy Development and Review Department led by Michael Kuhn

This study provides information on official financing for developing countries, with the focus on low- and lower-middle-income countries. It updates and replaces *Multilateral Official Debt Rescheduling: Recent Experience* and reviews developments in direct financing by official and multilateral sources.
$20.00 (academic rate: $12.00; paper)
1994. ISBN 1-55775-378-4. **Stock #WEO-1394.**

Officially Supported Export Credits: Recent Developments and Prospects
by Michael G. Kuhn, Balazs Horvath, Christopher J. Jarvis

This study examines export credit and cover policies in the ten major industrial countries.
$20.00 (academic rate: $12.00; paper).
1995. ISBN 1-55775-448-9. **Stock #WEO-595.**

Available by series subscription or single title (including back issues); academic rate available only to full-time university faculty and students.

Please send orders and inquiries to:
International Monetary Fund, Publication Services, 700 19th Street, N.W.
Washington, D.C. 20431, U.S.A.
Tel.: (202) 623-7430   Telefax: (202) 623-7201
Internet: publications@imf.org

OCCASIONAL PAPER 156

The ESAF at Ten Years
Economic Adjustment and Reform in Low-Income Countries

Staff of the International Monetary Fund

INTERNATIONAL MONETARY FUND
Washington DC
December 1997

© 1997 International Monetary Fund

Cataloging-in-Publication Data

The ESAF at ten years : economic adjustment and reform in low-income
  countries / staff of the International Monetary Fund — Washington DC
  : International Monetary Fund, 1997.
       p.   cm. — (Occasional paper, ISSN 0251-6365 ; 156)

   ISBN 1-55775-693-7

   1. Structural adjustment (Economic policy) — Developing countries·
2. International Monetary Fund. 3. Economic assistance — Developing
countries. I. International Monetary Fund. II. Occasional paper (International Monetary Fund) ; no. 156.
HC59.7.E83 1997

Price: US$18.00
(US$15.00 to full-time faculty members and
students at universities and colleges)

Please send orders to:
International Monetary Fund, Publication Services
700 19th Street, N.W., Washington, D.C. 20431, U.S.A.
Tel.: (202) 623-7430   Telefax: (202) 623-7201
E-mail: publications@imf.org
Internet: http://www.imf.org

recycled paper

Contents

Boxes

Tables

Figures

The following symbols have been used throughout this paper:

. . .   to indicate that data are not available;

——   to indicate that the figure is zero or less than half the final digit shown, or that the item does not exist;

–   between years or months (e.g., 1994–95 or January–June) to indicate the years or months covered, including the beginning and ending years or months;

/   between years (e.g., 1994/95) to indicate a crop or fiscal (financial) year.

"Billion" means a thousand million.

Minor discrepancies between constituent figures and totals are due to rounding.

The term "country," as used in this paper, does not in all cases refer to a territorial entity that is a state as understood by international law and practice; the term also covers some territorial entities that are not states, but for which statistical data are maintained and provided internationally on a separate and independent basis.

Preface

Since 1986, the IMF has been supporting the adjustment and reform programs of its low-income member countries with financial resources on highly concessional terms through the Structural Adjustment Facility (SAF) and Enhanced Structural Adjustment Facility (ESAF). As their names suggest, these facilities were intended to back fundamental reform in the structure and institutions of the economies concerned, as well as strong macroeconomic policies, with the objectives of promoting higher economic growth and external viability in a balanced manner.

This paper is a summary of the latest periodic review of experience under SAF- and ESAF-supported programs (the last comparable study was published in 1993). It provides an overview of policies and economic developments in 36 countries during 1986–95, pulls together the main lessons from this experience, and sets out proposals for strengthening the design and implementation of future programs. The report draws on a number of background studies, which will also be published shortly. The review was directed by Susan Schadler, Senior Adviser in the Policy Development and Review Department, under the general guidance of the department's Director, Jack Boorman. The principal author of the summary report was Hugh Bredenkamp, Chief of the Policy Review Division. The staff team comprised Sharmini Coorey, Jorg Decressin, Louis Dicks-Mireaux, Zia Ebrahim-zadeh, Ali Ibrahim, Kalpana Kochhar, Jean Le Dem, Mauro Mecagni, Steven Phillips, and Tsidi Tsikata. A background study on revenue and expenditure policies in SAF- and ESAF-supported programs was prepared by staff of the Fiscal Affairs Department, under the direction of George Abed, Senior Adviser.

The authors are grateful to numerous colleagues in the Fund for detailed comments on the paper; to Kirsten Fitchett, Emmanuel Hife, and Kadima Kalonji for research assistance; to Lourdes Alvero, Julia Baca, and Olivia Carolin for secretarial assistance; and to Esha Ray of the External Relations Department for editorial assistance.

The opinions expressed in the paper are those of the authors and do not necessarily reflect the views of the IMF or of its Executive Directors.

I Overview

For over 10 years, the IMF has supported adjustment and reform programs in many of its low-income members through two facilities established specifically for that purpose—the Enhanced Structural Adjustment Facility (ESAF) and its precursor the Structural Adjustment Facility (SAF) (see Box 1). By the end of 1994, 36 countries had availed themselves of these facilities, in support of 68 multiyear programs (see Appendix).[1] This study summarizes the findings of a review of the experience under these programs and of economic developments in the countries that undertook them. Drawing on a number of detailed studies,[2] it surveys the policies that have been implemented with SAF/ESAF support, assesses economic developments, and identifies possible modifications to the focus and design of ESAF-supported programs that could strengthen economic performance. Although the study is naturally concerned with the IMF's activities, all the countries under review also received policy advice, technical assistance, and financial support for their programs from the World Bank and other agencies and donors in the international community.

The last review of this kind covered the experience of 19 countries through mid-1992.[3] It concluded that the experience under SAF/ESAF-supported programs had been generally favorable. Macroeconomic policies had been strengthened, and significant structural reforms undertaken. Together with sharply increased net resource transfers to the countries concerned and other exogenous developments, these policy advances had contributed to improvements in most indicators of economic performance: growth in output and export volumes, in particular, had strengthened, and inflation had fallen. The record had been uneven, however. Not all poli-

---

[1]This review covers only countries that began ESAF-supported programs before December 31, 1994, on the grounds that the experience of those starting later than this date would be too recent to evaluate fairly. All SAF and ESAF multiyear arrangements approved before December 31, 1994, are covered.

[2]Bredenkamp and Schadler (forthcoming) and Abed and others (forthcoming).

[3]Schadler and others (1993).

> **Box 1. The Enhanced Structural Adjustment Facility**
>
> In the mid-1980s, the IMF recognized that its low-income member countries needed access to highly concessional financial resources to support medium-term structural adjustment programs. It therefore set up the Structural Adjustment Facility (SAF) in 1986, and the Enhanced Structural Adjustment Facility (ESAF) one year later. In 1994, the ESAF was extended and enlarged, and in 1996 the basis for the continuation of ESAF operations in the twenty-first century was agreed upon. Commitments of assistance from the SAF ceased in 1993. ESAF arrangements are intended to support especially vigorous adjustment programs with a higher level of financial assistance than was available under the SAF. Loan commitments are made for a three-year period, in support of three successive annual programs. They carry an annual interest rate of 0.5 percent and repayments are made semiannually, beginning 5½ years and ending 10 years after disbursement. Seventy-nine IMF member countries are currently eligible for ESAF assistance.

cies had been implemented as envisaged, and a difficult world economic climate and deteriorating terms of trade had adversely affected outcomes in key respects. As many as half of the countries reviewed had failed to make discernible progress toward external viability, although almost all had halted the deterioration in their debt situations. Relatively little had been achieved in the reform of banking systems and, especially, of public enterprises. On the basis of that review, it was concluded that:

- The objectives and design of programs supported by concessional ESAF resources were appropriate; the importance of a medium-term perspective for adjustment was reconfirmed, as was the emphasis on structural reform and institution building to support strong macroeconomic policies.
- More ambitious fiscal adjustment was required to reduce excessive deficits and to sustain the

improvements in competitiveness that had been achieved. This extra adjustment should come through fundamental reforms of expenditure control and tax systems.

- A more forceful effort was needed—in close collaboration with the World Bank—to address the lagging reforms of public enterprises and to press ahead with bank restructuring, improvements in bank supervision, and the transition to indirect instruments of monetary control.
- The increased emphasis on social issues was welcome. It was important to protect the more vulnerable social groups from the impact of adjustment policies and, to this end, the IMF should work closely with the World Bank on the design of social safety nets.
- The excessive debt burdens still facing many low-income countries warranted further action by the international community, including through the flexible implementation (and possibly further enhancement) of Paris Club concessions for low-income countries that maintained sound policies.[4]

The present study begins with a brief description of the conditions prevailing prior to SAF/ESAF-supported programs. In Section II, it recalls the main elements of the implied strategy for adjustment and reform and comments on the economic and political environment within which programs had to be implemented. Section III reviews the record with regard to policies—fiscal consolidation and restructuring, inflation control, and structural reform—and the resulting trends in economic growth and countries' external positions. The study concludes that most countries pursuing reform and adjustment programs with the support of the SAF and ESAF have strengthened their economies materially over the past 10 years. Fiscal imbalances have been reduced, and macroeconomic policies have eradicated almost all instances of high inflation. Many improvements in economic structure that the facilities were intended to promote appear to have taken root, and to be spreading, as the pace of structural reform has accelerated in recent years. In most of the countries under review, these policy gains appear to have helped to improve growth and living standards and to bring about a strengthening of external positions. Nevertheless, progress in a number of areas—macroeconomic and structural—has fallen short of program objectives and, most important, of what is needed for countries to reach their growth potential. Progress in

reducing intermediate inflation rates, creating more outward-oriented economic conditions, and moving toward external viability has also been uneven.

In light of these findings, the final section of the study draws lessons from the ESAF countries' experience and identifies various possible ways in which ESAF-supported programs might be reoriented, and in some respects redesigned, to achieve the two key objectives of the ESAF—sustained higher growth, with an improvement in living standards, and progress toward external viability.[5] These two goals are found to be mutually reinforcing and achievable through a common set of policies. Several aspects of ESAF-supported programs are considered: the need for further and more growth-enhancing fiscal adjustment that would also improve prospects for viability; the case for more decisive disinflation as a spur to growth and measures to achieve it; steps to advance structural reforms in two areas where performance has continued to lag—the public enterprises and banking systems; and, finally, modifications to promote more continuity in policy implementation.

The aim in most of this analysis is to step back from the program-by-program detail and look rather at how far countries progressed between the beginning of their SAF/ESAF-supported adjustment (which, by and large, means since the mid-1980s) and 1995, the most recent year for which comprehensive data exist. This choice reflects, first, the view that adjustment and reform are a continuing process, and do not begin or end with specific programs; second, that the full effects of policies may emerge only gradually, and with an uncertain lag; and, third, that there is now a sufficient span of experience with adjustment in the countries under review to allow a more extended perspective than was possible at the time of the last ESAF review. The present study deploys a variety of before-and-after, cross-country (see Box 2), and control-group comparisons to examine the links between policies implemented and outcomes achieved.

There has been much controversy over the appropriate approach to evaluating IMF- (and World Bank–) supported programs. Some evaluations have focused on the question of whether economies grew more rapidly (or had more favorable outcomes for other key variables) as a result of their choice to enter into an IMF arrangement.[6] This study does not attempt to establish the extent to which policies or outcomes were "caused" by SAF/ESAF support and conditions. Rather it assumes that the basic strategy

---

[4]Such action was taken—first, with the introduction by the Paris Club of highly concessional terms in December 1994 (the so-called Naples terms), and subsequently by agreement on the debt initiative for the heavily indebted poor countries sponsored by the World Bank and the IMF.

[5]In this study, the terms "ESAF countries" and "ESAF users" are used interchangeably to refer (solely) to the countries under review.

[6]Bredenkamp (forthcoming) discusses these methodological issues and refers to some key papers on the subject.

Box 2. The Countries Under Review

For the purposes of exposition and analysis, it has proven useful in this study to divide the 36 countries under review into five regional groupings, as follows:

CFA Africa	Other Africa	Asia	Western Hemisphere	Transition Economies
Benin	Burundi	Bangladesh	Bolivia	Albania
Burkina Faso	The Gambia	Nepal	Guyana	Cambodia
Côte d'Ivoire	Ghana	Pakistan	Honduras	Kyrgyz Republic
Equatorial Guinea	Guinea	Sri Lanka	Nicaragua	Lao People's
Mali	Kenya			Democratic Republic
Niger	Lesotho			Mongolia
Senegal	Madagascar			Vietnam
Togo	Malawi			
	Mauritania			
	Mozambique			
	Sierra Leone			
	Tanzania			
	Uganda			
	Zimbabwe			

In many contexts, these groupings were found to represent quite well the trends or specific characteristics in the constituent countries, while bringing out interesting or important differences *between* the groups. There were numerous instances, however, where substantial diversity—or some notable outliers—were evident within the groups, and the report comments on these cases where they occur. In general, considerable care has been taken—including through comparisons of means and medians, and using formal significance tests where relevant—to avoid drawing spurious inferences from group averages.

for growth and adjustment underlying the ESAF—which is based on a large body of analytical and empirical literature that draws on the experience of all developing countries—is the right one, and concentrates on assessing how well that strategy was reflected in the design and execution of programs. The study also seeks evidence on how much progress has been made in strengthening economic performance in ESAF countries and how the basic strategy can be refined and improved.

This review of SAF/ESAF-supported programs conducted by IMF staff will be complemented by an independent evaluation currently being undertaken by a panel of outside experts. The external evaluators will use a case-study approach to examine three topics in detail: (1) developments in countries' external positions; (2) social policies and the composition of government spending; and (3) the determinants and influence of differing degrees of national ownership of ESAF-supported programs.

II Initial Conditions and the Setting for Adjustment

Before turning to the record of adjustment and reform undertaken in ESAF countries, it is useful to recall why countries embarked on this process, and what they hoped to achieve. This section looks first, in broad terms, at the nature of the economic difficulties that countries faced prior to their first SAF/ESAF-supported program, since these naturally determined much of what followed. The objectives and key components of the strategies designed to address those problems are then summarized. The final element considered is the background—both domestic and global—against which policies were implemented.

Initial Conditions

Countries seeking support under the SAF and ESAF had typically accumulated deep-seated economic problems over an extended period. Most came to the IMF in circumstances not of sudden macroeconomic or financial instability but rather of persistently weak growth, often chronically high inflation, and fragile external positions. Development strategies, based commonly on pervasive state intervention in the economy, public ownership, and protectionism, had left a dismal legacy. Distortions and rigidities were stifling entrepreneurship and promoting waste and corruption. They also aggravated the vulnerability of economies that were unusually prone to adverse economic shocks. In many countries, especially in Africa, these profound weaknesses had been masked during much of the 1970s by heavy foreign borrowing on the back of improving terms of trade. When commodity prices turned down sharply and interest rates rose in the early 1980s, both the debts and the policies they had financed became manifestly unsustainable.[7]

The immediate need in most cases was to bring some order to countries' external cash flow positions, through a combination of debt relief or rescheduling and new resource flows. Even though many countries had already begun to adjust in the context of programs supported by stand-by arrangements, their external situations prior to SAF/ESAF-supported programs remained precarious: current account deficits (excluding official transfers) averaged 12–14 percent of GDP, scheduled debt service was typically 35–40 percent of exports, and official reserves were uncomfortably low, given the volatility of these countries' foreign exchange earnings. External imbalances were particularly severe among future ESAF users in Central America and parts of Africa, much less so in Asia.

Net resource transfers did pick up sharply in the context of SAF/ESAF-supported programs. By this time, however, it was widely recognized that the debt crisis of the early 1980s was not a temporary problem of liquidity shortage—a matter of tiding over until the next upturn in commodity prices—but a true watershed. Countries had become locked in a cycle of low saving, weak external positions, and low growth, with each element constraining the others. In the years leading up to their first SAF/ESAF arrangement (by and large, the early to mid-1980s), most were experiencing stagnant exports and declining living standards, with saving rates averaging only about 8 percent of GDP.

Certainly, the early 1980s were lean years for the developing world as a whole. But future SAF/ESAF users were on average falling further behind other developing countries in terms of per capita income during this period (Table 1): their saving rates were half the average of other developing countries, and they had larger budget deficits, higher inflation, higher levels of external debt, more distorted exchange systems, faster population growth, and more adverse social indicators (such as education, health, and life expectancy). It was apparent that fundamental economic reform was required to reverse these trends and deliver a lasting improvement in growth and the external finances.

---

[7]See Schadler and others (1993) for a fuller description of the state of countries' economies prior to embarking on SAF/ESAF-supported adjustment programs.

Table 1. Economic and Social Indicators in ESAF and Other Developing Countries
(In percent a year, unless otherwise indicated)

	ESAF Countries		Non-ESAF Developing Countries[1]	
	1981–85	1991–95[2]	1981–85	1991–95[2]
Real per capita GDP growth	−1.1	0.0	0.3	1.0
Inflation[3]				
Mean	94.4	44.9	23.5	139.9
Median	11.7	11.6	9.1	10.3
Gross national saving (in percent of GDP)	8.0	9.9	18.6	17.4
Budget balance[4] (In percent of GDP)	−9.1	−5.6	−6.8	−4.8
Export volume growth	1.7	7.9	4.4	5.7
Debt-service ratio (actual) (in percent of exports of goods and nonfactor services)	27.9	25.7	18.8	15.7
External debt (face value, in percent of GNP)	81.9	154.2	55.7	75.6
Gross reserves (in months of imports)	2.0	3.5	4.7	5.6
Premium in parallel market exchange rate				
Mean	230.5	18.3	49.0	201.2
Median	28.6	8.2	53.2	211.0
Population growth	2.8	2.5	2.4	2.2
Life expectancy (years at birth)	51.5	55.0	59.7	63.6
Infant mortality (per thousand live births)	111.9	87.5	71.8	52.7
Illiteracy (In percent of population age 15 or above)	54.8	47.3	32.2	23.0

Sources: Bredenkamp and Schadler (forthcoming); International Monetary Fund, *World Economic Outlook* and *International Financial Statistics*; and World Bank, *World Debt Tables* and Social Indicators of Development.

[1]Developing countries as defined in *World Economic Outlook*, excluding countries classified as "high income" by the World Bank and SAF/ESAF users.

[2]1991–94 for some variables.

[3]End of period when available, period average otherwise.

[4]Overall balance, including grants as revenue.

The Adjustment Strategy

SAF/ESAF-supported adjustment programs varied widely in their emphasis and detail, in keeping with the differing circumstances of individual countries. But countries' common problems—and the universal underlying aim of achieving higher sustainable economic growth—resulted in reform strategies that shared certain core objectives.

First, to raise saving rates. The very low saving rates in ESAF countries were reflected in a combination of low investment ratios and high current account deficits. Since public dissaving was seen both as a root of this problem and as the most likely source of an early improvement in national saving rates, fiscal adjustment was at the heart of almost all SAF/ESAF-supported programs. Supporting policies, to bolster private saving, included financial sector reform and a shift from negative to positive real interest rates. The basic aim was to shift the macroeconomic balances underlying current account deficits in favor of greater investment.

Second, to secure macroeconomic stability. Although only 9 of the 67 three-year SAF/ESAF arrangements covered by this review began with initial inflation rates in excess of 40 percent, most ESAF countries—with the exception of those in the CFA franc zone and some in Asia—had experienced volatile inflation for some years, with rates seldom falling into the single-digit range. This instability was viewed as disruptive, and a deterrent to investment. Programs aimed to reduce it by bringing inflation to low (single-digit) levels and by putting the government budget (a chronic source of financial instability) on a surer footing. Low inflation was also considered an important factor in improving conditions for the poorest sectors of the population.

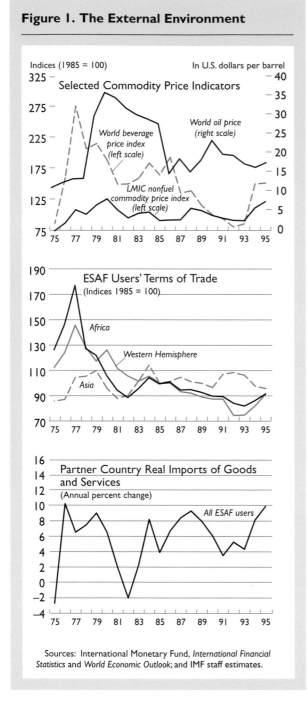

Figure 1. The External Environment

Selected Commodity Price Indicators

Indices (1985 = 100)

In U.S. dollars per barrel

World beverage price index (left scale)

World oil price (right scale)

LMIC nonfuel commodity price index (left scale)

ESAF Users' Terms of Trade
(Indices 1985 = 100)

Africa

Western Hemisphere

Asia

Partner Country Real Imports of Goods and Services
(Annual percent change)

All ESAF users

Sources: International Monetary Fund, *International Financial Statistics* and *World Economic Outlook*; and IMF staff estimates.

Third, to liberalize and open economies to foreign trade. ESAF economies were generally inward-oriented with distorted internal relative prices. Producers faced substantial protection from external competition and disincentives against export activity. Programs sought to eliminate systemic anti-export bias through removal of exchange and trade restrictions (particularly quantitative import restric-

tions), exchange rate unification, tariff reform, liberalization of export price and marketing regimes, and public enterprise reform. In addition, in many cases, real devaluations of the domestic currency—secured by fiscal adjustment—aimed at enhancing the outward orientation of the economy.

Fourth, to reduce government intervention and promote well-functioning markets. The state needed to cease controlling prices, foreign exchange, and product marketing and by and large to withdraw from ownership and control of the means of production. Instead, its challenge was to establish a legal and institutional framework conducive to private business, where contracts could be enforced and property protected. The development of the financial sector was encouraged through a combination of financial and operational restructuring, privatization, and more effective supervision. Deregulation of pricing and marketing, public enterprise and banking system reform, and privatization were thus important structural components of SAF/ESAF-supported programs. The sequencing of reforms in these areas posed particularly difficult issues.

Fifth, to reorient government spending and restructure revenues. "Government," if represented by the share of its expenditure in GDP, was not unusually large in ESAF countries, but it was doing many of the wrong things. An excessive portion of government spending was devoted to subsidies for consumers and state-owned firms, wages for inefficient (or, in some cases, nonexistent) civil servants, ill-chosen capital projects, and the military. Programs aimed increasingly to reorient spending from areas with relatively low social and economic rates of return—unproductive spending—to activities with high rates of return, such as primary education and basic health care. Revenue systems to finance these expenditures also needed to be rendered more efficient, through the simplification of tax and tariff structures, a move toward modern tax instruments such as the value-added tax (VAT), and more effective tax and customs administration.

Sixth, to mobilize external resources. A key part of the strategy under the ESAF was to support countries' reform efforts by temporarily easing the external financing constraint and to move them toward viability in part through reducing reliance on debt-creating inflows and, in some cases, debt burdens. Policies to this end included the clearance of payments arrears, agreements on debt reschedulings and debt relief, a shift to more concessional financing, and a rebuilding of official reserves.

The Setting for Adjustment

Reforms of this scope and magnitude would be challenging in the best of circumstances, and the environment within which policymakers had to implement ESAF-supported programs often complicated their task.

During the late 1980s and early 1990s, most countries had to contend with a sizable deterioration in their terms of trade as they embarked on their first SAF/ESAF-supported programs. The many countries for which tea, coffee, or cocoa was the principal export—almost one-third of all ESAF users—suffered from a 60 percent drop in world beverage prices between 1986 and 1992 (Figure 1). Other nonfuel commodity prices—and, more generally, the growth of demand in ESAF users' export markets—weakened from 1988 through the industrial country recession of 1991–93.

Roughly one in four ESAF users also experienced severe civil strife or war during the late 1980s and early 1990s, in some cases associated with transition to more pluralistic political systems. In such circumstances, it was difficult to formulate policies, still less to sustain their implementation, and this was a factor contributing to the interruption or breakdown of a number of programs. In addition, many countries suffered from natural disasters during this time, including recurrent drought in sub-Saharan Africa and cyclones and flooding in Bangladesh and Nepal.

On the whole, market conditions improved for ESAF users after 1993. Nonfuel commodity prices (especially beverage prices) and the growth of global demand picked up markedly during 1994–95. At the same time, world energy prices remained subdued, at levels 20–30 percent below their peak in 1990. The prevalence of civil conflict also appeared to diminish in the mid-1990s, albeit with some striking exceptions (Burundi, Pakistan, Sierra Leone, and Sri Lanka). This generally more favorable climate seems to have continued in 1996, and is likely to have contributed to the widespread improvement in growth in ESAF countries during 1994–96.

ESAF countries suffered throughout the adjustment period, however, from restricted access to industrial country markets for key export products—particularly in agriculture, textiles, and clothing. Various international agreements defining market access, and granting preferences in some cases, contributed to segmenting markets and discouraging export diversification. Whether trade barriers were eased or intensified over time for ESAF users is difficult to determine: some preferential trading schemes have been broadened, with liberalizing effects; by contrast, some ESAF countries were adversely affected by increased protection in textiles and agriculture.

III What Has Been Achieved?

Progress with regard to the strategy for adjustment and reform can be assessed both on the basis of policies implemented and outcomes achieved. The experience of SAF/ESAF-supported programs—and the countries that undertook them—is reviewed below from both perspectives. Fiscal policies, inflation, structural reforms, and the degree of openness are examined first, before turning to the outcomes for economic growth and countries' external positions. Because adjustment in the six transition economies under review began comparatively late (see Box 3 for a synopsis) and historical data are generally lacking for these countries, most of the analysis that follows relates to the nontransition countries.

Macroeconomic Stabilization

Fiscal Consolidation

In the broadest terms, fiscal adjustment in the ESAF countries appears to have proceeded in three phases since the beginning of the 1980s. The first phase, prior to the inception of the SAF in 1986, was marked by early attempts to tackle the most egregious fiscal imbalances—typically to be found in non-CFA Africa and the Western Hemisphere. These efforts, often made in the context of programs supported by standby arrangements with the IMF, met with some success (Figure 2). Progress slowed markedly, however, during much of the late 1980s and early 1990s. Asian and Western Hemisphere countries continued to trim budget deficits over this period, but African countries saw their budget positions hold steady at best, with deteriorations in most CFA franc zone countries. Progress resumed only after 1994, as countries took advantage of an upturn in export demand, growth, and the terms of trade to trim budget deficits, mainly by containing expenditure as output increased.[8]

The average SAF/ESAF-supported program aimed, over a three-year horizon, to cut primary budget deficits (in relation to GDP, excluding grants and privatization receipts) by a little under half—or 3 percentage points of GDP.[9] African countries sought greater-than-average adjustment, including in programs supporting the major devaluation of the CFA franc in 1994 (Figure 3). On average, the greatest adjustment was targeted in cases where initial imbalances were the most severe (Figure 4).

The relative reliance on targeted expenditure restraint and revenue increases to bring about this adjustment varied widely, depending to some degree on initial conditions. Thus, although programs envisaged cuts in noninterest expenditure relative to GDP of about 2 percentage points on average over three years, almost half targeted increased or unchanged spending from preprogram levels. The deepest cuts—averaging more than 2½ percentage points over three years—were sought in Africa, where initial spending levels were highest (the transition economies excepted). In all other regions, the principal source of fiscal adjustment was to be increased revenues. Across the regions (again, other than the transition economies) the aim was to raise revenue-GDP ratios by about 1 percentage point over three years. The constellation of revenue targets (see Figure 4) implied some degree of convergence in revenue-GDP ratios over time: programs aimed to maintain (or, in some cases, reduce) these ratios where the initial tax burden was relatively high, and boost them in countries where initial revenues were below average.

Looking more closely at the modalities of adjustment within spending and revenue totals, the diversity across countries increases still further, but a few important patterns can be discerned:[10]

---

[8]The CFA franc zone countries achieved significant savings in the government wage bill by containing nominal wage growth following their 1994 devaluation.

[9]Unless otherwise specified, the observations in this section are based on a restricted sample of 28 (out of 36) countries and 47 (out of 68) SAF/ESAF-supported programs, because of the absence of three-year-ahead fiscal targets for some programs.

[10]These findings are taken from Abed and others (forthcoming), who examine revenue and expenditure policies in SAF/ESAF-supported programs in more detail, based on one-year-ahead or within-year targets. An analysis on three-year-ahead targets, to be consistent with the rest of this section, was not possible at this level of disaggregation, since medium-term program targets were either not set or not reported in the necessary detail. Three-year-ahead targets were generally more ambitious than nearer-term targets.

Box 3. Adjustment in ESAF-Supported Transition Economies

The demise of central planning and the transition to a market-based economy began at different times for the six transition countries under review: in 1986 for the Lao People's Democratic Republic, 1989 for Vietnam, 1990 for Mongolia, and 1992 for Albania and the Kyrgyz Republic; Cambodia—still struggling with armed internal conflict—did not undertake comprehensive adjustment until 1993. ESAF-supported programs began in 1993 and 1994 in all but one of the six countries. The Lao People's Democratic Republic, the exception, began adjustment under a SAF arrangement in 1989, followed by an ESAF arrangement in 1993. ESAF-supported programs in these countries were, in many respects, a continuation and a deepening of adjustment efforts initiated at the beginning of transition. Although their strategies included the same core elements as in other ESAF countries (see section on "The Adjustment Strategy" above), adjustment programs in the transition economies tended to place greater emphasis on certain areas, consistent with their different circumstances.

• *Rapid stabilization* was a central objective, to be achieved mainly through strong fiscal adjustment and tight control of credit, particularly to public enterprises. Stabilization efforts were most successful in Albania and the Indochinese economies, all of which reduced inflation to low levels, initially through a credit-based approach backed in Indochina by wage controls. During 1992–95, following initial stabilization, Cambodia, the Lao People's Democratic Republic, and Vietnam maintained stable nominal exchange rates (with official rates generally within 1 percent of the parallel market rate) through tight fiscal and monetary policy. Although Mongolia and the Kyrgyz Republic also made notable progress in reducing inflation in 1994–95, their inflation rates remained relatively high (53 percent and 32 percent, respectively, at the end of 1995), mainly because of difficulties in curbing fiscal deficits and controlling credit growth to public enterprises.

• *Strong fiscal adjustment,* particularly through tax and public enterprise reform, was crucial. Budget deficits were reduced sharply in Albania, the Lao People's Democratic Republic, and Vietnam. In Albania, measures to improve tax and customs administration were delayed, and fiscal adjustment relied mainly on programmed reductions in current spending, facilitated by the decline in unemployment (reflecting greater private sector activity) and reforms in the budget process.

Government employment was reduced by close to a third from mid-1992 to February 1995, spending was shifted toward investment, direct subsidies were virtually eliminated by 1995, and other current expenditures were scaled back considerably. Tax reforms were introduced early (1988–89) in the Lao People's Democratic Republic and Vietnam, and later in Cambodia. By 1994–95, revenues had strengthened considerably in all three countries, aided in Vietnam by the improved financial performance of state enterprises. Fiscal deficits were kept to moderate levels, initially by lowering the real wage bill (partly through retrenchment, with labor later being absorbed by the growing private sector), lowering subsidies and transfers to public enterprises, and reducing capital outlays and social services. The compression of capital and social spending was subsequently reversed as revenues were raised. Reform efforts failed to increase revenues in the Kyrgyz Republic and Mongolia, partly due to tax arrears and poor tax administration, and overall fiscal deficits were markedly higher.

• *Wide-ranging structural reforms,* particularly public enterprise reform and privatization, received strong emphasis. In Vietnam, state enterprises were given substantial management autonomy in 1988–89, while policies were adopted to increase competition (by liberalizing imports and encouraging foreign direct investment), harden budget constraints (by eliminating most direct subsidies and directed credit), and subject enterprises to uniform rules of taxation. As a result, the net budgetary contribution of enterprises rose to over 10 percent of GDP by 1994–95, partly through increased profits from the oil sector. Similar efforts were undertaken in the Lao People's Democratic Republic and Cambodia. Although a majority of small and medium-sized enterprises were privatized in Albania, the Kyrgyz Republic, and Mongolia by the end of 1995, ESAF-supported programs called for further restructuring and privatization of strategic enterprises. In all six countries, weak banking systems remain a concern. In addition, a need for further reforms in the legal and institutional framework was identified in programs, especially those governing land in Albania and the Kyrgyz Republic. By the end of 1995, all six countries had undertaken extensive liberalization of prices, trade, and foreign investment and had relatively few exchange restrictions on current transactions.

• First, most programs targeted a significant shift from current to capital spending: two-thirds of programs envisaged increased capital expenditure, while almost 60 percent planned cuts in current spending relative to GDP.

• Second, of the saving sought in current spending, roughly half was to come from the govern-

ment wage bill and half from subsidies and transfers (through, for instance, reduced support for public enterprises and better targeting of consumer subsidies).

• Third, most programs in recent years included pledges to strengthen health and education spending, although this objective was seldom

Figure 2. Fiscal Trends in ESAF Countries
(Averages, in percent of GDP)

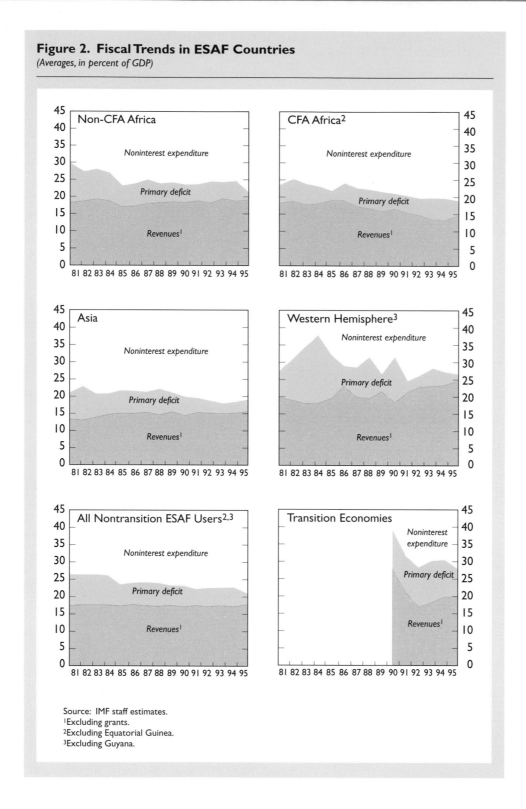

Source: IMF staff estimates.
[1]Excluding grants.
[2]Excluding Equatorial Guinea.
[3]Excluding Guyana.

quantified; they also commonly incorporated specific safety net measures for vulnerable groups to mitigate the short-term impact of price increases or reduced employment opportunities.

• Fourth, on the revenue side, programs typically aimed to shift the burden from nontax to tax revenues, from direct to indirect taxation (often through the introduction or expansion of a VAT),

Figure 3. Fiscal Adjustment in SAF/ESAF-Supported Programs: Averages by Region[1]
(In percent of GDP)

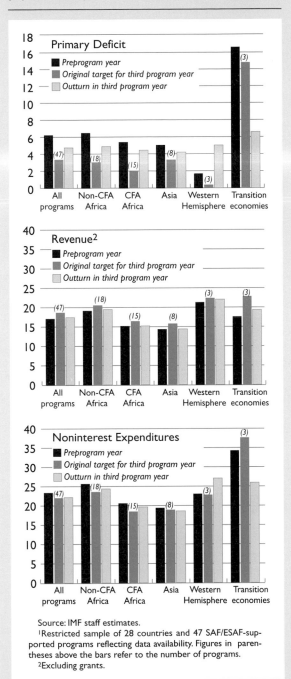

Source: IMF staff estimates.
[1]Restricted sample of 28 countries and 47 SAF/ESAF-supported programs reflecting data availability. Figures in parentheses above the bars refer to the number of programs.
[2]Excluding grants.

Figure 4. Fiscal Adjustment in SAF/ESAF-Supported Programs: By Initial Conditions[1]
(In percent of GDP)

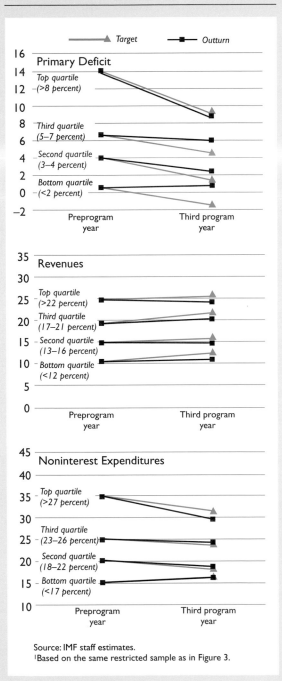

Source: IMF staff estimates.
[1]Based on the same restricted sample as in Figure 3.

and to boost tax receipts from international trade; the latter was sought in some cases as a matter of expediency, but in others it was simply a product of expected increases in imports, im-

proved customs administration, or the planned tariffication of quantitative trade restrictions.

On average, only about half of the targeted reduction in primary budget deficits was achieved (see

Figure 3). Performance varied widely, however, with almost half of all programs achieving no improvement in the primary balance over three years. The largest shortfalls, relative to target, appeared in the Western Hemisphere countries, where deficits actually increased as a percentage of GDP (though this partly reflects upward revisions to recorded deficits in the preprogram year). African countries also tended to miss program targets by wide margins, but nevertheless succeeded in reducing their budget deficits from preprogram levels. Revenues fell short of target in roughly two-thirds of all programs, and on average (in relation to GDP) were barely changed from preprogram levels. Somewhat surprisingly, however, deficit overruns were not significantly correlated with revenue shortfalls, reflecting a common tendency for expenditures to be curtailed in programs where revenues failed to meet expectations. The brunt of this expenditure restraint was typically borne by capital spending, which came in below target in three-quarters of the programs experiencing revenue shortfalls (whereas current spending was cut in only one-third).[11] By contrast, overshooting of deficit targets was more typically associated with expenditure overruns, the latter dominating in two-thirds of such cases.[12]

Where program objectives were not met, the reasons were often complex. On the revenue side, targets for direct and indirect taxes were, on average, achieved. The ambition to raise tax receipts from foreign trade, however, was only partially realized in most cases. It appears that early tariff rate reductions were often not accompanied by the planned elimination of import duty exemptions, or by effective measures to tackle evasion. In some cases (notably in Africa), there were also delays in converting quantitative restrictions to tariffs. In an attempt to compensate for tax shortfalls, countries often resorted to one-off measures to boost nontax revenues, increased profit transfers from central banks being a common device.

Expenditure overruns were most prevalent in African and Western Hemisphere countries. Governments frequently failed to scale back civil service headcounts as intended, trying instead to trim wage rates (in conflict with another oft-stated objective:

retaining and motivating good quality civil servants). Subsidy costs also tended to exceed targets in these countries, in all likelihood reflecting their limited progress in reforming public enterprises. More generally, ESAF countries' expenditure management suffered from weak budgetary institutions—owing in part to a scarcity of trained personnel—with poor systems for budgeting and monitoring of expenditures, and widespread use of extrabudgetary funds.

As regards the evolving composition of government spending in ESAF countries, the record is, on the whole, reasonably positive (Figure 5). Relative to the pre-SAF/ESAF period, the desired shift from current to capital expenditure did occur, albeit to a lesser extent than had been hoped. The tendency to sacrifice capital spending as revenues fell short meant that, rather than rising as intended, capital spending did no more than hold steady as a share of GDP in the nontransition economies as a whole, and declined slightly among ESAF users in Africa.[13] More encouragingly, the limited data that are available suggest that roughly three-quarters of countries succeeded in raising expenditure on health and education since their SAF/ESAF-supported adjustment began, including (on average) in Africa. Similarly, in the area of military spending there was a broad-based shift in the desired direction, with declines observed since the pre-SAF/ESAF period in 12 of the 15 countries for which data are available, from an average of almost 3 percent to about 2½ percent of GDP.

Inflation Control

The diversity of experiences among ESAF countries in reducing inflation is so marked as to preclude generalizations about the sample as a whole. Among regional groupings, however, some clear patterns emerge (Figure 6).[14]

First, countries in the CFA franc zone stand apart, having succeeded in maintaining inflation consistently in the low single-digit range since the mid-1980s, reflecting their use of the exchange rate peg to the French franc as an anchor. The 50 percent devaluation of the CFA franc in January 1994 triggered a price level adjustment in that year, but by 1995 inflation was already back to about 7 percent on average, and it fell further in 1996. ESAF countries in Asia have also had generally stable inflation

---

[11]The tendency to sacrifice capital before current spending may arise from the perception that cuts in public investment are politically less costly. For evidence, see Haggard and others (1995).

[12]This assortment of outcomes—with some programs recording expenditure overruns and others a combination of revenue and expenditure shortfalls—explains why, in the aggregate (see Figure 3), expenditures appear roughly in line with targets on average, while revenues are lower than targeted. Dicks-Mireaux and others (forthcoming) provide detailed analysis and statistical testing of these findings.

[13]These averages conceal some notable successes in raising capital spending, however. In Bolivia, Ghana, Mozambique, Nicaragua, and Uganda, the share of capital spending in GDP has increased by at least 4 percentage points since the pre-SAF/ESAF period.

[14]References in this section to "low" inflation mean an annual rate below 10 percent, "intermediate" means 10–40 percent, and "high" means above 40 percent.

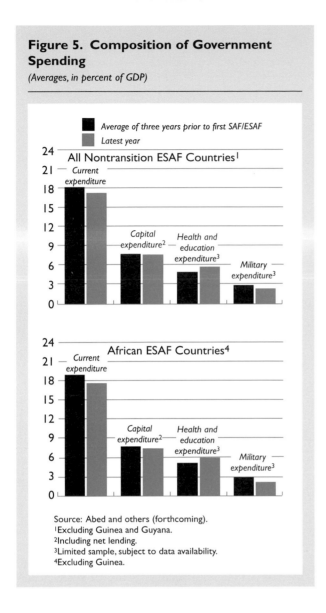

Figure 5. Composition of Government Spending

(Averages, in percent of GDP)

■ Average of three years prior to first SAF/ESAF
▦ Latest year

All Nontransition ESAF Countries[1]

Current expenditure

Capital expenditure[2]

Health and education expenditure[3]

Military expenditure[3]

African ESAF Countries[4]

Current expenditure

Capital expenditure[2]

Health and education expenditure[3]

Military expenditure[3]

Source: Abed and others (forthcoming).
[1]Excluding Guinea and Guyana.
[2]Including net lending.
[3]Limited sample, subject to data availability.
[4]Excluding Guinea.

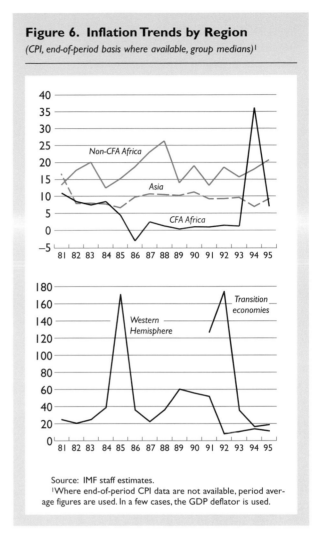

Figure 6. Inflation Trends by Region

(CPI, end-of-period basis where available, group medians)[1]

Non-CFA Africa

Asia

CFA Africa

Western Hemisphere

Transition economies

Source: IMF staff estimates.
[1]Where end-of-period CPI data are not available, period average figures are used. In a few cases, the GDP deflator is used.

over the past decade, fluctuating within a fairly narrow range around 10 percent.

The three ESAF users in the Western Hemisphere other than Honduras had witnessed very high inflation (above 100 percent) at some point in the past decade, but all extinguished it successfully (Bolivia in 1986 and Nicaragua and Guyana in 1992) and had reached rates in the neighborhood of 10 percent by 1995.[15] Dramatic disinflation was also achieved in the six transition economies. Following the price surges commonly associated with liberalization, all

but Mongolia quickly brought inflation down into the intermediate range, and by 1995 Albania, Cambodia, and Vietnam had rates close to or below 10 percent.

Inflation performance has been most mixed, however, in non-CFA Africa. In a handful of cases— The Gambia, Guinea, Lesotho, Mauritania, and Uganda—a good deal has been accomplished in recent years. These countries each had average inflation rates of below 10 percent during 1993–95— compared with rates during the late 1980s that averaged 37 percent, and exceeded 100 percent in Uganda. The region as a whole, however, saw no downward trend in inflation during the 10–15 years to 1995. Indeed, the average rate rose during the first half of the 1990s, to over 20 percent by 1995. Several countries witnessed sharp declines in inflation in 1996, although it is too early to say how much of this drop reflects the generally favorable supply con-

---

[15]Bolivia and Nicaragua had largely defeated their near-hyperinflations in earlier programs supported by stand-by arrangements with the IMF, but they consolidated this progress in their subsequent SAF- and ESAF-supported programs.

Figure 7. Inflation Targets, by Degree of Initial Inflation[1]

(Group medians, excluding CFA countries)

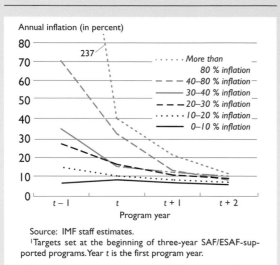

Source: IMF staff estimates.
[1]Targets set at the beginning of three-year SAF/ESAF-supported programs. Year *t* is the first program year.

Figure 8. Inflation Target and Outturns[1]

(Group medians, in percent; excluding CFA countries)

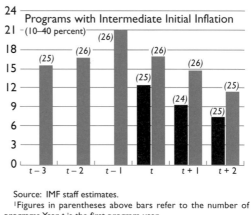

Source: IMF staff estimates.
[1]Figures in parentheses above bars refer to the number of programs. Year *t* is the first program year.

ditions and how much a durable strengthening of macroeconomic policies.

How does this experience compare with what was envisaged in SAF/ESAF-supported programs? Programs typically aimed to bring inflation down to the single-digit range over the three-year arrangement period, with the pace determined to a large extent by the initial level of inflation (Figure 7). In the event, programs had greatest success in tackling high and very high inflations (Figure 8). For the most part, however, the intended transition to low inflation was not achieved. Setting aside the CFA franc zone cases, fewer than two programs in five had single-digit inflation by the third program year. This is not much more than the proportion (30 percent of programs) that *already* had single-digit inflation in the year before the program started. Thus, almost as many countries moved up from the low to the intermediate range during programs as achieved the reverse.

In the majority of those starting with initial inflation in the intermediate range (26 programs, or half of all non-CFA cases), less than one-half of the decline in inflation targeted for the first year was achieved. The picture by the third year was only somewhat better, and there is no systematic evidence of further gains made beyond the program period. Moreover, although inflation rates did tend to decline during programs, it was typically from a peak following several years of rising inflation (see Figure 8): hence the earlier observation that many countries made no perceptible progress in reducing inflation over the longer term. Section IV, considers why many ESAF users have remained stuck in the intermediate inflation range (Table 2), and what this implies for program design.

Structural Reform

At the time of the last review, looking back over the first six years of experience with SAF/ESAF-supported programs, it was concluded that progress in structural economic reform among the countries involved had been profound but uneven. Important gains had been achieved in the areas of exchange and trade liberalization, price-setting and marketing, and the freeing of interest rates. But little had been accomplished in other areas, notably in the restructuring and reform of public enterprises and banking systems.

Four years on, the assessment must be similarly qualified. On the positive side, reforms continued to

Table 2. Progress on Inflation Since the Pre-SAF/ESAF Period[1]
(In percent)

	Average Inflation During Three Years Prior to First SAF/ESAF Program	Average Inflation, 1993–95
CFA franc zone Africa, median	1.4	16.5[2]
Other ESAF users		
"Stronger performers"[3]		
Albania	170.4	17.6
Bangladesh	10.2	4.7
Bolivia	3,471.2	10.1
Gambia, The	34.6	1.4
Guinea	71.8	4.2
Guyana	63.6	10.6
Lesotho	14.4	8.0
Mauritania	8.8	4.4
Nepal	11.0	8.2
Sierra Leone	70.3	24.0
Sri Lanka	6.9	8.7
Uganda	155.3	8.3
"Weaker performers"		
Burundi	8.8	14.3
Ghana	19.6	44.2
Honduras	23.0	22.9
Kenya	7.4	22.7
Lao People's Democratic Republic	18.2	13.8
Madagascar	11.6	35.6
Malawi	19.4	53.1
Mongolia	177.0	100.8
Mozambique	32.7	56.0
Pakistan	5.4	11.4
Tanzania	33.9	26.9
Zimbabwe	20.2	21.9

Source: IMF staff estimates.

[1]Excluding countries that did not begin their first SAF/ESAF-supported program until 1994 (Cambodia, Côte d'Ivoire, the Kyrgyz Republic, Nicaragua, and Vietnam).

[2]This figure reflects the CFA franc devaluation in early 1994; the 1995 median was 6.4 percent.

[3]Countries that achieved average single-digit inflation during 1993–95, or (in the case of Albania, Bolivia, Guyana, and Sierra Leone) that had brought inflation down very sharply from high preprogram levels.

move ahead on all fronts and in all countries, to varying degrees. Equally important, there are few instances of substantial policy reversals. Thus, although the process has been long and drawn out in many cases, the countries concerned now have economies that are significantly more market driven and flexible than they were 10 years ago. There are also signs that the pace of structural reform has picked up in recent years, especially in Africa (Figures 9 and 10). It remains the case, however, that reforms affecting bank soundness and public enterprises lagged far behind other areas and fell short of program ambitions: these are also among the areas in which African economies compare least favorably with other ESAF countries. (The judgments in this section regarding the extent and pace of structural reform are based primarily on "policy indices," the construction of which is summarized in Box 4.)

The deregulation of pricing and marketing was among the earliest of structural reforms to be implemented in SAF/ESAF-supported programs (and some countries had made significant advances in prior adjustment programs). Major successes were achieved early on, particularly in the important markets for agricultural products. Progress since then has continued; by 1995 instances of the most extensive intervention had been eliminated, although one-third of ESAF countries still had controls on a few staple foodstuffs, transportation, utilities, petroleum

Figure 9. Status of Structural Reform in ESAF Countries
(Indices of structural reform)

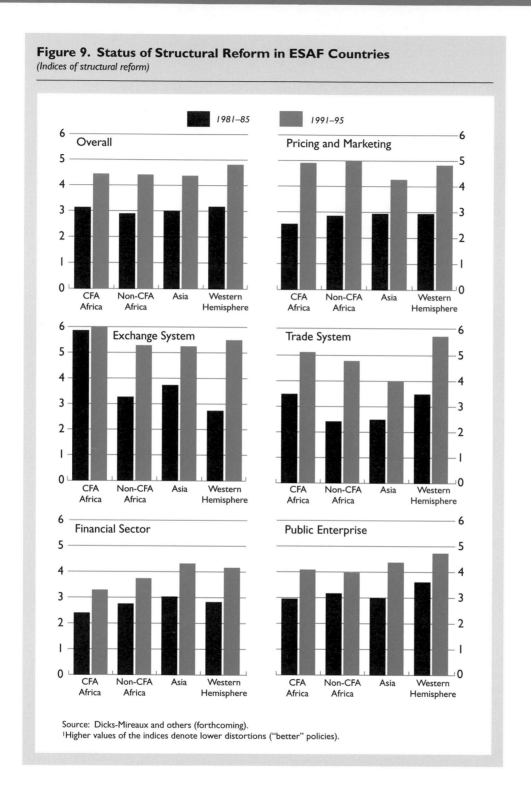

Source: Dicks-Mireaux and others (forthcoming).
[1] Higher values of the indices denote lower distortions ("better" policies).

products, and some construction materials. There has also been a widespread shift to more rational mechanisms for setting prices that remain subject to controls, with petroleum prices now commonly linked to world prices, and utility rates typically set on a cost recovery or long-run marginal cost basis. One important area where the pace of reform accelerated in recent years is in the pricing and marketing of export products, which were heavily controlled in almost half of all nontransition ESAF countries in

Figure 10. The Pace of Structural Reform
(Change in indices of structural reform)[1]

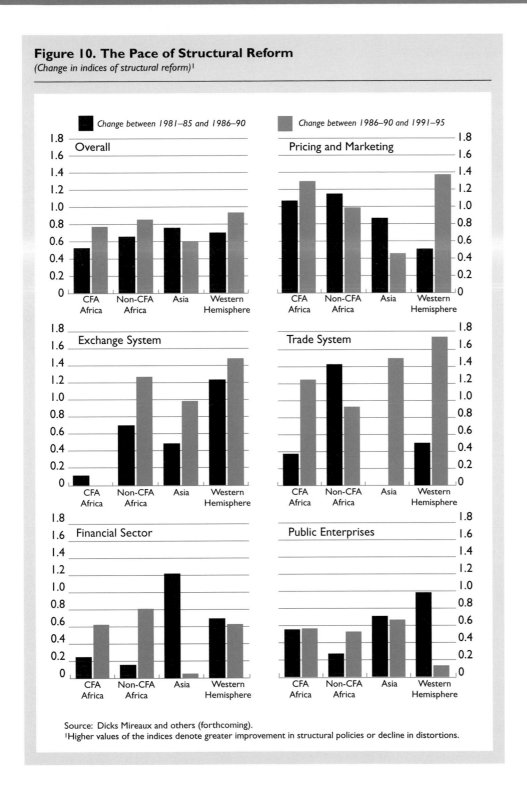

Source: Dicks Mireaux and others (forthcoming).
[1]Higher values of the indices denote greater improvement in structural policies or decline in distortions.

the early 1980s and which are now universally subject, at most, to light or moderate intervention. In general, with a few exceptions, price reform is an area where Africa has outpaced other ESAF countries since the early 1980s.

Rapid progress has also been commonplace in the reform of ESAF countries' exchange systems. Already by 1990, extensive use of surrender requirements and controls on the allocation of foreign exchange was confined to only four of the nontran-

---

Box 4. Indices of Structural Reform

The five indices of structural reform shown in Figures 9 and 10 are each based on a number of criteria:
• *Pricing and marketing*. The extent of price controls and state intervention in marketing of fertilizers, petroleum products, major foodstuffs, and export products.
• *Exchange system*. The level of the premium in the parallel exchange market and the extent of surrender requirements and nonmarket foreign exchange allocation.
• *Trade system*. The coverage of quantitative restrictions and the level and dispersion of tariffs.
• *Financial sector*. The presence or otherwise of controls on credit or interest rates; real interest rates and interest rate spreads that are above or below certain thresholds; quantitative measures of financial intermediation, private sector access to credit, and financial deepening; and the existence or otherwise of a diversified banking system and markets for interbank funds, government or central bank securities, and stocks.
• *Public enterprise sector*. Measures of public enterprises' share in total output and total credit, of their overall financial balance, and of net financial flows from government.

The detailed methodology for scoring against and weighting these criteria is explained in Dicks-Mireaux and others (forthcoming).

---

sition ESAF countries (Bangladesh, Mauritania, Tanzania, and Zimbabwe).[16] By 1995 such distortions had been eliminated in all nontransition countries except Madagascar, and currently all except Burundi, Lesotho, Mauritania, and Mozambique have accepted the obligations of Article VIII of the Fund's Articles of Agreement.[17] Foreign exchange markets in many countries remain subject to restrictions on capital transactions, however, as indicated by the persistence of parallel market premiums exceeding 10 percent in two-thirds of Asian and non-CFA African ESAF countries in 1995.

The easing of trade barriers was somewhat slower in coming, beginning typically in the late 1980s, but accelerating in the early 1990s. Non-CFA African countries had the most severe initial distortions in this area, but subsequently made faster progress than any other region, and by 1995 almost all had put in place regimes that were in many respects less

protective than the average Asian ESAF user.[18] In the CFA countries, the pace of trade reform benefited from the impetus provided by the 1994 devaluation of the CFA franc and by new regional initiatives aimed at expanding trade links in that part of the world. Overall, significant progress was achieved in curtailing quantitative restrictions: the number of countries making extensive use of such highly distorting instruments declined from 14 in the early 1980s to 7 by 1990 and zero by 1995. The rationalization and reduction of tariff rates typically proceeded more slowly. The pace picked up in the early 1990s with important reforms in a number of countries (Benin, Ghana, Guinea, Honduras, Kenya, and Togo), although many countries supplemented tariffs with other taxes, customs fees, and duties targeted at imports. Notwithstanding the generally encouraging trends, there is great scope for further gains in trade reform through tariff reductions: as of 1995, trade regimes remained "moderately restrictive" in half of all nontransition ESAF countries.[19]

A more sobering impression emerges from the experience with public enterprise reform. This has been an important element in SAF/ESAF-supported programs, since the losses imposed by public enterprises on the state budget and the banking system have been of macroeconomic proportions. Although in some countries the planned measures were piecemeal—aimed at selected problem enterprises—as many as two-thirds of the countries under review developed comprehensive public enterprise reform plans, typically in collaboration with the World Bank. The key elements of the strategy were as follows:
• *Hardening budget constraints* on public enterprises, by limiting their recourse to capital transfers, direct subsidies, and net lending from government and to credit from the banking system.
• Creating the conditions for more *management accountability* in public enterprises, either by entering into "performance contracts" with existing managers or by contracting out management responsibilities to the private sector.
• Enhancing *competition* to encourage efficiency gains in public enterprises and to pave the way for privatization, through the lifting of restrictive regulations on pricing and investment, and removal of de jure barriers to entry.
• *Privatization* of selected (usually small and medium-sized) enterprises; divestment plans typically excluded "strategic" enterprises—those in

---

[16]Countries in the CFA franc zone had foreign exchange systems that were free of restrictions on current transactions throughout the period under review.

[17]Among ESAF transition countries, the Krygyz Republic and Mongolia have also accepted the obligations of Article VIII.

[18]The indices of trade reform do not, however, capture use of nontariff import charges (see below).

[19]In this context, "moderately restrictive" means a tariff structure with average tariff rates of 20–25 percent (maximum 30–40 percent) and few exemptions.

utilities, telecommunications, transportation, heavy industry, and agricultural processing and marketing—which were usually targeted instead for restructuring under state control.

- Building *social and political consensus* for the reforms, including through the process of negotiating policy framework papers with World Bank and IMF staff (and dialogue during staff visits more generally) and by provision of social safety nets.[20]

Overall, the implementation of public enterprise reform has been slow, uneven, and subject to extensive slippages. The size and financial burden of public enterprises (according to the limited available data) have been reduced in roughly half of the nontransition ESAF countries since the early 1980s, and the number of countries with a severe burden in this respect has fallen sharply. However, despite the finding of the last review that this is an area where greater efforts were needed, only in non-CFA Africa is there any evidence of an accelerated pace of reform in the 1990s. Even in non-CFA Africa, progress has been variable: based on available indicators, half of the countries appear to have made little or no progress during the past 10 years.

Poor results can be traced to the fact that the biggest problems—both from a financial and a resource allocation perspective—typically reside in the strategic sectors, where the standard approach has had least effect. Many countries (especially the transition economies) have made significant progress in privatizing small and medium-sized enterprises, but few (Bolivia and Ghana are exceptions) have divested large enterprises in the strategic sectors. Meanwhile, attempts at restructuring the large enterprises have not delivered the desired results. Managers do not appear to have changed their ways in response to the introduction of performance contracts, which have often been poorly designed. And governments have tended to replace direct budgetary support with quasi-fiscal assistance such as tax concessions and loan guarantees, thereby reducing pressure on the enterprises to reform. It is encouraging that recognition of these weaknesses appears to be growing, and recent programs have tended to put greater emphasis on privatization of strategic enterprises, including through leasing arrangements.

Reforms of the financial system in SAF/ESAF-supported programs have had three broad and complementary aims: to move from state to market allocation of credit; to substitute indirect for direct instruments of monetary control; and to strengthen banks' financial positions on a durable basis. In the event, achievements have been mixed, with least progress in what is perhaps ultimately the most important aspect: bank soundness. Reforms to liberalize interest rates were enacted early and are now widespread, encompassing two-thirds of nontransition countries in 1995 (with remaining controls confined largely to Africa). As a result, the prevalence of negative real interest rates has diminished sharply outside non-CFA Africa. The development of financial markets—for interbank funds, government securities, and stocks—and the transition to indirect instruments of monetary control have also proceeded well, beginning in the late 1980s (Asian countries made particularly strong and rapid progress here). The number of countries with formal quantitative controls on credit dropped from almost half of all nontransition countries in 1990, and all but five countries in the early 1980s, to only seven by 1995.

Weaknesses in the banking systems in ESAF countries, however, remain pervasive. Though data are extremely scarce, the extent of balance sheet problems has become increasingly apparent over the past decade as banks' principal clients, the public enterprises, suffered from the terms of trade declines of the late 1980s and the squeezing of financial aid from state budgets. Banking (liquidity) crises have been avoided in most countries, probably owing to the perception of implicit government guarantees, but banks' ability to mobilize and allocate resources efficiently has been severely impaired in cases where loan portfolios are fundamentally unsound. At the root of these difficulties has been—in addition to the continuing financial problems of borrowers in the public enterprise sector—a combination of governmental interference in bank operations, weak managers and management systems, and poor regulatory and supervisory frameworks.

Most countries have adopted multiyear bank restructuring plans, in the context of ESAF-supported programs, aimed at addressing inadequacies in each of these areas. The dominant approach has involved government assumption of problem loans and recapitalization, some cost-cutting and downsizing of operations, the introduction in state banks of performance or management contracts to improve decision making, and the strengthening of supervision. Privatization has been limited, as has resort to bank liquidations (except in some CFA countries). Although many of these programs are ongoing, or are too recent to allow an assessment, the results of those in the vanguard have not been encouraging. The fiscal costs, where they are known at all, have been large—on the order of 15–25 percent of GDP in some cases. Yet progress has been slow and fitful, and it has rarely been possible to point to significant

---

[20]All five of the countries examined in the case studies reported in Decressin and others (forthcoming) provided some form of assistance—usually severance benefits, but sometimes also retraining support—for employees laid off during restructuring of public enterprises.

improvements in the functioning of banks. Reforms appear to have been held back by a dearth of local banking skills, a failure to expand competition in the banking sector, and an unwillingness of governments to stop pressuring banks to lend to uncreditworthy public enterprises.

There has been increasing recognition that an important element in the move to market-based economies is the strengthening of property rights and other aspects of good governance. Legal systems and practices are needed to define clearly and enforce property rights, to ensure respect for contracts, and to deter corruption and abuse of authority. ESAF-supported programs have made a positive contribution in this regard, both directly (promoting reform of land tenure systems and more liberal and transparent foreign investment codes, for instance) and indirectly (by reducing the extent of the distortions and regulations that feed corruption). Assessing overall progress in this area is particularly difficult, however. Dicks-Mireaux and others (forthcoming) report some evidence, based on ratings by commercial agencies according to various "economic security" criteria.[21] These suggest a mixed picture among ESAF countries: property rights appear to have improved in recent years (comparing the early 1990s with the late 1980s) in two-thirds of countries, but deteriorated in one-third. The improvements seem to have been concentrated in Asian and Western Hemisphere countries, although some countries in Africa (Ghana, Tanzania, and Uganda) have also made considerable progress in this area.

Openness

This survey of evolving policies tells a story of qualified progress over the past decade among countries pursuing SAF/ESAF-supported programs. There were consistent but often hesitant advances in most policy areas, disappointments in some respects and in some countries, but signs of a general strengthening of the adjustment effort in the early 1990s. Progress in increasing the outward orientation of ESAF countries' economies—an important strategic objective—was similarly modest, but with signs of an improving trend in recent years.

Liberalization of exchange and trade regimes, nominal depreciation, and fiscal adjustment were reflected in a steady and sizable depreciation of the real exchange rate across all regions from 1985 onward (Figure 11). Real depreciation was particularly

sharp in the Western Hemisphere and least pronounced in CFA Africa until the devaluation of the CFA franc at the beginning of 1994. Notwithstanding substantial cross-country variation, parallel market premiums on the whole also declined markedly over this period as exchange regimes were liberalized. Regional differences also narrowed significantly, reflecting marked progress in those regions—non-CFA Africa and Western Hemisphere—that had the most distorted exchange regimes in the early 1980s, and comparatively little progress in Asia.[22]

These developments contributed to a sizable expansion from the mid-1980s onward in the degree of openness—as measured by the level of foreign trade in relation to GDP—in non-CFA Africa and the Western Hemisphere. In Asia, where the trade ratio is smaller owing to the much larger size of these countries, the increase has been less pronounced, as overall output grew in line with relatively rapid growth in trade.[23] In CFA Africa, foreign trade flows picked up following the devaluation in 1994.

A somewhat different regional picture, however, emerges from an analysis of trade volumes. In all regions, with the striking exception of Asia, export volumes had been stagnant or declining during the early 1980s and picked up only modestly in the second half of the 1980s (Figure 12). On average, countries in Africa and the Western Hemisphere incurred major losses in export market share throughout the 1980s. These losses were stemmed in the early 1990s, however, as export volume growth in the two regions accelerated to over 7 percent, and significant gains in market share were recorded by a number of countries (including Ghana, Kenya, and Tanzania). By contrast, export market share rose steadily and markedly in Asia from 1985 to 1995.

Stronger export growth and increased resource transfers allowed import volumes to rebound in Africa in the mid- to late 1980s, following a period of severe compression. In Asia and the Western Hemisphere, import growth was subdued or declining until the early 1990s, when it rose sharply as a counterpart to booming exports in these regions.

Economic Growth

This broad picture is closely mirrored in ESAF countries' growth performance over time. From

---

[21]The criteria are the quality and acceptance of the tools of law and order, the quality of public administration and extent of government corruption, and contract and expropriation risks to foreign investors.

[22]Countries in the CFA franc zone had negligible premiums throughout, owing to the absence of significant exchange restrictions in CFA franc regime.

[23]The average population in Asian ESAF countries is 6 to 15 times larger than the average population in African or Western Hemisphere ESAF countries.

Figure 11. Share of Trade in GDP and Exchange Rates

(Sample medians)

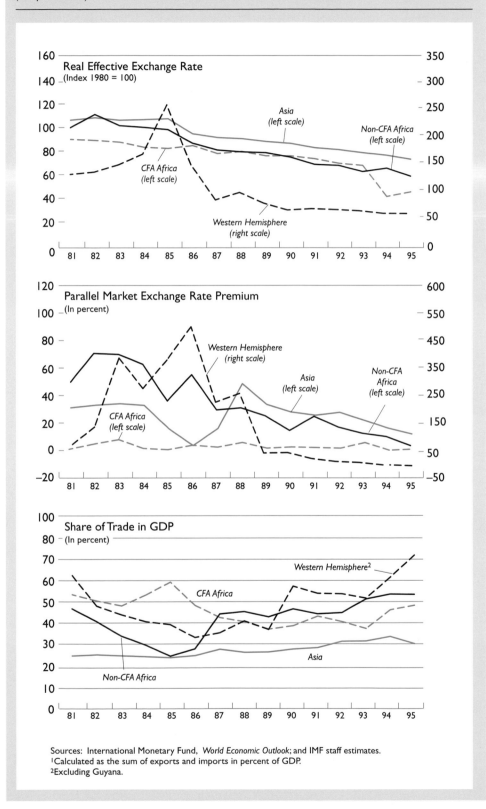

Sources: International Monetary Fund, *World Economic Outlook*; and IMF staff estimates.
[1]Calculated as the sum of exports and imports in percent of GDP.
[2]Excluding Guyana.

Figure 12. Trends in External Trade
(Sample medians)

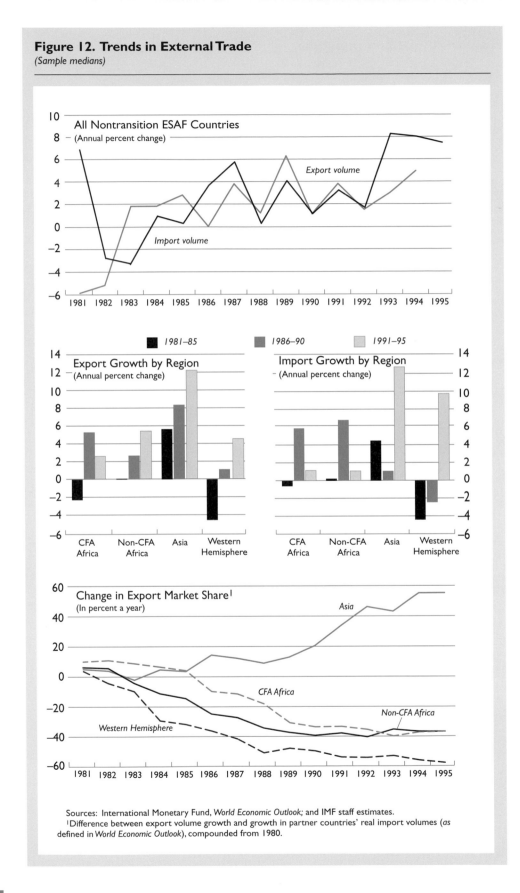

Sources: International Monetary Fund, *World Economic Outlook;* and IMF staff estimates.
[1]Difference between export volume growth and growth in partner countries' real import volumes (*as defined in World Economic Outlook*), compounded from 1980.

Figure 13. Real Per Capita GDP Growth
(In percent a year)

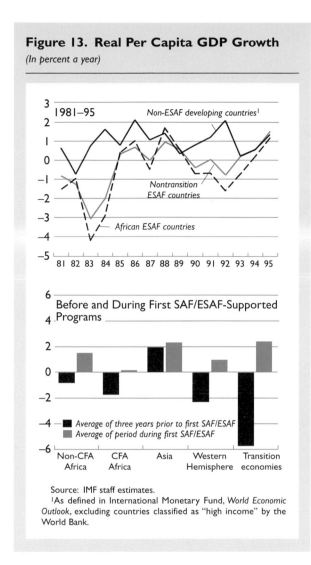

Source: IMF staff estimates.
[1]As defined in International Monetary Fund, *World Economic Outlook*, excluding countries classified as "high income" by the World Bank.

Figure 14. Growth, Saving, and Investment
(Period averages)

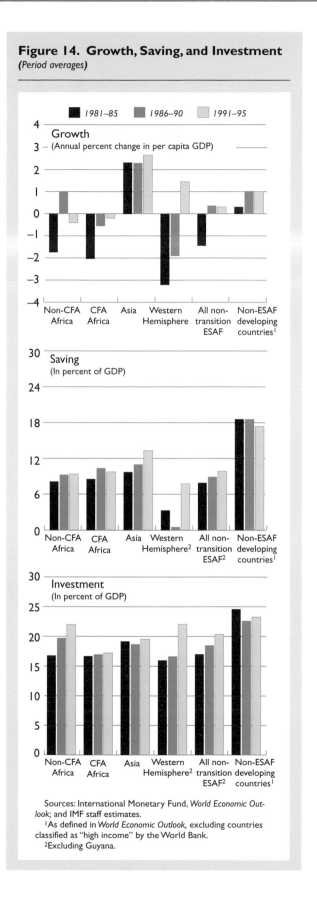

Sources: International Monetary Fund, *World Economic Outlook*; and IMF staff estimates.
[1]As defined in *World Economic Outlook*, excluding countries classified as "high income" by the World Bank.
[2]Excluding Guyana.

the trough of the early 1980s, when real per capita GDP declined at an average of almost 1½ percent a year in nontransition ESAF countries, growth rose to a modest positive rate of around 0.3 percent a year in the early 1990s (Figure 13).[24] During 1994–95—aided by a sharp rise in world demand, improved terms of trade, and the realignment of the CFA franc—average per capita growth exceeded 1 percent, and it remained strong in 1996.

The improving trend also helped to narrow the gap between growth in ESAF users and other developing countries. In the early 1980s, annual average

[24]The turnaround is greater still when expressed in terms of median growth rates, which rose from –1.9 percent a year in 1981–85 to 0.6 percent a year in 1991–95. The difference reflects a more asymmetric distribution of growth rates in the recent period.

Figure 15. Social Indicators of Development
(Period averages)

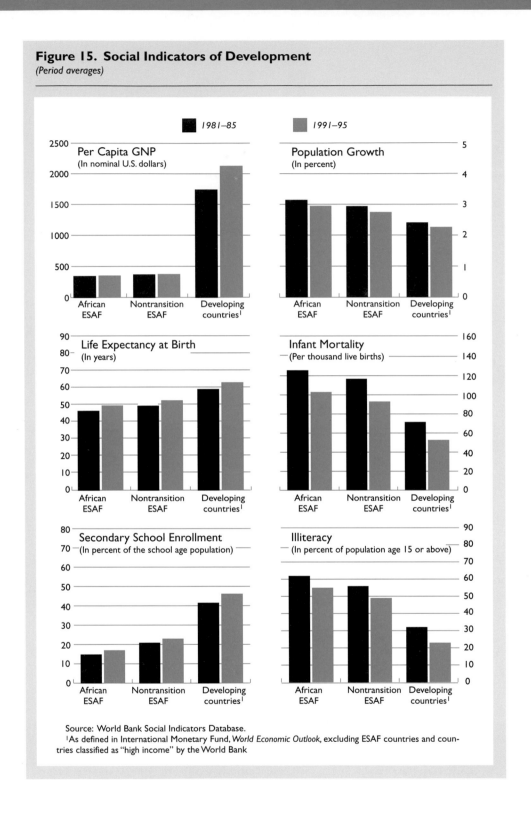

Source: World Bank Social Indicators Database.
[1] As defined in International Monetary Fund, *World Economic Outlook,* excluding ESAF countries and countries classified as "high income" by the World Bank

per capita growth in non-ESAF developing countries exceeded that in nontransition ESAF countries by around 2.2 percentage points: this differential had been more than halved, to 0.9 point, by 1991–95. The turnaround in growth typically began remarkably quickly as countries embarked on their first SAF/ESAF-supported programs (see Figure 13, bottom panel). Saving and investment rates in

ESAF countries showed some measure of convergence too with respect to other developing countries, although ESAF users continue to have much lower saving rates than other countries (Figure 14).

Important as these gains are, there are other perspectives that suggest a less sanguine assessment. First, and most obviously, since ESAF countries' output expanded less rapidly than in the rest of the developing world over the past decade, their average level of per capita income (which was only about one-quarter the average in other developing countries in the early 1980s) fell further behind. Other development indicators depict an improvement in living standards in ESAF countries since the early 1980s but, again, without narrowing the gap vis-à-vis the other countries (Figure 15).

Second, not all countries or regions within the ESAF group shared in the recovery to the same extent. The turnaround in economic growth was most pronounced among the four Western Hemisphere countries, especially Bolivia and Guyana. By contrast, ESAF users in Africa—the poorest in the sample—saw, on average, a smaller degree of convergence toward the developing country mean (see Figure 14). The averages, however, even within Africa, mask a large dispersion—one that widened significantly between the early 1980s and early 1990s. Of the 22 African ESAF countries, as many as 7—Equatorial Guinea, Ghana, Guinea, Lesotho, Mozambique, Tanzania, and Uganda—had real per capita GDP growth that exceeded the average of all developing countries over the 10 years ending in 1995. In some, the excess was by a wide margin.[25]

This prompts the question of what motivated the recovery in growth among ESAF users over the past 10 years. How much was due to good fortune, and how much to good policies? In Coorey and Kochhar (forthcoming), the comparative growth experience of ESAF and other low- and middle-income developing countries is examined using a standard empirical model based on the now extensive literature on this subject. This study reveals, importantly, that the behavior of growth in ESAF countries—its responsiveness to policies, terms of trade shocks, differences in social and demographic factors, and so on—does not differ fundamentally from that in other

developing economies: ESAF countries are not "special" in this respect.[26]

The estimated relationships are subject to sizable margins of error and, as is common with this kind of analysis, they leave a large portion of the variation in growth over time and across countries unexplained.

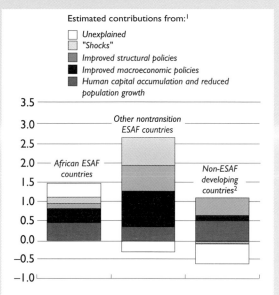

Figure 16. Explaining Increases in Growth Since the Early 1980s
(Change in annual average real capita GDP growth between 1981–85 and 1991–95)

Source: Coorey and Kochhar (forthcoming).

[1]Estimated contributions to changes in growth rates are derived from an econometric equation relating per capita GDP growth to a range of determinants estimated on pooled annual data from 1981 to 1995 for 84 low- and middle-income developing countries. In this figure, "macroeconomic policies" combine the effects of changes in inflation and the budget balance; "structural policies" combine openness to foreign trade, size of government, and economic security; "shocks" include changes in the terms of trade and dummies for weather and war or civil unrest. The unshaded portion in each bar is the portion of the change in growth that the estimated equation does not explain. The total change in growth between 1981–85 and 1991–95 is equal to the difference between the height of the bar above and below the zero axis.

[2]The 84 low- and middle-income developing countries, excluding ESAF countries.

---

[25]Uganda's real per capita GDP growth averaged 3.7 percent a year between 1986 and 1995, compared with an average of 0.9 percent for all developing countries. All four Asian ESAF users also had growth well in excess of the developing country average over this period. Although full time-series data are not available for the transition economies, those in Indochina (Cambodia, the Lao People's Democratic Republic, and Vietnam) recorded average real per capita growth of over 4 percent during 1991–95.

---

[26]Formally, in a growth equation estimated on pooled data for a large sample of developing countries, the hypothesis of stable parameters between the ESAF sample and other developing countries could not be rejected by the data. Also, a dummy variable distinguishing ESAF from other countries was not significant. The policy and other variables used in this analysis are listed in the notes to Figure 16.

Table 3. Per Capita GDP Growth in 1991–95: Differentials Relative to Non-ESAF Developing Countries[1]

(Percentage points, annual averages)

	African ESAF Countries	Other ESAF Countries
Differential in real per capita GDP growth	–0.6	1.8
Of which, due to:[2]		
Macroeconomic policies	0.2	–0.2
Structural policies	–0.4	0.0
Population growth	–0.8	–0.2
Human capital	–1.2	–0.1
"Catch-up"	1.5	0.7
Shocks	0.1	0.2
Unexplained	0.0	1.3

Source: Coorey and Kochhar (forthcoming).

[1]The sample of 84 low- and middle-income developing countries used in the growth regression, excluding ESAF countries.

[2]See Figure 16, footnote 1, for an explanation of these estimates. The "catch-up" term represents the estimated amount by which growth in the countries concerned would exceed that in non-ESAF developing countries due solely to lower initial income levels, if all other factors were equal.

Figure 17. Balance of Payments Developments

(Sample medians)

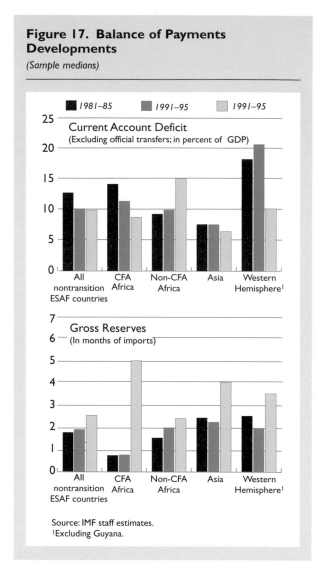

Source: IMF staff estimates.
[1]Excluding Guyana.

Nevertheless, they suggest that about half of the rise in per capita GDP growth in the nontransition ESAF countries between the early 1980s and the early 1990s may be attributed to strengthened policies. Structural reform and financial consolidation—reduced fiscal deficits and, in a few countries, lower inflation—both contributed to this result (Figure 16). When compared with other developing countries over the same period, ESAF countries' generally more successful efforts at macroeconomic stabilization were an important element behind the convergence in per capita growth rates between the two groups. Human capital accumulation (proxied by increases in life expectancy) and reduced population growth also figured prominently in the gains in growth among developing countries since the early 1980s, in ESAF and non-ESAF countries alike.

The empirical model sheds some light on why average growth among ESAF users in Africa in particular has continued to lag behind that in other countries, notwithstanding some narrowing of the gap over time. Continuing weaknesses in structural policies are part of the story, as is apparent from Figure 16. However, using non-ESAF developing countries as a benchmark for comparison, it appears that by the early 1990s, the dominant factors holding back relative growth performance in Africa were more rapid population growth and inadequate investment in human capital (Table 3).[27] These impediments more than offset the growth advantage that African ESAF countries are estimated to have solely by virtue of their lower initial level of development (labeled "catch-up" in Table 3). These findings, which are consistent with those of other studies, highlight the importance of policies aimed at raising health and education standards in these countries. At the same time, given that the impact of such policies will be felt only gradually, this analysis brings into

---

[27]Although the latter is proxied in the equation for growth by life expectancy, it can be interpreted as encompassing general standards of health and education. Empirical studies of growth commonly find an important influence from primary and secondary education levels.

Table 4. External Debt: Some Long-Run Comparisons

(In percent unless otherwise indicated)

	ESAF Users[1]		Low-Income Countries		All Developing Countries[2]	
	1985	1995	1985	1995	1985	1995
Total external debt						
In billions of U.S. dollars	81.6	161.0	198.3	534.8	1,028.3	2,065.7
In percent of GNP	71.1	87.8	24.7	38.7	34.0	39.6
Share of public and publicly guaranteed debt	77.1	82.2	74.7	81.9	71.0	70.1
Of which, shares held by:						
Bilateral creditors	48.8	43.6	44.0	42.9	28.8	39.1
Multilaterals (excluding IMF)	20.2	44.1	17.3	27.8	9.0	16.1
IMF	10.1	5.8	9.9	3.3	5.3	4.2
Private creditors	20.9	6.5	28.8	26.0	56.9	40.6
Concessional debt as share of total[3]	47.2	65.9	39.4	42.0	16.6	21.1
Average grant element in new borrowing[4]	50.0	61.7	29.9	29.6	15.1	20.2

Sources: World Bank, Debtor Reporting System; and IMF staff calculations.

[1] Excluding transition economies.

[2] World Bank definition, including ESAF countries.

[3] Loans with an original grant element of at least 25 percent.

[4] Grant element equals commitment value minus discounted present value of contractual debt service; expressed in percent of amount committed.

stark relief the challenge facing African countries if they are to narrow the gap in per capita income levels vis-à-vis the rest of the world.

External Viability

The relatively poor response of saving rates to rising growth and improved policies in ESAF countries has meant that current account deficits were barely reduced, on average, over the past decade (Figure 17). Consequently, the stock of ESAF users' external debt—about 80 percent of which is public or publicly guaranteed—almost doubled between 1985 and 1995.[28] By comparison with prior history, a much larger portion of this debt was provided on concessional terms by multilateral creditors, while private creditors substantially reduced their exposure to ESAF countries (Table 4).

Data on overall external financing flows, although sketchy, suggest that ESAF countries in non-CFA Africa and the Western Hemisphere were the principal beneficiaries of official flows—both transfers and loans—over the past 10 years (Table 5). Relative to the size of their economies, total financing flows to countries in these regions increased markedly between the early 1980s and early 1990s, with a rising proportion in the form of official transfers. By contrast, Asian and CFA countries obtained stable or declining amounts of external financing (relative to their GDP) and relied much less heavily than the other regions on debt relief and arrears as a source of funds. Except in Asia and the transition economies, private capital flows, although rising in recent years, remained small in relation to total financing needs. ESAF users in all regions achieved a substantial increase in official reserve coverage, particularly during the early 1990s (Figure 17).

These tendencies were to a large extent already apparent at the time of the previous ESAF review. That review concluded that only about half of the then 19 ESAF users had succeeded in making progress toward external viability (see Box 5 on definitional issues), although almost all had halted the trend deterioration in their external debt situations. In Tsikata (forthcoming), this analysis is brought up to date and extended to the now larger sample of countries. Possible factors underlying relative progress across countries are also considered, albeit in rather broad terms, given that this will be the subject of a detailed study in the external evaluation of the ESAF (see above).

As in the last review, the present study gauges progress toward external viability primarily on the basis of indicators of the debt burden and the degree of reliance on exceptional financing, with some reference also to indicators of "external vulnerability." However, the emphasis here is shifted away from measures based on debt stocks. Nominal debt stock ratios give a misleading picture when average repayment terms become increasingly concessional, as they

---

[28] This increase is less than the debt buildup experienced by all low-income countries over the same period (170 percent), but is similar to the average for developing countries as a whole.

Table 5. Net External Flows to ESAF Countries

(Annual averages; in percent of GDP)

	1981–85	1986–90	1991–95
Non-CFA Africa			
Official transfers	5.0	7.7	10.2
Net flows on long-term debt[1]	4.7	5.9	5.0
Debt relief and arrears[2]	2.7	4.0	5.5
Net foreign investment[3]	2.0	2.7	11.2
Net credit from IMF	0.4	0.1	0.2
CFA Africa[4]			
Official transfers	7.0	6.9	6.3
Net flows on long-term debt[1]	6.5	4.3	2.8
Debt relief and arrears[2]	2.9	4.2	4.4
Net foreign investment[3]	3.2	2.6	1.5
Net credit from IMF	0.9	−0.2	0.3
Asia (nontransition)			
Official transfers	3.1	2.3	1.7
Net flows on long-term debt[1]	3.7	3.6	2.5
Debt relief and arrears[2]	0.1	0.0	0.0
Net foreign investment[3]	2.7	2.6	7.4
Net credit from IMF	0.2	0.0	0.1
Western Hemisphere[5]			
Official transfers	2.0	6.0	8.1
Net flows on long-term debt[1]	6.9	14.1	5.0
Debt relief and arrears[2]	7.5	9.8	19.2
Net foreign investment[3]	1.9	3.9	13.0
Net credit from IMF	0.2	0.1	0.5
Transition economies			
Official transfers			8.6
Net flows on long-term debt[1]			3.6
Debt relief and arrears[2]			1.3
Net foreign investment[3]			19.4
Net credit from IMF			0.9

Sources: IMF staff estimates; and World Bank, Debtor Reporting System.
[1]Excluding borrowing from the IMF.
[2]Rescheduling, change in arrears and debt cancellation.
[3]Net foreign direct investment and portfolio equity flows.
[4]Excluding Equatorial Guinea.
[5]Excluding Guyana.

have done for ESAF countries since the mid-1980s (see Table 4); and historic time series for debt in present value terms are not available. Instead, two measures of the debt-service burden are considered—specifically, the ratio to exports (an indicator of the "foreign exchange" burden of debt) and the ratio to GDP (an indicator of the "internal transfer" burden).[29]

In relation to exports of goods and services, scheduled debt service has been on a fairly consistent downward trend for the average nontransition ESAF country since the mid-1980s, from a median of 40–45 percent then, to about 28 percent in 1995 (Figure 18). For the ESAF users classified as heavily indebted poor countries (HIPCs), the decline has been similar but at a level about 5 points higher.[30]

---

[29]The internal transfer burden is sometimes alternatively referred to, in countries where the bulk of external debt is public, as the "fiscal" burden, and measured in relation to fiscal revenues. The debt-service-to-revenue ratio may, however, *understate* the debt burden when government revenues are unsustainably high as a share of GDP; conversely, when the fiscal system is in disarray and revenues are "too low," it can *misidentify* as a debt problem

what is more properly viewed as a problem of fiscal administration. Using the ratio of debt service to GDP is a way of avoiding this potential difficulty.

[30]Note that the coverage of the HIPC group in Figure 16 excludes transition economies and Tanzania, owing to problems of data availability and reliability.

There is, however, no discernible trend over the long run in measures of the "internal" burden of foreign debt: average scheduled debt service stayed within ranges of 4–5 percent of GDP (8–9 percent for HIPCs) for most of the last 10 years. This disparity between the external and internal perspectives on the debt burden is a reflection of the marked rise in the share of exports in ESAF countries' GDP.

Focusing on individual country experiences since the pre-SAF/ESAF period, out of 27 countries where data permit an assessment, 12 can be said to have made "clear" progress toward external viability—defined as an improvement (or maintenance at low levels) in all three of the principal indicators: the ratios of debt service to exports and GDP and the ratio of exceptional financing to exports (see Table 6 for country coverage and exclusions). In another 10 countries, "limited" progress was achieved, meaning that no more than one of the indicators showed a deterioration since the pre-SAF/ESAF period. In all but 2 of these 10 cases, the ratios of debt service to exports and GDP both improved, and only reliance on exceptional financing failed to move in the desired direction (see Table 6).

Thus, 22 out of 27 countries appeared to have made some measure of progress toward external viability. Bearing in mind that changes in methodology make comparisons difficult, this suggests some improvement on the findings of the last ESAF review, where only half of the countries were considered to have advanced in relation to the external objective. It remains true, however, that many of the countries that progressed continue to have heavy debt burdens: 13 out of the 22 had scheduled debt service in excess of 25 percent of exports in 1995. Looking at two measures of external vulnerability—export diversification and reserve coverage—13 of the 22 countries appear to have strengthened their position over the last 10 years, with neither indicator worsening and at least one improving (see Table 6).[31]

At the other end of the spectrum are five countries (Honduras, Kenya, Madagascar, Sierra Leone, and Zimbabwe) where no apparent progress was made toward external viability during the period under review.[32] What explains the disappointing results in these cases, by comparison with the more successful ones? Several hypotheses were examined.

---

[31]Countries that may have weakened in this respect are Malawi, Mauritania, Senegal, and Togo; for others, the direction of change is unclear.

[32]Failure to make progress does not necessarily mean that these countries now face an unsustainable debt situation: for example, Kenya (a HIPC) and Zimbabwe (a non-HIPC) have had relatively moderate debt burdens throughout the period since their SAF/ESAF-supported adjustment efforts began. More generally, debt sustainability must be assessed on a forward-looking basis.

- First, that those making more progress might have obtained more favorable borrowing terms. This is not supported by the data. The average grant element in new borrowing incurred since a country's first SAF/ESAF-supported program was 63 percent for those that made "clear" progress toward external viability, 67 percent for countries achieving "limited" progress, and 54 percent for the "no" progress group. These differences are not statistically significant.
- Second, that the most successful might have received higher official transfers. While the scale of official transfers has varied widely across countries, it appears that the groups making progress toward viability did receive more transfers on average than those that did not: in

Figure 18. Alternative Measures of the Debt-Service Burden
(Sample medians)

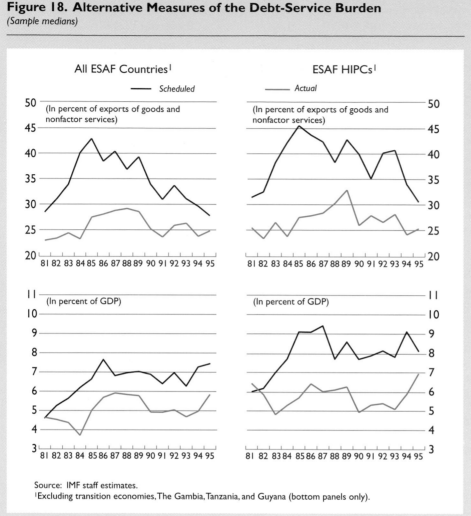

Source: IMF staff estimates.
[1]Excluding transition economies, The Gambia, Tanzania, and Guyana (bottom panels only).

relation to the initial (pre-SAF/ESAF) debt stock, such transfers averaged 12 percent a year in the "clear" and "limited" progress groups, and 4½ percent a year in the "no" progress group. These differences may be linked to comparative policy performance.[33]

- Third, that maintaining smaller current account deficits might have been a determining factor. In fact, the reverse appears to be true: measuring current account deficits in relation to initial-

period debt stocks, the averages are 20 percent for the "clear" progress group, 16 percent for the "limited" progress cases, and 7 percent for the countries making "no" progress.

- Fourth, that countries making most progress may be those achieving higher rates of economic growth, particularly in favor of exports, and hence more rapid expansion in the resource base available to support external debt. This appears to be the critical factor. Since the pre-SAF/ESAF period, real GDP and export volumes have grown at annual rates 3–6 percentage points faster, on average, among countries making "clear" progress toward viability than among "no" progress countries (Figure 19).

Thus, far from being conflicting objectives, it appears that strong (export-led) growth and greater progress toward external viability are complemen-

---

[33]Two pieces of evidence can be offered on this point: first, since beginning SAF/ESAF-supported adjustment, the proportion of years in which annual programs were completed was much less (about 35 percent) for the "no" progress group than for the other groups combined (about 55 percent); and second, the "no" progress group achieved significantly less fiscal adjustment than the "clear" progress group over the same period (see Figure 19).

Table 6. Indicators of Progress Toward External Viability[1]
(In percent unless otherwise indicated)

| | Scheduled Debt Service in Relation to | | | | Exceptional Financing Ratio[4] | | Export Concentration[5] | | | Reserve Coverage[6] | | |
| | Exports[2] | | GDP | | | | Fell | Un-changed | Rose | Rose | Un-changed | Fell |
	Pre-SAF/ ESAF[3]	1993–95	Pre-SAF/ ESAF[3]	1993–95	Pre-SAF/ ESAF[3]	1993–95						
Clear progress[7]												
Bangladesh	30.3	12.8	2.1	1.3	0.0	0.0	•			•		
Benin	48.6	30.1	6.0	4.6	40.7	13.0			•	•		
Bolivia	80.0	39.4	12.2	7.6	46.4	14.9	•				•	
Burkina Faso	29.0	21.9	3.2	2.8	11.2	2.3			•	•		
Gambia, The	44.9	25.7	7.2	4.5	38.0	−0.3	•			•		
Lesotho	41.0	14.9	3.5	2.8	0.0	0.0	•			•		
Malawi	47.5	27.8	13.6	10.8	5.5	−2.4	•					•
Mauritania	34.5	32.7	17.5	15.1	13.3	7.6	•					•
Nepal	6.7	10.7	0.7	1.6	0.0	0.0			•	•		
Pakistan	35.8	27.6	4.5	4.5	0.4	0.0			•	•		
Sri Lanka	21.3	12.5	5.5	4.3	0.0	0.0			•	•		
Uganda	67.8	38.5	4.8	4.2	5.2	0.9	•			•		
Mean	40.6	24.5	6.7	5.4	13.4	3.0						
Limited progress[7]												
Burundi	49.9	34.3	4.9	4.0	0.0	2.3	•			•		
Equatorial Guinea	59.6	35.2	18.8	16.3	−34.1	28.4	•				•	
Ghana	45.3	27.1	5.0	6.4	−14.3	−0.7	•			•		
Guinea	32.9	29.6	9.7	6.2	3.6	14.7	•			•		
Guyana	96.8	27.7			4.5	8.0	•			•		
Mali	42.0	37.4	7.5	7.4	20.3	20.7			•	•		
Mozambique	291.7	136.4	13.3	33.1	278.2	197.1	•			•		
Niger	44.7	32.7	9.6	4.9	14.9	23.0	•			•		
Senegal	24.7	22.9	7.2	6.1	11.0	16.4			•		•	
Togo	44.5	39.6	14.8	9.0	13.3	34.3			•			•
Mean	73.2	42.3	10.1	10.4	29.7	34.4						
No progress[7]												
Honduras	37.6	38.1	11.0	13.1	13.5	7.3	•			•		
Kenya	25.7	29.2	5.6	8.8	0.0	1.0	•					•
Madagascar	79.3	63.7	11.1	12.7	47.5	51.3	•				•	
Sierra Leone	51.6	59.0	5.5	9.3	21.3	39.8			•	•		
Zimbabwe	20.7	24.6	6.3	9.5	0.0	0.0	•			•		
Mean	43.0	42.9	7.3	10.2	20.0	17.8						

Source: IMF staff estimates.

[1]Excluding transition economies. Côte d'Ivoire and Nicaragua are excluded because their ESAF programs had been in place for less than three years at end-1995, and Tanzania because of severe deficiencies in official export data.

[2]Exports of goods and nonfactor services. For Lesotho, the denominator includes workers' remittances because of the dominance of this item in the country's foreign exchange earnings.

[3]Annual average for three years preceding first SAF/ESAF program.

[4]The sum of net change in arrears, rescheduling, and debt cancellation, as a ratio to exports of goods and nonfactor services.

[5]Change between 1985 and 1995 in share of total exports accounted for by the largest three export products.

[6]Change between 1985 and 1995 in official reserves, in months of imports. The indications for individual CFA countries (Benin, Burkina Faso, Côte d'Ivoire, Equatorial Guinea, Mali, Niger, Senegal, and Togo) are not as meaningful as for the other countries because of the pooling arrangements in the CFA.

[7]Countries that made "clear progress" are those that showed improvement in all three indicators, or (in the case of Nepal) that maintained indicators at low levels. Countries that made "no progress" are those where at least two indicators worsened. Countries with a mixed record are designated "limited progress."

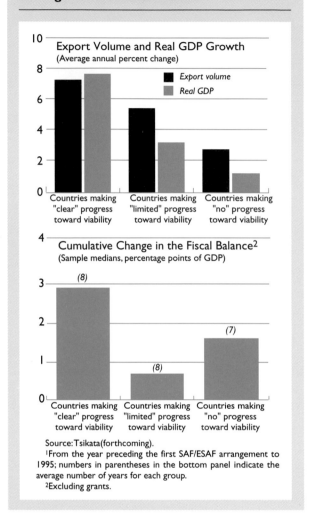

Figure 19. Growth of Export Volume and of Real GDP, and Change in Fiscal Balance During the SAF/ESAF Period[1]

Export Volume and Real GDP Growth
(Average annual percent change)

■ Export volume
▨ Real GDP

Countries making "clear" progress toward viability
Countries making "limited" progress toward viability
Countries making "no" progress toward viability

Cumulative Change in the Fiscal Balance[2]
(Sample medians, percentage points of GDP)

Countries making "clear" progress toward viability   (8)
Countries making "limited" progress toward viability   (8)
Countries making "no" progress toward viability   (7)

Source: Tsikata (forthcoming).
[1]From the year preceding the first SAF/ESAF arrangement to 1995; numbers in parentheses in the bottom panel indicate the average number of years for each group.
[2]Excluding grants.

tary.[34] This raises the question, however, of why debt management policies did not succeed in all countries in keeping debt accumulation in close correspondence with the evolving path of exports and output. If they had, even the slower-growing economies could have avoided a deterioration in

their external debt situation. Did countries borrow more than anticipated in SAF/ESAF-supported programs? Were borrowing plans based on overoptimistic assumptions—for instance, regarding export growth? Or was it that large amounts of debt were accumulated outside the context of programs (that is, either between programs or when programs had broken down)?

The evidence suggests that the problem does not appear to be one of widespread overshooting of borrowing plans. Among a sample of those that had made "limited" or "no" progress toward external viability, formal program limits on external borrowing (which apply only to nonconcessional borrowing) were found to have been almost universally respected.[35] Likewise, projections of overall official borrowing were met or *undershot* in more than three-quarters of the cases examined. Nor is there evidence of systematic overprediction of exports, if one controls for broad policy implementation: there is a slight (but statistically significant) pattern of overprediction on a full sample, but within the set of programs completed without interruption, exports were as likely to exceed as to fall short of target.[36]

What is less clear is that borrowing is curtailed significantly when policy implementation falters. The proportion of programs where official borrowing projections were undershot was no higher among interrupted programs than among programs that were completed without interruption. In a similar vein, the average rate of increase in the debt stock during program interruptions (at 7.7 percent a year) was slightly higher than in years when programs were on track (7.4 percent a year). Half of the 14 countries examined were borrowing at a faster pace during interruptions than during "on track" years.[37] Thus, one likely explanation for lack of progress toward external viability, in cases where it occurred, is that export growth (and perhaps economic activity more generally) suffered more than the country's access to external financing when policies weakened.

---

[34]Tsikata (forthcoming) reports additional evidence in support of this observation. It is shown there that progress toward external viability is not associated with import compression: as noted above, those making most progress toward this goal had, on average, the highest annual rate of import growth.

[35]Such targets were found to be quite stringent, often disallowing new nonconcessional borrowing altogether, though their coverage was limited (inter alia due to the exclusion of long maturities).

[36]An "uninterrupted program" is defined as one where the supporting arrangement ran its full course and where delays (if any) in completing reviews did not exceed six months (see the section on "Sustaining Programs").

[37]These 14 cases were those that had, at some point, experienced program interruptions of at least a year.

IV   Lessons for Program Design

Countries undertaking programs of adjustment and reform supported by the SAF and ESAF have brought their economies a long way from the doldrums of the early 1980s. Real per capita output growth among nontransition ESAF users has, on average, caught up with that in other developing countries. The social indicators in most countries have improved. Roughly three-quarters of ESAF users have moved closer to external viability. Budget deficits have been trimmed, and instances of very high inflation have been virtually eliminated. Developments in the last one to two years have been even more encouraging: while this may owe something to the favorable global environment, the liberalization and restructuring undertaken over the past decade give grounds for believing that durable gains in economic potential have been achieved in the countries under review.

Notwithstanding these gains, ESAF countries remain among the poorest in the world, and must aim for *faster* economic growth than other developing countries on a sustained basis if they are to close the enormous gap in living standards.[38] This is not in prospect so long as their investment and domestic saving rates continue to fall short of those in the rest of the developing world. Bolder strategies are called for to lift countries onto a higher growth path. This review has confirmed that the achievement of sustained, outward-oriented growth is also critical in accelerating progress toward external viability. Hence, the two principal goals of the ESAF are mutually supporting and can be achieved through a common set of policies, combined with access to financing on appropriate terms and debt relief where necessary.

At the heart of a strengthened approach must be greater efforts to cut government budget deficits, which in 1995 still averaged 7–8 percent of GDP (overall, before grants) in the countries under review. Numerous empirical studies have concluded that public saving is the most—possibly the only—

effective policy instrument to influence national saving directly in the near term.[39] This study finds that weak fiscal discipline inhibits growth through other channels as well—by contributing to chronic inflation, weak external positions, and stop-go policy implementation. With these interrelationships in mind, proposals for strengthening ESAF-supported programs have been grouped under four broad headings: (1) the key elements of a stronger and reoriented fiscal adjustment effort; (2) a more resolute approach to reducing inflation; (3) a more focused and concerted push on key structural reforms; and (4) steps to reduce the incidence of major policy slippages and encourage more sustained policy implementation. These proposals are discussed in turn.

Growth-Enhancing Fiscal Adjustment

By and large, fiscal adjustment thus far in ESAF-supported programs has been modest, and future programs should aim to bring about more decisive deficit reduction. For many countries, simply meeting targets more or less as ambitious as those set in the past would represent a major advance, while for others the objectives themselves should be more ambitious. The means to achieve the required additional adjustment, however, may also have important implications for economic growth, as well as for the path of adjustment itself. In many countries, the bulk of deficit reduction will have to come from structural reform on the expenditure side, in the civil service and public enterprises in particular. Since such reforms may be costly in the short term (requiring redundancy payments, for instance), it should not always be expected that budget deficits will be reduced in the first program year. A general aim, however, should be to cut deficits and raise national saving rates significantly over the course of a three-year pro-

---

[38]As is well established in the literature, GDP growth is highly correlated with improved living standards and reductions in poverty (see Jayarajah and others (1996)).

[39]For a survey of this evidence, see Goldsbrough and others (1996). The main factor driving private saving appears to be the growth of income, implying that strategies to raise growth will indirectly stimulate private saving.

gram. As programs are implemented, policies should be adjusted as necessary to ensure this result.

The Tax Burden

There are no established standards for what would constitute an "appropriate" tax burden in ESAF countries. Revenue objectives need to be related to some notion of the adequacy and efficiency of government spending and, more generally, the appropriate size of government. There is evidence, however, that the capacity to raise revenue efficiently tends to rise with the level of economic development. For ESAF countries, revenue-GDP ratios in excess of about 20 percent would be higher than expected, given their level of development.[40] Accordingly, some ESAF countries with ratios much above this level should probably aim to *reduce* the revenue burden over time. Conversely, there are cases—notably those countries in which taxes amounted to less than 10 percent of GDP in 1995—where higher revenues should be feasible, both as part of an additional fiscal adjustment effort and to support a higher level of productive government expenditure in the medium term.

For most ESAF users, however, the share of tax revenues in GDP is already comparable to that in other developing countries. This suggests that these countries should be focusing their tax reform efforts on simplifying and rationalizing tax *systems* to make revenues more robust and minimize distortions (Box 6), rather than to boost the overall tax take. In the process, resort to short-term ad hoc revenue measures—often made out of budgetary necessity—should be viewed as strictly temporary and not as a substitute for fundamental reform of tax policy and administration.

Capital Spending

Deficit reduction achieved through cuts in capital spending would not raise public saving. Whether capital spending in the public sector is too high or too low in ESAF countries is a difficult judgment and one that would need to be made case by case. But it seems clear that repeatedly squeezing capital spending ad hoc when revenues fall short of target, as has been common practice, is not the appropriate way for such important allocative decisions to be made. This problem could be addressed in program design by (1) incorporating in budgets more cautious assumptions regarding the feasible pace of tax reforms (or the response of revenues to reforms); and (2) putting high-priority capital spending in a "core" budget, to be protected against adverse contingencies.

---

[40]See Abed and others (forthcoming). The "level of development" is broadly equated here with per capita income levels.

Box 6. Strengthening Tax Systems

The review of tax policies in ESAF countries in Abed and others (forthcoming) suggests some important priorities for tax reform in future programs:
- First, a well-designed, broad-based *consumption tax such as the VAT* appears to be the surest instrument for achieving a rapid strengthening of the revenue base, in a way that minimizes disincentives to save and invest. It can also lay the groundwork for improving other taxes, such as those on international trade. The tax should have a single rate (or at most two rates) and the fewest possible exemptions.
- Second, as domestic tax reforms take effect, *import tariffs* should be reduced to moderate or low average rates, and the dispersion narrowed so as to reduce arbitrary and excessive rates of effective protection. *Export duties* should be avoided.
- Third, reforms of *taxes on incomes and profits* should focus on simplification and base broadening, to allow needed reductions in overly high marginal tax rates. These reforms should usually be complemented by a simplified (generally presumptive) tax regime for small businesses and the informal sector.
- Fourth, significant gains in revenue performance are attainable from improvements in *tax and customs administration,* such as streamlined procedures, special attention to large taxpayers, improved audits, and computerization. Such reforms have long gestation lags, however, and need to be started early and sequenced carefully if they are to pay dividends during a program period.

Social Spending

Spending on health and education, though conventionally classified as government consumption, is more in the nature of investment (in human capital). Provided the resources are used effectively, such spending is growth enhancing. Like productive capital spending, therefore, high-priority expenditures on health and education should be protected in a "core" budget.[41] To ensure this, considerable improvements are needed in the quality and availability of expenditure data on a functional basis, together with information on the efficiency of such expenditure. This should be a focus of technical assistance and new donor financing. Such efforts would complement World Bank plans to enhance its monitoring of the "outputs" from social spending (school enrollment, literacy rates, access to safe water, and so on) and may lead to a better understanding of the links between input and output indicators.

---

[41]The reference to prioritization here is important: it would not necessarily be desirable to include, for instance, spending on university education or specialized curative health services in the core budget.

Closer monitoring is also needed to allow effective evaluation of social safety net measures incollaboration with the World Bank and other institutions. While such measures now feature prominently in many ESAF-supported programs, little followup information has been provided regarding their impact on the targeted population groups.

Other Current Spending

This leaves three areas where progress to date has not been adequate and a clear break from the past is essential to bring about the needed reduction in budget deficits.

- *Civil service wage bills.* Attempted reforms in this area have been partial, prone to reversal, and frequently reliant on cuts in wages rather than staff numbers. Thus, the quality and efficiency goals essential for long-term savings have not been met. The design of these reforms lies within the World Bank's mandate, but conditionality in IMF programs should attach greater weight to the achievement of headcount reductions and reforms of the civil service wage structure that would produce durable—if not immediate—budget savings, while improving the efficiency of the civil service.
- *Public enterprises.* The opportunity costs imposed by public enterprises on the state budget are not limited to the recorded subsidies and transfers. They extend to tax breaks, quasi-fiscal assistance—through directed loans from state banks, for instance—and tax revenues that would accrue if the assets were put to more productive use. Budgetary concerns are thus one of several reasons to intensify public enterprise reform in ESAF-supported programs.
- *Military spending.* In line with the global trend, military spending tended to decline during ESAF-supported adjustment and is now estimated to absorb around 2 percent of GDP or less in approximately half of all ESAF countries. In a good number of countries, however, a much higher level of resources continues to be devoted to the military, suggesting the potential to achieve significant economies in this area. Such opportunities should be seized, as and when the social and political climate permits.

Expenditure Management

Finally, improved budgeting and expenditure control systems are needed, both to promote the desired expenditure restructuring and to allow closer adherence to overall fiscal targets. There is a strong advantage to addressing problems in this regard at an early stage. Programs could therefore make greater use of prior actions to encourage progress in a number of areas, including measures to provide appropriate incentives for officials charged with implementing the reforms, and to ensure transparency and accountability in expenditure management.

More Decisive Disinflation

Experience suggests strongly that those countries with inflation stuck in the intermediate range are sacrificing growth. Although the empirical estimates are inevitably imprecise, the present study and others have found that costs appear to mount once inflation exceeds single-digit levels.[42] The analysis in this study suggests that the negative relationship (plotted in Figure 20) is significant even after controlling for supply shocks (such as weather and the terms of trade) and other determinants of economic growth; that it is proportional—so that reducing inflation from 30 percent to 10 percent may be just as beneficial as reducing it from 90 percent to 30 percent; and that it applies in ESAF countries just as in other developing countries. In contrast to some earlier findings (particularly those drawn from studies that impose a linear form on the inflation-growth relationship), these results seem to hold even when all cases of high inflation are excluded from the analysis.

The *nature* of this relationship is uncertain and probably complex: growth may benefit from low inflation directly, through improved resource allocation and higher investment, or indirectly as a result of the broad-based reforms that are typically needed to sustain low inflation. Thus, the full effects are likely to accrue only in response to an anti-inflation strategy that is comprehensive and consistent. Nevertheless, the potential gains from policies that achieve and maintain low inflation appear to be substantial, not only for output growth but also for the distribution of income: inflation tends to be a regressive tax, especially in low-income countries, where inflation hedges for the poor are scarce.

Potential Costs of Disinflation

Disinflation is traditionally considered to impose short-run output losses on the economy. This depends on the circumstances, however. There is evidence that costs are lower at higher initial levels of inflation: thus, those with most to gain in the long run—

---

[42]See Phillips (forthcoming) for a detailed review of the evidence on these points and on the other empirical findings and analytical issues referred to in this section. A similar conclusion was reached in "The Rise and Fall of Inflation—Lessons from the Postwar Experience" (see International Monetary Fund (1996), especially pages 116–22).

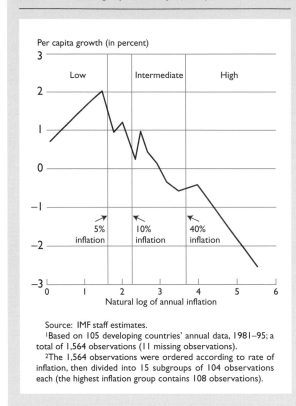

Figure 20. Association of Real Per Capita GDP Growth with Log Inflation[1]

(Mean values within groups ranked by inflation)[2]

Source: IMF staff estimates.
[1]Based on 105 developing countries' annual data, 1981–95; a total of 1,564 observations (11 missing observations).
[2]The 1,564 observations were ordered according to rate of inflation, then divided into 15 subgroups of 104 observations each (the highest inflation group contains 108 observations).

those in or above the higher end of the intermediate inflation range—may also have least to lose in the short run. The degree of inflation inertia that generates the short-run losses is also likely to be less in ESAF countries, with typically large informal sectors, than in more developed economies. Finally, even if there is a short-run cost from the demand squeeze, this may be more than offset by accompanying supply-side effects when disinflation is part of a broader policy package supported by external financing (as is the case in ESAF-supported programs).

What is the evidence? Except in countries with low initial inflation (which have tended not to target disinflation), growth typically rose *immediately* in SAF/ESAF-supported programs (Figure 21). Looking closer at programs according to the degree of disinflation achieved, the record shows that even countries that halved their inflation rates in the course of a program had on average faster growth than during the preprogram period. This supports the notion that trade-offs between growth and inflation, if they exist, are dominated by other factors. It does not appear, then, that concerns about short-run out-

put effects should deter countries from a bolder effort to reduce inflation; still less do they justify postponing disinflation indefinitely, as has happened in several cases.

Another consequence of disinflation is the need for the public sector to adjust to the loss of seigniorage, either by tapping other revenue sources or through expenditure savings. For countries with initial inflation in the 30–40 percent range (where seigniorage appears to be maximized), reaching 5–10 percent inflation could require the government to find compensating fiscal adjustments of as much as 2 percent to 2½ percent of GDP. This amount is sizable, but should be achievable if—as has been emphasized—low inflation is part of a strategy that would extend to fundamental tax and expenditure reform.

Implications for Program Design

SAF/ESAF-supported programs have in fact consistently targeted single-digit inflation. But the record in achieving this objective has, with few exceptions, been poor, both during and outside programs. The sharp downturn in inflation in 1996 in a number of countries is welcome, but—set against the trend of the previous 10 years—does not dispel concerns about program performance in this area.

Why have programs so often failed to deliver low inflation? One obvious answer would be that financial ceilings—in particular, on credit expansion—have not been respected. Overshooting of targets for net domestic assets (NDA) has indeed been common (Table 7). However, Phillips (forthcoming) finds no systematic link between adherence to program targets for NDA, on the one hand, and the record on meeting monetary growth and inflation targets on the other. Projected money growth was exceeded in 13 of the 14 programs where first-year NDA ceilings were met, reflecting unanticipated balance of payments inflows.[43] Inflation overshot in 10 of these programs, and in fact did so even more frequently than when NDA ceilings were exceeded.

These findings point to two possible weaknesses in program design. First, programs may have underestimated the extent of fiscal adjustment needed to reach low inflation. The evidence does not show a clear relationship between inflation overshooting and deviations from fiscal targets in the programs under review. But the poor record on inflation calls strongly into question whether the fiscal targets

---

[43]The data are not adequate to identify the precise source of these inflows. As indicated in Table 7, they appear *not* to reflect unanticipated official borrowing. The bulk is recorded in the miscellaneous (residual) category "net private capital and balance of payments errors," the nature of which is highly uncertain.

Figure 21. Real Per Capita GDP Growth in SAF/ESAF Programs¹
(Median; percent change over previous year)

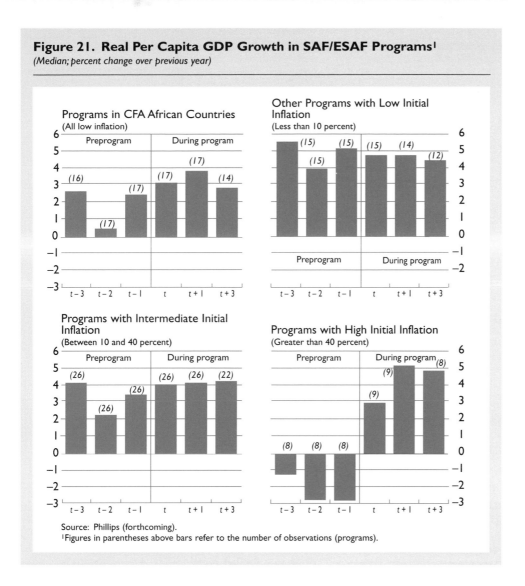

Source: Phillips (forthcoming).
¹Figures in parentheses above bars refer to the number of observations (programs).

themselves were too loose to achieve the inflation objective, regardless of the stance of credit policy. It is striking that the stronger performers on inflation (countries that achieved average inflation of 10 percent or less during 1993–95) had reduced their primary fiscal deficits to less than one-third of the average level prevailing in other countries (Table 8). These findings add to the case for stronger fundamental fiscal reforms to achieve lower deficits on a sustainable basis.

Second, the large majority of programs lacked an effective nominal anchor, relying on NDA ceilings alone to enforce monetary discipline. To some degree, this may have reflected a recognition that the likely fiscal stance would be incompatible with a nominal anchor, particularly in light of concerns about competitiveness. However, unless supported by a commitment to a nominal exchange rate peg, or

explicit inflation targets, NDA ceilings leave open a wide range of outcomes in which net foreign assets, money supply, and inflation may all exceed projections.[44] Only 8 of the 35 SAF/ESAF-supported programs with intermediate or high initial inflation had a nominal anchor, in all but two cases an exchange rate peg. These programs delivered better-than-average inflation performance. By contrast, as many as one in five programs explicitly geared nominal ex-

---

[44]In principle, inflation control could be achieved with commitments to NDA ceilings and a pure floating regime for the exchange rate (no discretionary intervention in the foreign exchange market), since the latter insulates the economy from accommodating external flows. Few governments would commit to a pure float, however, and there is no example of such a regime among the countries under review. Chile provides an example of the successful use of preannounced inflation targets as a nominal anchor.

Table 7. Deviations from Inflation Targets, by Net Domestic Assets Performance

(Cases of intermediate and high initial inflation; first program year)

	Inflation	Broad Money	Net Domestic Assets	Net Foreign Assets	Current Account Balance	Net Private Capital, and Balance of Payments Errors	Public External Borrowing
		(Deviation from targeted percentage change)			(Deviation from target, as percent of GDP)		
Net domestic asset growth limit respected (14 cases)							
Mean	9.0	16.2	−22.5	38.7	2.4	7.1	−2.1
Median	3.1	16.1	−7.2	24.7	1.3	4.9	−1.9
Of which:							
Intermediate inflation (9 cases)							
Mean	11.7	11.9	−22.9	34.9	0.5	3.8	−0.1
Median	6.0	6.2	−7.4	17.2	0.5	5.2	−1.7
Net domestic asset growth limit exceeded (21 cases)							
Mean	15.3	26.9	53.8	−26.9	1.1	1.8	−0.8
Median	4.9	14.6	14.5	−6.5	0.6	0.0	−0.7
Of which:							
Intermediate inflation (17 cases)							
Mean	4.4	13.1	30.4	−17.3	1.0	2.8	−0.2
Median	4.4	13.6	9.5	−5.4	1.3	0.2	−0.6

Source: IMF staff estimates.

change rate policy to a real exchange rate objective, and these had particularly poor inflation performance (Figure 22).[45]

Programs should not continue to claim single-digit inflation as one of their intended results unless they are designed in such a way that, if the program is fully implemented, this outcome is reasonably assured. The programs under review did not, with hindsight, provide that assurance. Given the strong case for single-digit inflation as an objective, the preferred solution would be the adoption of a significantly bolder approach than has been common hitherto. The goal need not necessarily be rapid disinflation but, particularly when initial inflation is in the intermediate range, it should be expected that it would be brought down to single-digit levels in the course of a three-year program.

The centerpiece in such an approach would be a greatly strengthened fiscal position, underpinned by basic reform of the state finances (including those of the public enterprises). A sufficiently ambitious pro-gram of this kind—which includes an inflation goal—should achieve low inflation without formally committing to a nominal exchange rate target or a monetary anchor. But experience suggests that including a formal anchor in such circumstances could add to the program's credibility and may speed the transition to low inflation. A nominal exchange rate peg or, alternatively, performance criteria for reserve money would serve this purpose. Either one could be adopted on a temporary basis, until such time as low inflation had been established. Each has pros and cons. The exchange rate anchor is more transparent and may be more effective in altering inflation expectations, but it may also be more difficult to exit from smoothly. Money supply targets, on the other hand, do not require the backing of foreign reserves needed for an exchange rate peg and allow the exchange rate to adjust flexibly in response to shifts in the terms of trade; but they can be difficult to manage when the demand for money is highly uncertain (as it often is during disinflation). These factors would need to be weighed case by case.

There can be no doubt that the prerequisites for adopting a formal nominal anchor—staunch adherence to fiscal discipline and minimal indexation—

---

[45]The shortcomings of anchorless programs were examined at length in Schadler and others (1995a and 1995b).

Table 8. Financial Policies and Inflation Performance, 1993–95[1]
(Percent per annum, means)

	Countries with Low Inflation[2]	Other ESAF Countries
Inflation	6.0[3]	33.2
Primary deficit[4] (in percent of GDP)	0.9	3.0
Broad money growth	18.3	38.7
Of which:		
Net domestic assets growth	11.5	20.5
Net foreign assets growth	6.8	18.2
Memorandum item:		
Real per capita GDP growth	2.0	0.2

Source: IMF staff estimates.

[1]Excluding countries that did not begin their first SAF/ESAF-supported program until 1994 (Cambodia, Côte d'Ivoire, Kyrgyz Republic, Nicaragua, and Vietnam).

[2]Those averaging single-digit inflation during 1993–95 (including Bolivia and Guyana, which averaged 10.1 percent and 10.6 percent inflation, respectively, in this period).

[3]Adjusted to exclude the 1994 outturns for the CFA countries, which were affected by the CFA franc devaluation in that year.

[4]Including grants. Excluding Guyana.

Figure 22. Inflation Performance With and Without Anchors[1]
(Sample medians; in percentage points)

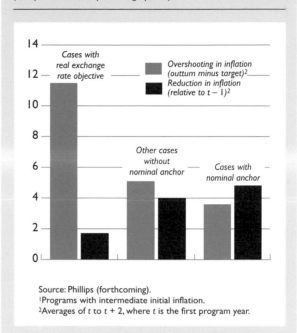

Source: Phillips (forthcoming).
[1]Programs with intermediate initial inflation.
[2]Averages of t to $t + 2$, where t is the first program year.

are exacting. There will therefore continue to be situations in which policies sufficiently strong to support a nominal anchor are judged to be beyond reach, at least in the near term. In these cases, programs should acknowledge that their ambitions, not only for inflation but probably also for growth, have to be correspondingly more modest. A more realistic assessment of inflation and growth prospects is needed to provide clearer guidance to national authorities on the additional adjustment needed to place their country on a higher growth trajectory.

Advancing Structural Reforms

Stronger macroeconomic adjustment would deliver a quicker and more pronounced supply response if accompanied by structural measures to encourage private investment and entrepreneurship. Most aspects of structural reform have some bearing on private sector development, and programs should continue to address structural weaknesses across a broad front, setting priorities on a case-by-case basis. Many ESAF countries have achieved a great deal already in areas such as the liberalization of prices and marketing and exchange system reform. Future programs should therefore be expected to devote increased attention to the "second generation" of reforms—those where progress has lagged, or where more can be done to raise countries' economic potential. These areas would include:

- *Trade liberalization.* There is increasing recognition of the important and wide-ranging benefits that result from opening economies to international trade and investment. The countries under review have made progress in this respect, but average tariff rates remain high and should be reduced and streamlined further, together with nontariff barriers.
- *Public enterprise reform.* Progress here has been limited, with the result that in most countries public enterprises continue to impede private sector development by preempting resources and hampering competition.
- *Bank restructuring.* Persistent weaknesses (operational and financial) in the banking sector are impairing efficient intermediation and thereby constraining business investment.
- *Strengthened property rights.* Clear and fair systems of property rights and adherence to the rule of law in business practices are prerequisites for a strong private sector. Many problems in this

regard can be traced back to excessive regulation, complex tax and tariff structures, and direct state involvement in commercial affairs. At the same time, governments need to help ensure the development of well-functioning markets to finance private activities. Hence, the most effective contribution the IMF can make is to continue supporting programs that address these root causes, some of the most important of which lie in the first three areas identified above.

The slow pace of reform of public enterprises and banking systems was emphasized in the last ESAF review. The present study has therefore investigated—through detailed examination of selected country cases—the possible reasons for persistently slow progress in these two critical areas. The aim was to identify what could be done in the context of future ESAF-supported programs to help accelerate reform, recognizing that the World Bank retains the lead role in advising on the design and implementation of reforms in both areas. Hence, the focus here is on those aspects of policy—the linkages between structural reform and macroeconomic policies—that fall within the IMF's area of responsibility. The analysis and findings are set out in Decressin and others (forthcoming).

Public Enterprise Reform

The limited success in hardening the budget constraints of public enterprises in ESAF countries, and especially the disappointing results from performance contracts, have led to increasing emphasis in recent reform programs on privatization and less on state-managed restructuring. Privatization may indeed be the only way that inappropriate financial links between corporations and the government can be severed once and for all. The shift in this direction is therefore welcome, and should be further encouraged.

Nevertheless, because most ESAF users can be expected to retain some enterprises under state ownership, more must be done to ensure that essential discipline can be imposed effectively on these enterprises, and the potential threat they pose to financial stabilization contained. There is no realistic prospect of meeting this goal, however, without the compilation of adequate financial data on public enterprises. Although this issue has long been highlighted by the IMF, little has been done in the context of ESAF-supported programs to press for data improvements in this area. Of the five country case studies examined (involving 18 annual SAF/ESAF-supported programs among them), only two instances could be found of structural conditions being applied to the collection of data on public enterprises.[46] Bolivia was the only one of these countries to have compiled financial data on all public enterprises with a reasonable degree of specificity and reliability. In the others, even information on the direct financial flows between public enterprises and the government was frequently unavailable or incomplete, and there were no data on nonbank borrowing (some of which may have been government guaranteed). Also unrecorded were the numerous forms of indirect or noncash support that governments commonly provided to favored public enterprises, such as implicit interest subsidies, loan or exchange rate guarantees, and relief or forgiveness on tax and loan liabilities. In short, the status quo in this area looks much the same as it did at the time of the last review four years ago: public enterprise data are generally adequate in Western Hemisphere countries but still extremely poor in most African countries.

This is an issue on which the IMF should take a more proactive role, in cooperation with the World Bank, by helping to marshall donors' financial and technical resources to assist countries in what is admittedly a complex and skill-intensive task and by applying conditionality to reinforce the importance of action in this area. The authorities could be encouraged to focus initially on a few key enterprises, expanding coverage as resources permit, but should aim to record not only enterprises' direct financial transactions with government and banks but also quasi-fiscal support, such as government guarantees for domestic borrowing.

One consequence of the lack of adequate financial data on public enterprises has been that IMF staff were generally not in a position to identify promptly serious emerging financial problems in specific enterprises, and hence to advise the World Bank and the national authorities on the choice of enterprises to be targeted for urgent reform.[47] Such problems were most severe in cases where the Bank was supporting reform through sectoral operations, which tended to focus on enterprises that were perceived as major bottlenecks to growth (public utilities and key export producers, for instance), rather than those that imposed the biggest financial drain on the state budget. Once equipped with the necessary information, IMF staff will need to play a more active role in such circumstances, where its central interest in the state

---

[46]The two instances were Bolivia (1988 ESAF) and Senegal (1995 ESAF). The other countries examined were Ghana, Mongolia, and Zimbabwe; see Decressin and others (forthcoming).

[47]In Ghana, earlier recognition of financial weaknesses in the state petroleum company (GNPC) might have brought this enterprise into the reform program before it put at risk the stabilization objectives of the IMF staff-monitored and ESAF-supported programs of the early 1990s.

finances and monetary conditions in the economy as a whole is at stake. In particular, programs should seek to monitor financial flows between public enterprises, the state budget, and the banking system more comprehensively, so that budget constraints can be hardened.

More generally, conditionality in ESAF-supported programs should continue to reinforce public enterprise reforms planned under the aegis of the World Bank. Particular attention could be paid to measures that promote competition, such as liberalizing the codes governing domestic and foreign direct investment and removing monopoly rights, since these help not only to exert some market discipline over public enterprises but also to create the right environment for privatization.

Restructuring Banking Systems

One manifestation of the inefficiencies and financial mismanagement in the public enterprise sector was a substantial accumulation of nonperforming loans in the banking systems of ESAF countries, often amounting to one-third or more of banks' total portfolios. This problem was related to, and compounded by, structural weaknesses in the banks' own management, many of which stemmed from too much government intervention in lending decisions and insufficient effective prudential regulation and supervision.

The five case studies examined suggest several reasons why progress in restructuring and reforming banking systems in ESAF countries has continued to falter.[48] Lack of political commitment—especially an unwillingness to cede political influence over banks' operations—was an important factor in countries in which progress has been particularly poor. A scarcity of banking expertise and skilled staff has also been a problem, one that can be remedied only with time, and a continuation of extensive technical assistance from the IMF and other institutions. On three counts, however, the IMF could take more direct action to improve performance in future ESAF-supported programs.

First, the *huge fiscal costs* held back reform in some instances (Tanzania provides a clear example). This appeared to result from a failure to articulate the complete strategy at the outset, which would have allowed costs to be better anticipated and financing identified.[49] There is scope for IMF staff to engage more actively in discussions with the World Bank and national authorities at the planning stage to ensure that *all* potential fiscal costs are assessed, including some that tend to be overlooked, such as running costs for loan recovery agencies. As well as reducing the likelihood that reforms would run into financial roadblocks once under way, more prior attention to these issues would have the important advantage of concentrating minds on the link between the pace of a planned strategy and its costs, and might in some cases lead to the adoption of a more ambitious (hence, typically, cheaper) approach than would otherwise have been selected. It could also help to ensure greater emphasis on design features—such as an appropriate "exit" (bank closure) strategy—that would serve simultaneously to promote substantive reform and save budgetary resources. In this regard, consideration could be given to sharing the costs of restructuring more broadly among shareholders, creditors, and depositors—among other things, to reduce risks of moral hazard.

Second, piecemeal implementation weakened the impact of reforms, leading in some cases to significant delays and even reversals. Proceeding, for instance, with financial restructuring (to tackle the "stock" problem) without reforming banks' operations or enforcing the new prudential and regulatory environment (the "flow" problem) tended to result in recurring bank distress.[50] Similarly, failure to upgrade the legal and judicial framework, to allow effective enforcement of contracts, resulted in low loan-recovery rates (as in Senegal and Tanzania), adding to the net cost and thereby hampering reform. The IMF could contribute to more comprehensive implementation by refocusing its conditionality in ESAF-supported programs. The case studies suggest that past use of structural performance criteria and benchmarks has not been very effective, at least in part because of its emphasis on approving plans and passing laws rather than on operational achievements. Instead, programs should monitor the adequacy of policies affecting the banking system and the ability of the authorities to enforce best practices.[51] Key aspects would include licensing and exit policies, lender-of-last-resort facilities, rules for loan classification and provisioning, capital standards, and the legal authority and capacity of supervisors to implement prudential regulations and impose penalties. Performance in these areas as well as in relation to the broader and longer-term goals of banking reform should be assessed in the context of program reviews.

---

[48]The five countries examined in this part of the study were Bolivia, Ghana, the Lao People's Democratic Republic, Senegal, and Tanzania.

[49]By contrast, the comparative success of banking reforms in Ghana and Senegal appears to owe much to their comprehensive initial planning.

[50]This occurred in Bolivia, the Lao People's Democratic Republic, and, to some extent, in Tanzania.

[51]Best practices could be drawn from Basle Committee's *Core Principles for Effective Supervision;* see Basle Committee on Banking Supervision (1997).

Third, *lack of progress in public enterprise reform* undermined bank restructuring efforts. Indeed, the problem of weak loan portfolios is unlikely to be solved on a lasting basis until the financial weaknesses in the public enterprise sector are satisfactorily addressed. If, as proposed above, information is compiled on the balance sheets and financial transactions of public enterprises, the interrelationships would become clearer, and this may help to promote more concerted strategies for the public enterprise and banking sectors.

Sustaining Programs

The preceding sections have examined the policies and outcomes in all ESAF countries and identified specific areas where the design of programs could be improved. This final section approaches program design from a different perspective—that of countries in which significant interruptions occurred in or between SAF/ESAF-supported programs. The concern in such cases goes beyond a desire solely to avoid breaks in IMF arrangements: if deviations from planned policies were sufficiently large to cause the IMF to withhold support, they could also have been harmful to investors' and market sentiment, and hence to economic performance. The resulting loss of credibility is costly even when policy adjustments are subsequently made to retrieve the ground lost during the interruption. In the analysis of this issue presented in Mecagni (forthcoming), two principal questions were posed: What were the main factors that gave rise to the interruptions? And could programs have been designed or monitored differently to reduce the frequency of interruptions without unduly compromising objectives?

To the extent that changes in design or monitoring could not be expected to eliminate interruptions, an important—and considerably more difficult—question is raised: would greater selectivity in approving arrangements help? This question is posed not so much from the perspective of whether it would limit the use of IMF resources in risky situations; rather, the issue considered is whether greater selectivity would encourage countries to commit themselves more forcefully to appropriate policies. While it is not possible to address this question empirically (the construction of a counterfactual would be too subjective to be useful), the concluding paragraph raises some considerations that bear on the question.

In this study, interruptions refer to delays of longer than six months between (1) a scheduled review and its actual completion, (2) two annual arrangements in a three-year arrangement, or (3) two three-year arrangements. Like any definition of interruptions, this one has an element of arbitrariness. However,

upon examination it appeared to capture situations where a clear lapse from the desired pace of adjustment occurred. By this definition, program interruptions have been numerous. Fifty-one significant interruptions of SAF- or ESAF-supported programs have occurred since the inception of the SAF in 1986, affecting 28 of the 36 countries under review. Only one-fourth of all three- or four-year arrangements were completed without significant interruption.[52] The high frequency of interruptions was a critical motivation for examining separately these particular experiences during SAF/ESAF-supported programs.

There is a temptation to think of interruptions as the result only of severe policy slippages. In fact, in almost one-third of the 51 episodes examined, the primary cause of the interruption was not the need to correct a significant policy slippage. About one-sixth of all interruptions stemmed from severe political upheavals that called into question the authority of the government to negotiate or provide a credible commitment to a program. In most of these cases, past policy slippages had occurred, but even in these the dominant factor underlying the interruption and its length was the need to resolve a political crisis before concerted attention could be given to the economic program. In another one-sixth of interruptions, past policies had been broadly satisfactory, but there were delays in agreeing on future policies. In most of these episodes, time was needed for the authorities to muster political support for certain measures or for the IMF and the authorities to agree on measures to address the effects of a recent unexpected external shock.

Thus, about two-thirds of the interruptions were strongly affected by serious slippages in past policies that either weakened the government's credibility or produced protracted disagreements between the IMF and the government on remedial measures. Not surprisingly, the evidence suggests that, on average, these interruptions were associated with significantly worse policies than uninterrupted programs (Figure 23 shows the comparative evidence for fiscal policies: the interrupted programs—those in black—clearly tend to fall in the left, or "worse," half of the distribution of fiscal outturns).

An examination of the interruptions attributable to policy slippages finds little support for the view that changes in program design could have made a significant difference to the occurrence or length of the interruption. Still, specific modifications are identified that might have helped in a handful of past episodes and that are worth considering for the fu-

---

[52]Excluded from these calculations were SAF arrangements that were replaced before completion with ESAF arrangements, arrangements that had an original duration of less than three years, and three-year arrangements that have not yet run their course.

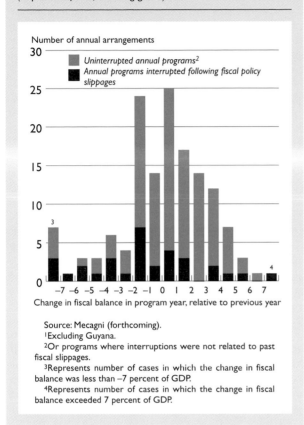

Figure 23. Frequency Distribution of Changes in the Fiscal Balance[1]

(In percent of GDP, excluding grants)

Number of annual arrangements

Legend:
Uninterrupted annual programs[2]
Annual programs interrupted following fiscal policy slippages

Change in fiscal balance in program year, relative to previous year

Source: Mecagni (forthcoming).
[1]Excluding Guyana.
[2]Or programs where interruptions were not related to past fiscal slippages.
[3]Represents number of cases in which the change in fiscal balance was less than –7 percent of GDP.
[4]Represents number of cases in which the change in fiscal balance exceeded 7 percent of GDP.

ture. These conclusions were reached by examining five possible weaknesses in program design that might have contributed to interruptions:

- Targets for macroeconomic policies were too ambitious.
- The program of structural reform was insufficiently prioritized.
- The provision of technical assistance was inadequate.
- IMF staff monitoring and consultation with authorities was too infrequent.
- Contingency planning was inadequate.

Identifying *overambitiousness in financial targets* is far from straightforward. What is achievable in one country at one time may not be a relevant benchmark for other countries with different capacities and constraints or even for the same country at another time. Still, a comparison of targets for key macroeconomic policy variables—such as the main fiscal aggregates—in interrupted annual arrangements with the average of those for all annual arrangements provides a crude test of the hypothesis

that interrupted programs were overly ambitious. By this standard, most of the annual targets for the programs interrupted due to policy slippages were not more ambitious than the "average" program, and the average targeted change adjusted for initial conditions in these interruption cases was not statistically different from that for all programs (Figure 24).[53]

Another approach to the overambitiousness hypothesis is to consider what the targets for interrupted programs would have been had the outcomes reflecting policy slippages been the original targets. This possibility was considered for the 13 interrupted programs where fiscal targets appeared from Figure 24 to be relatively ambitious (that is, for programs above and to the right of the regression line). In 10 of these cases, the fiscal deficit actually deteriorated, at times by several percentage points of GDP. In 7 cases, the policies implemented resulted in the accumulation of external arrears. In another 4 instances, "lowering the bar" to match the actual outcomes would have implied accepting inflation either rising or stuck in the 20–30 percent range. In sum, it appears that easing targets to match outcomes would in most cases have implied endorsement of deteriorating macroeconomic conditions.

There is also little evidence in favor of the hypothesis that *overly ambitious or insufficiently prioritized structural reforms* were a key cause of interruptions. First, interruptions were linked far more frequently and directly to slippages in macroeconomic policies than to those in structural policies. While structural policies were often not implemented as expected (interruptions linked to policy slippages followed periods in which, on average, over two-thirds of structural benchmarks and about half of the structural performance criteria had been missed), only in a few instances could the proximate cause of the slippage be seen as structural in nature. Second, taking structural benchmarks and performance criteria as an indication of the prioritizing of structural reforms, programs where past policy slippages were the major influence on interruptions typically had no more such conditions than the average for all programs: programs interrupted due to policy slippages had on average two- three structural performance criteria and six- seven structural benchmarks, in line with the wider sample.[54]

---

[53]This result was obtained by regressing the targeted change in the fiscal balance (excluding grants) on the previous year's fiscal balance and a constant, for all annual SAF/ESAF-supported programs for which data are available (excluding some extreme outliers). A dummy variable for years in which a program was interrupted because of policy slippages was found to be statistically insignificant.

[54]For these purposes, reflecting data availability, the wider sample was taken to be all ESAF-supported programs approved since 1991.

Figure 24. Targeted Change in Fiscal Balance in Interruptions Affected by Policy Slippages[1,2]

(In percent of GDP, excluding grants)

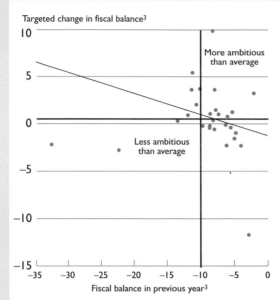

Source: Mecagni (forthcoming).

[1]The horizontal and vertical lines shown correspond to the average values of the variables in the control group of annual programs not affected by interruptions.

[2]The regression line shows the estimated relation between targeted change in fiscal balance, initial imbalance, and a constant for the sample of all annual programs. The sample excludes seven outlier observations.

[3]Using the initial fiscal balance as estimated at the time the program was formulated, which in some cases differs from the final data.

Closely linked to the question of whether policy programs were overly ambitious is that of the *adequacy of technical assistance*. All of the countries supported through the ESAF have poor administrative capacity, and more technical assistance, if properly received and utilized, would help realize stronger adjustment. In at least four countries, however, it appears that administrative constraints were so severe as to be a key factor behind the interruption of a program—that is, the pace of reform consistent with ESAF support required greater administrative capacity than existed. In at least two of these four cases (Burkina Faso and Mozambique), efforts to provide technical assistance met with less than complete cooperation from officials. In the Lao People's Democratic Republic, despite a substantial technical assistance effort (covering fiscal, monetary, and statistical issues), the reform agenda still

far exceeded implementation capacity. These cases illustrate the limits to what technical assistance can achieve in the short term, with or without the full co-operation of the authorities. However, Equatorial Guinea provides an example where, at least with the benefit of hindsight, it can be said that the IMF could have been more proactive in pressing the authorities to request and work with technical assistance teams.

Because ESAF arrangements are subject to requirements for relatively infrequent formal monitoring (by comparison with stand-by and extended arrangements), it is reasonable to ask whether *more frequent monitoring* could have helped forestall emerging slippages. A comparison between ESAF-supported countries and countries receiving IMF support among the Baltic countries, Russia, and other countries of the former Soviet Union is telling. The number of resident representatives, the frequency of staff visits, and the total staff resources per country have all been considerably greater in these countries than in ESAF countries. Moreover, quarterly test dates and formal quarterly (or even more frequent) review requirements have existed in all stand-by and extended arrangements with the Baltic countries, Russia, and other countries of the former Soviet Union, while ESAF arrangements have had only half-yearly test dates and reviews.[55] Although causality cannot be inferred, the much lower frequency of interruptions (5 out of 29) in arrangements with the Baltic countries, Russia, and other countries of the former Soviet Union than in SAF or ESAF arrangements (51 out of 68) is striking.

It is reasonable to suppose, therefore, that more intensive program monitoring— through quarterly test dates (and disbursements), more frequent reviews, and perhaps more widespread assignment of resident representatives to ESAF countries—might help in some instances to keep governments' attention focused on the requirements of adjustment policies and to prompt an early response to emerging problems. This approach could be applied flexibly, for use particularly in cases where a solid track record has not been established or where the IMF and the authorities consider that it would help sustain program implementation.

The potential importance of *contingency planning* depends on the extent to which unexpected developments, such as the terms of trade or weather-related

---

[55]In fact, annual ESAF arrangements have no test date or disbursement at end year, implying that during the second half of each program year there is no direct penalty for poor policy performance—a penalty applies only indirectly, through the prospect of more difficult negotiations and perhaps harsher corrective measures to secure approval of the subsequent annual arrangement.

shocks, significantly influenced the slippage in policies. For the most part, other than the instances of major political upheavals referred to earlier, exogenous shocks were not important causes of interruptions. They were a contributory factor, however, in eight cases. Of these programs, even though the risk of the external disturbance had been recognized ex ante, only four had an in-built contingency mechanism. Those that did not were not necessarily flawed: the implicit assumption was that unless the program were modified by a subsequent review, the effects of any disturbance would have been offset fully by additional policy adjustment. In no case, however, did these programs anticipate how such adjustment would be brought about. In at least two of these cases—Equatorial Guinea and Guinea—remedial measures (primarily, administered price adjustments) were eventually implemented. These measures would appear to have been good candidates for inclusion in a list of contingent commitments, in the sense that they could be implemented readily and were quick acting.

In sum, none of the aspects of program design examined provides a compelling explanation of program interruptions related to policy slippages. A few changes to the design or monitoring of programs may help to improve implementation, particularly a more proactive approach to the provision and coordination of technical assistance, insisting on the demonstration of countries' cooperation before some programs are approved, and more frequent monitoring and assignment of resident representatives (although the potential benefits would need to be weighed against the costs). Greater use of contingency planning may also be desirable in some circumstances, bearing in mind the risk that it may overburden programs. But in few cases is it obvious that these kinds of modification would have been sufficient to avert or considerably shorten a program interruption.

The implication is that, in fact, most program interruptions have been the result of factors outside the IMF's control—that is, major political upheavals (of the kind described at the beginning of this section) and flagging commitment. Discontinuities or weaknesses in policy management appear to have been related in roughly a dozen cases to less severe forms of political disruption, including routine elections, transitions to multiparty political systems, and social unrest. These events typically resulted in government overspending and a general distraction of the decision-making authority. However, in more than one-third of the interruptions no unusual event of this kind occurred during the period leading up to the interruption. For most of these, myriad influences were at play in the failure to implement policies as planned: lack of public support for adjustment policies, disagreements within narrower political circles, reluctance of the authorities to confront special-interest groups, poor organization, and governance-related weaknesses.

It is these conditions that raise questions about whether greater selectivity in approving arrangements would help reduce shortfalls in meeting policy commitments that ultimately produce interruptions. Specifically, by withholding IMF support for programs until authorities have demonstrated a reasonable ability to deliver agreed policy changes, could the implementation record be strengthened? Several considerations are relevant. First, policy slippages frequently occur around elections—a time when selectivity issues are particularly sensitive. Greater selectivity would probably require stronger assurances than have been provided in the past of the authorities' ability to implement policies during election cycles. Second, past interruptions are an imperfect guide to the likelihood of future interruptions. Only about half of the countries that had interruptions had more than one. Third, staff-monitored programs were almost as likely to be followed by an interrupted arrangement, or no arrangement at all, as they were to precede a program completed without interruption. These observations suggest that while greater selectivity may help build countries' resolve to implement programs as agreed, establishing the criteria for greater selectivity would be far from straightforward. Without greater selectivity, however, interruptions are likely to remain a feature of the ESAF experience, as the IMF continues to assist members at the margins of commitment and in the midst of difficult political transitions to start the adjustment process or push ahead with reforms already begun.

Appendix. Annual Arrangements Under the SAF and ESAF[1]

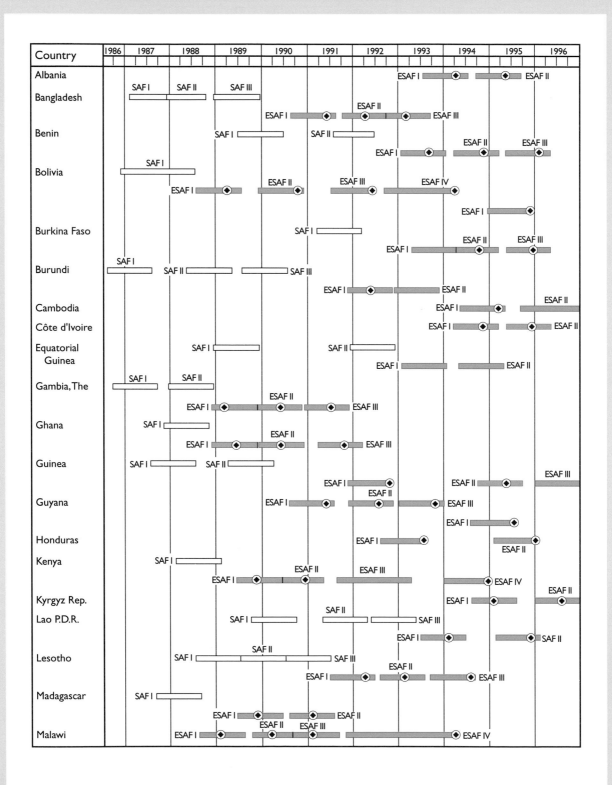

Appendix *(concluded)*

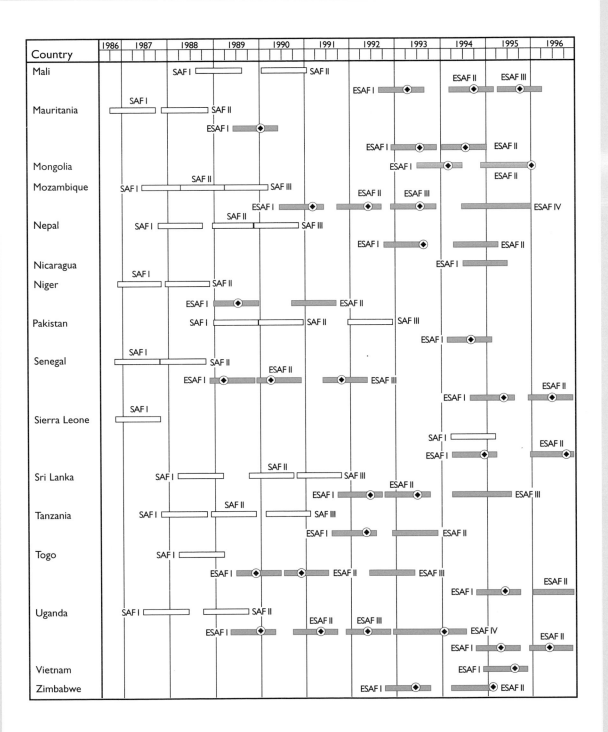

[1]Countries for which an ESAF arrangement was approved before December 31, 1994. The symbol   in the ESAF bars indicates when a review was completed.

References

Abed, G., and others, forthcoming, *Fiscal Reforms in Low-Income Countries: Experience Under IMF-Supported Programs* (Washington: International Monetary Fund).

Basle Committee on Banking Supervision, 1997, *Core Principles for Effective Supervision,* Consultative Paper (Basle).

Bredenkamp, H., forthcoming, "Methodological Issues," in *Economic Adjustment and Reform in Low-Income Countries: Studies by the Staff of the IMF,* ed. by H. Bredenkamp and S. Schadler (Washington: International Monetary Fund).

_____, and S. Schadler, eds., forthcoming, *Economic Adjustment Reform in Low-Income Countries: Studies by the Staff of the IMF* (Washington: International Monetary Fund).

Coorey, S. and K. Kochhar, forthcoming, "Economic Growth: What Has Been Achieved and How?" in *Economic Adjustment and Reform in Low-Income Countries: Studies by the Staff of the IMF,* ed. by H. Bredenkamp and S. Schadler (Washington: International Monetary Fund).

Decressin, J., L. Dicks-Mireaux, Zia Ebrahim-zadeh, and A. Ibrahim, forthcoming, "Moving Ahead with Structural Reform," in *Economic Adjustment and Reform in Low-Income Countries: Studies by the Staff of the IMF,* ed. by H. Bredenkamp and S. Schadler (Washington: International Monetary Fund).

Dicks-Mireaux, L., J. Le Dem, K. Kochhar, and S. Phillips, forthcoming, "The Policy Record," in *Economic Adjustment and Reform in Low-Income Countries: Studies by the Staff of the IMF,* ed. by H. Bredenkamp and S. Schadler (Washington: International Monetary Fund).

Goldsbrough, D., S. Coorey, L. Dicks-Mireaux, B. Horvath, K. Kochhar, M. Mecagni, E. Offerdal, and J. Zhou, 1996, *Reinvigorating Growth in Developing Countries: Lessons from Adjustment Policies in Eight Countries,* IMF Occasional Paper 139 (Washington: International Monetary Fund).

Haggard, S., J-D. Lafay, and C. Morrisson, 1995, *The Political Feasibility of Adjustment in Developing Countries,* Development Center Studies (Paris: Organization for Economic Cooperation and Development).

International Monetary Fund, 1996, *World Economic Outlook, October 1996: A Survey by the Staff of the International Monetary Fund,* World Economic and Financial Surveys (Washington).

Jayarajah, C., W. Branson, and B. Sen, 1996, *Social Dimensions of Adjustment: World Bank Experience, 1980–93* (Washington: World Bank).

Mecagni, M., forthcoming, "The Causes of Program Interruptions," in *Economic Adjustment and Reform in Low-Income Countries: Studies by the Staff of the IMF,* ed. by H. Bredenkamp and S. Schadler (Washington: International Monetary Fund).

Phillips, S., forthcoming, "Inflation: The Case for a More Resolute Approach," in *Economic Adjustment and Reform in Low-Income Countries: Studies by Staff of the IMF,* ed. by H. Bredenkamp and S. Schadler (Washington: International Monetary Fund).

Schadler, S., F. Rozwadowski, S. Tiwari, and D. Robinson, 1993, *Economic Adjustment in Low-Income Countries: Experience Under the Enhanced Structural Adjustment Facility,* IMF Occasional Paper 106 (Washington: International Monetary Fund).

Schadler, S., A. Bennett, M. Carkovic, L. Dicks-Mireaux, M. Mecagni, J. Morsink, and M. Savastano, 1995a, *IMF Conditionality: Experience Under Stand-By and Extended Arrangements—Part I,* IMF Occasional Paper 128 (Washington: International Monetary Fund).

_____, 1995b, *IMF Conditionality: Experience Under Stand-By and Extended Arrangements—Part II,* IMF Occasional Paper 129 (Washington: International Monetary Fund).

Tsikata, T., forthcoming, "Progress Toward External Viability," in *Economic Adjustment and Reform in Low-Income Countries: Studies by the Staff of the IMF,* ed. by H. Bredenkamp and S. Schadler (Washington: International Monetary Fund).

Recent Occasional Papers of the International Monetary Fund

156. The ESAF at Ten Years: Economic Adjustment and Reform in Low-Income Countries, by the Staff of the International Monetary Fund. 1997.

155. Fiscal Policy Issues During the Transition in Russia, by Augusto Lopez-Claros and Sergei Alexashenko [forthcoming].

154. Credibility Without Rules? Monetary Frameworks in the Post–Bretton Woods Era, by Carlo Cottarelli and Curzio Giannini. 1997.

153. Pension Regimes and Saving, by G.A. Mackenzie, Philip Gerson, and Alfredo Cuevas. 1997.

152. Hong Kong, China: Growth, Structural Change, and Economic Stability During the Transition, by John Dodsworth and Dubravko Mihaljek. 1997.

151. Currency Board Arrangements: Issues and Experiences, by a staff team led by Tomás J.T. Baliño and Charles Enoch. 1997.

150. Kuwait: From Reconstruction to Accumulation for Future Generations, by Nigel Andrew Chalk, Mohamed A. El-Erian, Susan J. Fennell, Alexei P. Kireyev, and John F. Wilson. 1997.

149. The Composition of Fiscal Adjustment and Growth: Lessons from Fiscal Reforms in Eight Economies, by G.A. Mackenzie, David W.H. Orsmond, and Philip R. Gerson. 1997.

148. Nigeria: Experience with Structural Adjustment, by Gary Moser, Scott Rogers, and Reinold van Til, with Robin Kibuka and Inutu Lukonga. 1997.

147. Aging Populations and Public Pension Schemes, by Sheetal K. Chand and Albert Jaeger. 1996.

146. Thailand: The Road to Sustained Growth, by Kalpana Kochhar, Louis Dicks-Mireaux, Balazs Horvath, Mauro Mecagni, Erik Offerdal, and Jianping Zhou. 1996.

145. Exchange Rate Movements and Their Impact on Trade and Investment in the APEC Region, by Takatoshi Ito, Peter Isard, Steven Symansky, and Tamim Bayoumi. 1996.

144. National Bank of Poland: The Road to Indirect Instruments, by Piero Ugolini. 1996.

143. Adjustment for Growth: The African Experience, by Michael T. Hadjimichael, Michael Nowak, Robert Sharer, and Amor Tahari. 1996.

142. Quasi-Fiscal Operations of Public Financial Institutions, by G.A. Mackenzie and Peter Stella. 1996.

141. Monetary and Exchange System Reforms in China: An Experiment in Gradualism, by Hassanali Mehran, Marc Quintyn, Tom Nordman, and Bernard Laurens. 1996.

140. Government Reform in New Zealand, by Graham C. Scott. 1996.

139. Reinvigorating Growth in Developing Countries: Lessons from Adjustment Policies in Eight Economies, by David Goldsbrough, Sharmini Coorey, Louis Dicks-Mireaux, Balazs Horvath, Kalpana Kochhar, Mauro Mecagni, Erik Offerdal, and Jianping Zhou. 1996.

138. Aftermath of the CFA Franc Devaluation, by Jean A.P. Clément, with Johannes Mueller, Stéphane Cossé, and Jean Le Dem. 1996.

137. The Lao People's Democratic Republic: Systemic Transformation and Adjustment, edited by Ichiro Otani and Chi Do Pham. 1996.

136. Jordan: Strategy for Adjustment and Growth, edited by Edouard Maciejewski and Ahsan Mansur. 1996.

135. Vietnam: Transition to a Market Economy, by John R. Dodsworth, Erich Spitäller, Michael Braulke, Keon Hyok Lee, Kenneth Miranda, Christian Mulder, Hisanobu Shishido, and Krishna Srinivasan. 1996.

134. India: Economic Reform and Growth, by Ajai Chopra, Charles Collyns, Richard Hemming, and Karen Parker with Woosik Chu and Oliver Fratzscher. 1995.

133. Policy Experiences and Issues in the Baltics, Russia, and Other Countries of the Former Soviet Union, edited by Daniel A. Citrin and Ashok K. Lahiri. 1995.

132. Financial Fragilities in Latin America: The 1980s and 1990s, by Liliana Rojas-Suárez and Steven R. Weisbrod. 1995.

131. Capital Account Convertibility: Review of Experience and Implications for IMF Policies, by staff teams headed by Peter J. Quirk and Owen Evans. 1995.

130. Challenges to the Swedish Welfare State, by Desmond Lachman, Adam Bennett, John H. Green, Robert Hagemann, and Ramana Ramaswamy. 1995.

129. IMF Conditionality: Experience Under Stand-By and Extended Arrangements. Part II: Background Papers. Susan Schadler, Editor, with Adam Bennett, Maria Carkovic, Louis Dicks-Mireaux, Mauro Mecagni, James H.J. Morsink, and Miguel A. Savastano. 1995.

128. IMF Conditionality: Experience Under Stand-By and Extended Arrangements. Part I: Key Issues and Findings, by Susan Schadler, Adam Bennett, Maria Carkovic, Louis Dicks-Mireaux, Mauro Mecagni, James H.J. Morsink, and Miguel A. Savastano. 1995.

127. Road Maps of the Transition: The Baltics, the Czech Republic, Hungary, and Russia, by Biswajit Banerjee, Vincent Koen, Thomas Krueger, Mark S. Lutz, Michael Marrese, and Tapio O. Saavalainen. 1995.

126. The Adoption of Indirect Instruments of Monetary Policy, by a staff team headed by William E. Alexander, Tomás J.T. Baliño, and Charles Enoch. 1995.

125. United Germany: The First Five Years—Performance and Policy Issues, by Robert Corker, Robert A. Feldman, Karl Habermeier, Hari Vittas, and Tessa van der Willigen. 1995.

124. Saving Behavior and the Asset Price "Bubble" in Japan: Analytical Studies, edited by Ulrich Baumgartner and Guy Meredith. 1995.

123. Comprehensive Tax Reform: The Colombian Experience, edited by Parthasarathi Shome. 1995.

122. Capital Flows in the APEC Region, edited by Mohsin S. Khan and Carmen M. Reinhart. 1995.

121. Uganda: Adjustment with Growth, 1987–94, by Robert L. Sharer, Hema R. De Zoysa, and Calvin A. McDonald. 1995.

120. Economic Dislocation and Recovery in Lebanon, by Sena Eken, Paul Cashin, S. Nuri Erbas, Jose Martelino, and Adnan Mazarei. 1995.

119. Singapore: A Case Study in Rapid Development, edited by Kenneth Bercuson with a staff team comprising Robert G. Carling, Aasim M. Husain, Thomas Rumbaugh, and Rachel van Elkan. 1995.

118. Sub-Saharan Africa: Growth, Savings, and Investment, by Michael T. Hadjimichael, Dhaneshwar Ghura, Martin Mühleisen, Roger Nord, and E. Murat Uçer. 1995.

117. Resilience and Growth Through Sustained Adjustment: The Moroccan Experience, by Saleh M. Nsouli, Sena Eken, Klaus Enders, Van-Can Thai, Jörg Decressin, and Filippo Cartiglia, with Janet Bungay. 1995.

116. Improving the International Monetary System: Constraints and Possibilities, by Michael Mussa, Morris Goldstein, Peter B. Clark, Donald J. Mathieson, and Tamim Bayoumi. 1994.

115. Exchange Rates and Economic Fundamentals: A Framework for Analysis, by Peter B. Clark, Leonardo Bartolini, Tamim Bayoumi, and Steven Symansky. 1994.

114. Economic Reform in China: A New Phase, by Wanda Tseng, Hoe Ee Khor, Kalpana Kochhar, Dubravko Mihaljek, and David Burton. 1994.

113. Poland: The Path to a Market Economy, by Liam P. Ebrill, Ajai Chopra, Charalambos Christofides, Paul Mylonas, Inci Otker, and Gerd Schwartz. 1994.

112. The Behavior of Non-Oil Commodity Prices, by Eduardo Borensztein, Mohsin S. Khan, Carmen M. Reinhart, and Peter Wickham. 1994.

111. The Russian Federation in Transition: External Developments, by Benedicte Vibe Christensen. 1994.

110. Limiting Central Bank Credit to the Government: Theory and Practice, by Carlo Cottarelli. 1993.

109. The Path to Convertibility and Growth: The Tunisian Experience, by Saleh M. Nsouli, Sena Eken, Paul Duran, Gerwin Bell, and Zühtü Yücelik. 1993.

Note: For information on the title and availability of Occasional Papers not listed, please consult the IMF Publications Catalog or contact IMF Publication Services.